MARY
QUEEN OF SCOTS

JENNY WORMALD

With a Foreword *and* Afterword *by*
ANNA GROUNDWATER

BIRLINN

This edition published in 2018 by
Birlinn Ltd
West Newington House
10 Newington Road
Edinburgh
EH9 1QS

www.birlinn.co.uk

Previously published in 2017 by
John Donald, an imprint of Birlinn Ltd

First published in 1988 by George Philip
Republished as a paperback in 1991 by Collins and Brown
Revised edition published in 2001 by Tauris Parke Paperbacks

ISBN: 978 1 78027 552 9

British Library Cataloguing-in-Publication Data
A catalogue record for this book is available on request
from the British Library

Typeset by 3btype.com
Printed and bound in Britain by Clays Ltd, Elcograf S.p.A.

Contents

Jenny Wormald in the BBC and Pioneer Productions programme
Bloody Queens
(Credit: BBC/Pioneer Productions/Seamus McCracken)

Appreciation

My mother Jenny had a fascinating relationship with Mary Queen of Scots and it was my privilege to watch that play out over the last three decades and more of her life. Especially so as the Preface to the original 1988 edition includes my brother Tom's and my first mentions in print. I well remember visiting the mound at Fotheringhay and Westminster Abbey at the time – and being disappointed that I was too small to see Mary's tomb properly! Mum had also featured in a *Timewatch* episode about Mary in 1987 commemorating the 400th anniversary of her execution, and came at it from a very different perspective from the other talking heads, including Gordon Donaldson and Antonia Fraser. That was when she made a comment that became stock-in-trade in the family – 'Darnley was . . . a weed!'

Mum's view of Mary was certainly both controversial and outspoken and, as Anna Groundwater highlights in her Foreword to this new edition, she sparked off an at times vociferous debate, the dynamics of which continue to this day. Despite her grumbling, I think she found that stimulating and sometimes even enjoyable, and so she could not really let it go. It also reached widely beyond academia: as an example of that, my copy of the 1988 edition contains a positive review of the book by Ruth Rendell, which perhaps inevitably focuses on the 'did she / didn't she' mystery around Darnley and the Casket Letters.

As with Mum's wider work to challenge the misconceptions about Scotland in the early modern era, it was her remarkable re-think of Scotland's nobility in the fifteenth and sixteenth centuries which allowed her to reassess Mary's performance as a ruler, and come to her ultimate conclusion of Mary's failure. That conclusion, while eliciting some fierce criticism, made her a welcome and lively addition to many articles, programmes and interviews. In common with all of Mum's work, these were never dull or ambiguous in terms of the views she expressed. I can still hear those ringing words 'tedious creature!'; yet when we went to visit the new statue of Mary at Linlithgow in late 2015, both my brother and I were surprised at the calmness of Mum's reaction, although she did mutter, 'well who else's heart would it be!' I think Anna captures the complex dynamic of Mum's opinions: it wasn't personal, she didn't dislike Mary *per se*, but she did think the romantic–tragic mythmaking made for very poor history. And that it was a waste of time when there was so much better history to study.

So Mum's approach to Mary was also very much rooted in her wider approach to historical study. Those who were taught by her will recognise that no-nonsense and forceful expression of views throughout the volume, but as always written in an engaging and approachable way. My brothers and I were lucky enough to have ready access to that no-nonsense approach, as were her many friends, colleagues and students over the years. This interaction not least led to the remarkable and deeply touching reaction at the time of her death, in which that relationship with Mary was one of the oft-repeated elements. Mum's posthumous appearance on the BBC and Pioneer Productions programme *Bloody Queens* gave her an excellent opportunity to put her message across one more time in person, as the republication of *A Study in Failure* now does in print.

The family are immensely grateful to Hugh Andrew, Mairi Sutherland and Tom Johnstone at Birlinn, and Anna Groundwater at the University of Edinburgh (where Mum happily spent the last years of her working life), for making the republication of *Mary Queen of Scots: A Study in Failure* possible. We hope that it continues to spark interest and debate as it has done since its original publication. As Anna makes very apparent, things have moved on in the thirty years since, and will continue to do so. Mum would be pleased with that. It is very heartening that there are so many themes and issues still to explore in the coming years. With that in mind, my brothers, Andrew and Tom, and I are very pleased to dedicate this new edition to Mum's memory.

Luke Wormald

Foreword

Jenny and Mary, A Complicated Relationship

The first publication of Jenny Wormald's *Mary, Queen of Scots: A Study in Failure* in 1988 was greeted by howls of outrage, and some more considered opinion. Both of which (I suspect) would have been received by the author with gleeful joy. Any outrage was a measure of the emotive nature of response to Mary's misfortunes that have dogged understanding of her reign. One only has to read customer reviews of the book on Amazon to see the intensely personal and empathetic identification of readers with Mary's fate that precludes disinterested judgement; more scholarly criticism too has occasionally succumbed to a tinge of the sentimental. But such reaction was also probably what Jenny was hoping for in stimulating, reinvigorating and redefining the terms of the debate.

The book was published as part of a 'Monarchs and Monarchies' series, of which Dr David Starkey was Series Editor, and was thus subject to that series' expectations of content and format (significantly, no footnotes). Its writing was done amidst a welter of books, dramatizations and speeches to commemorate the 400th anniversary of Mary's execution. From the first pages, Wormald spells out her objectives. This was not to be a personal biography: instead the focus was to be on Mary's actions as monarch, as queen, during her personal reign, 1561 to 1567. As such, Wormald did not set out to write 'a definitive study of the reign', but to 'open up the lines of enquiry sketched out here', to encourage debate, and thus a more 'objective assessment' of Mary's monarchical abilities (p. 12). It is important to remember this, in terms of what Wormald was trying to achieve here. To some extent the book can be seen as an extended opinion piece – 'a polemical book-length essay', as *The Telegraph* called it – and it needs to be read in that spirit.

Crucially, Wormald intended 'a study of Mary as queen rather than a woman of great misfortune' (p. 11). She puts Mary the monarch centre stage, not Mary the drama queen, 'the pantomime villainess or fairy queen' (p. 10). Wormald then locates that stage within its longer-term Stewart contexts (for they most certainly did not begin and end with Mary), and its wider geographical European setting. What was happening in Scotland was not just 'a little local Scottish drama' but part of an era of revolution and reformation – 'Scotland was only one of eight countries . . . which experienced upheaval and revolt.' Against that background, the book was to be 'about Mary as a mid sixteenth-century monarch' (p. 11). In particular, Wormald wanted to address the *entire* personal rule, rescuing the then 'neglected' first four years. The reign needed also to be situated within an analysis and understanding of the 'nature of Scottish monarchy', with Mary as one in a long line of Stewart kings. This was 'a question not answered by the superficial assumptions about the impossible Scottish nobility' (p. 12) usually found in books about Mary, many of them by Tudor or English historians with little understanding or knowledge of the different forms of Stewart Scottish government.

Wormald's wishes for debate were fulfilled. Debate is certainly what the book prompted. Review titles encapsulated this furore, including Maurice Lee's 'The Daughter of Debate: Mary Queen of Scots after 400 years', and 'A New Case for the Prosecution', Michael Lynch's rebuttal of Wormald's interpretations of the evidence. Several critics highlighted the 'prosecutorial' character of her argument, 'relentlessly pressed' (Maurice Lee). Much cited was Wormald's pithily phrased, and thus memorable, condemnation of Mary's abilities, found unconvincing by some – her repeated use of words such as 'lamentable' and 'ludicrous'. Where were the extenuating personal and contextual circumstances? What about the more admirable aspects of her reign? For Lynch and others, this was all too black and white.

Wormald certainly leaves us in no doubt as to her opinion of Mary's abilities as ruler. That's partly what makes this book as refreshing to read now as it was then. There's no cloying romanticism here. From the start, her central criticism is clear: Mary provides us with 'the unique spectacle of an adult reigning monarch who did not want to reign' (p. 13). Throughout the text Mary is repeatedly portrayed as a 'queen reluctant to rule' (p. 108). The fundamental reason for this, Wormald thinks, was Mary's 'indifference, even a degree of antagonism' to Scotland. 'For Mary, Scotland was a poor relation of France' ranking 'only third in her interests as queen' (p. 37) behind England, and her first husband's kingdom, France. This was fatal since the 'Scottish kingdom's pride in itself had been largely invested in the monarchy. By dissipating this investment she made her first, and her greatest political error' (p. 38).

Instead of concentrating on fulfilling her duties as monarch, and ruling Scotland properly, Mary's overriding ambitions were personal: that is, to succeed (the still young, but unmarried and childless) Elizabeth I as English queen, at the same time as putting 'marriage before monarchy' (p. 107). The problems she ran into were not simply the result of her gender, and Wormald passes over, in a way that would not be possible now, the impact of being a female ruler in a patriarchal society: her 'success or failure was a matter not of sex, but of personality and political intelligence. Rulers who let their hearts rule their heads tended to court disaster, be they male or female . . . It is therefore Mary the political animal, not Mary the female of the species, which has to be assessed' (p. 36), Mary the monarch not Mary the female monarch. Problematically, for Mary, Wormald concludes that she was 'of little wit and no judgement', and that she 'never stopped at one mistake where two were possible' (pp. xx, 136). Mary failed too, says Wormald, in her duties as a Catholic monarch in a kingdom in which the Protestant reformers had only recently overthrown the Catholic Church. A damning summation of the case for the prosecution, in which you can hear Wormald's own sometimes acerbic tones ringing from the page.

Black and white indeed. But arguably, the case had to be stated in such strong words to enable Wormald to reframe the debate away from the previous equally polarized focus on Mary the person, innocent victim, Catholic martyr or guilty adulteress, and the two big mysteries – the questions over Mary's implication in Darnley's murder, and the authenticity of the Casket Letters. This would free up Wormald to evaluate Mary's abilities as a ruler, rather than her personal morality, innocence or guilt; and to do it within the terms of the reign's specifically Scottish context and recent historiography.

That historiography was built partly on Wormald's own huge contribution to the 1970s and 1980s reimagining of how medieval and early modern Scottish government, and Stewart personal monarchy, worked – a contribution succinctly outlined in Steve Boardman's and Julian Goodare's introduction to the *festschrift* published for Jenny's seventieth birthday (*Kings, Lords and Men in Scotland and Britain, 1300–1625: Essays in Honour of Jenny Wormald*). For Wormald, it was important not to assess Mary in terms of what could be expected of an English monarch acting within Tudor systems of government, but instead within an understanding of Scottish social structures, the co-operation that Scottish kings could usually (though not always) expect from their nobles, and a general acceptance of Stewart dynastic rights to the monarchy. Crucially this was to avoid the notion that Scottish government was somehow less effective than English government because it lacked that kingdom's bureaucratic development. Instead Wormald was to argue that if Mary had understood how to rule in the way her Stewart forebears had, and her son James was to, there was nothing inherently to stop her ruling effectively. Mary was to be evaluated on her ability to use personal relationships, and kinship networks within a decentralized kingdom, to effect her will. If she failed in this, it was her own failure, and not merely that of disruptive nobles. For Wormald, however, Mary disastrously involved herself in factional politics, instead of rising above them to secure her authority. Mary allowed her monarchy to get too personal.

This argument is pursued through the introductory chapter, which crisply outlines the development of, and problems with, an often partisan historiography of Mary's reign. From the moment of her forced abdication, it was in someone's political or religious interests to legitimize or castigate her deposition, and ultimately her execution. But whereas '[v]iolence, sexual scandal and murder' (p. 6) had been seized on by her detractors in the later 1500s to condemn her actions as ruler, these aspects of her life now became the principal focus of her biographers, in particular her guilt or innocence, rather than just how good she was at being a queen. Chapter 2 lays the foundation for Wormald's argument in the strengths and record of Stewart government from 1424 against which Mary is to be measured. The next two chapters delineate the diplomatic and political upheavals, wars and growing Protestantism of her minority to show what she will have to deal with on assuming her personal reign. A crucial chapter then follows looking at Mary's performance in government over the first few years of what Wormald calls relative 'normality' after her 'reluctant' return to Scotland in 1561 (p. 11). She notes the lengthy gap between the death of Mary's mother, the regent Marie de Guise, in June 1560, the rebellious Reformation parliament of August 1560, and Mary's arrival at Leith in August 1561. Chapter 6 deals principally with the years of crisis, 1565 to 1567, the disastrous marriages, the murders, the confrontation with an outraged nobility at Carberry Hill, and her eventual deposition. A final brief chapter considers her flight to England, the subsequent lengthy incarceration, and her involvement in plots to restore her to the Scottish throne and to take over Elizabeth's. Given that Wormald's opinion is made clear throughout, there is a necessarily concise conclusion: 'Mary was a tragic figure . . . because she was one of the rare – strangely rare – cases of someone born to supreme power who was wholly unable to cope with its responsibilities' (p. 199).

Subsequently, Wormald continued that level of criticism in answers to journalists on yet more cinematic treatments of the passion and drama of Mary's life. Playing to the press, she used typical phrases such as 'tedious creature' or noted her 'baleful legacy'; in 1997, as three films loomed, she said 'I can't understand why anyone would want to make a film about such an overrated woman . . . She didn't have much of a head to begin with' (*The Sunday Times*, 21 December 1997); and in 2013, 'Those of us today [who regard] Mary Queen of Scots as a distinctly tedious pain in the neck can only groan at yet another romantic outburst' (*Sunday Herald*, 4 August 2013). In response to the suggestion by an MSP in 2008 that Mary's remains be transported from Westminster Abbey to Falkland Palace, Wormald reiterated her opinions on Mary's merits, noting that she was 'much keener on becoming queen of England than she ever was of being queen of Scotland. It seems appropriate to leave her alone' (*The Times*, 13 October 2008). Wormald maintained her position on Mary until the last, appearing in BBC 2's *Bloody Queen*, posthumously broadcast in February 2016. Talking about James' relationship with Mary, she thought 'the last thing he wanted was a discredited mother back – messing things up and getting in the way', but ended in grudging approval of the manner of Mary's death: 'In a sense, it's a terribly fitting kind of end, because like so much of Mary Queen of Scots' life, it's theatrical. And very good theatre this time.'

The vehemence of Jenny's characterization and denunciation of the unfortunate queen in interviews or later writings seems to me stimulated by her impatience, not only with Mary herself (though undoubtedly she was deeply irritated by her), but also with a sentimentalized Scottish fascination with failure, something that she addressed with Tom Devine in their co-edited *Oxford Handbook to Modern Scottish History* (2012). They attacked the 'passion for romance, invented or quasi-real . . . in the obsession with that lamentable figure, Mary, Queen of Scots' in which 'the equally lamentable Bonnie Prince Charlie runs her a close second'. The problem with this is that it means too many 'Scottish historians have spent proportionately too much time on a minor issue, at the expense of infinitely more important and interesting ones' (*Oxford Handbook*, p. 12). Elsewhere she has said 'I can't really particularly explain her [Mary's] fascination except that the Scots seem to quite like terrific failures provided they are romantic, like Bonnie Prince Charlie. The real Mary cuts a very poor figure' (*The Scotsman*, 21 August 1997). And she's not without support in this view: as Rosemary Goring wrote in 2012, 'I suspect the attraction of Mary and the Young Pretender goes deeper than we'd like to think. Their popularity can't be explained simply by a lack of interest in more recent or subtle events. Their turbulent, in many ways pitiful lives create a magnetic spell that seems unbreakable. Scots, it would appear, love heroic failure . . . Self-pity, *schadenfreude* and a need for entertainment may explain the enduring fascination with Mary Stuart and her ilk.' Noting scholars like Wormald who 'seek out fresh facts and new insights to jolt history out of its rut', she wished 'If only they could have the same effect on a nation that should be awarded a first-class degree in sentimentality' (*The Herald*, 27 September 2012). Wormald would no doubt have agreed.

Her principal aim here was to get away from an overly partisan or romanticized historiography of Mary that privileged a personal engagement with the subject over a more objective assessment of her abilities as a ruler. For Wormald, 'The business of the historian is not to love or to hate Mary Stuart, to judge her as a saint or a criminal, but to ask about the success or failure of her rule' (p. 10) – and not to focus debate solely on her involvement or otherwise with Darnley's murder, or the reality of her relationship with Bothwell. Wormald recognized that contemporarily people liked Mary – but, as she said elsewhere, that is not the benchmark that Mary as ruler should be measured against, either then or now. Interviewed in *The Scotsman* in 1997, Wormald observed that Mary 'was probably a nice woman, she might have been a good companion to take out to dinner, and there are records of her personal charm, but as a queen, her lack of interest in her country is quite staggering by any standards. The trouble is that most stories of her don't tell that' (*The Scotsman,* 21 August 1997). And in her review of John Guy's biography of Mary, Wormald recognized that Mary 'was no doubt nice to know, for some people and for some of the time' but asked 'does that rescue her as a ruler?' (*The Evening Standard*, 19 January 2004). Some of her critics have perhaps missed this point: they have taken overly personal exception to her criticism of Mary. It was not that Jenny didn't like Mary: it was just that what she found is 'someone neither "bad" nor "mad", but simply very sad' (p. xx).

So why, if Wormald found Mary so lamentable, is the book being republished now, especially given the plethora of subsequent biographies, including some by esteemed scholars (of which more in the Afterword)? Partly this is because public interest in Mary,

Queen of Scots, remains as fervent as ever – for instance, at least three treatments of her life are planned for the Edinburgh Festival this summer (2017). More significantly in scholarly terms, however, in the years since 1988 there has been no new biography of Mary by a *Scottish History* specialist, except for Julian Goodare's excellent *Oxford Dictionary of National Biography* entry. Given Wormald's strictures about the necessity of placing Mary's reign within the revised historiography of the Stewart monarchy in Scotland, this concern remains important and somewhat unfulfilled. The vitality of what she has to say about Mary's reign, in relation to those specifically Scottish and Stewart contexts, remains as refreshing and significant as ever. Whether you disagree with or endorse her conclusions, no one could write it like Jenny. Where other biographies have necessarily had to run the gamut of the 'did she / didn't she' school, Wormald's provocative opinion piece continues to refocus attention on Mary the monarch, and to stimulate debate.

The opportunity for republication arises out of a gap for Mary on the bookshelf of Birlinn's 'Stewart Dynasty in Scotland' series. The original text is reproduced here in its unfootnoted glorious entirety, with this Foreword, an Additional Bibliography, and an Afterword in which subsequent work on Mary is considered, and lines for further research suggested. It had been previously republished in paperback in 2001, with an inexplicably erroneous rear cover blurb, and lurid subtitle, *Politics, Passion and a Kingdom Lost*. Here the original subtitle is restored. Where necessary, errors highlighted by Michael Lynch in the hardback, not addressed in 2001, have now been corrected.

This republication comes eighteen months or so after Jenny's untimely death in December 2015. Some wonderful obituaries have reminded us of her formidable body of work, and the seismic impact she had on the reframing of the historiography of medieval and early modern Scotland, and its monarchs. One by Professor Dauvit Broun in *The Herald* observed that Jenny 'was the most original Scottish historian of the last century, giving the subject an international profile in a way that would previously have been regarded as inherently impossible'. Noting her early work on bonds of manrent, he said 'Wormald's genius was to see the potential of this material to speak to wider historical concerns about the nature of political culture and society . . . and to articulate this in ways which engaged not only with other historians with no knowledge of Scottish history, but with other disciplines too'. '[H]er work was grounded both on her understanding of the documents themselves and their local context, and on her imagination in seeing what this could mean more broadly.' Jenny, as Felicity Heal recalled in *The Guardian*, 'challenged the parochialism of many earlier accounts of the rule of the Stuart kings', and placed Scotland, 'and the writing of its history, in the European main-stream'. For a fuller appreciation of Jenny's enormous intellectual contribution to Scottish and British history, read Boardman's and Goodare's introduction to their edited *festschrift*. As these editors observe, Jenny 'launched an often brutally witty iconoclastic assault on hoary misconceptions about the medieval and early modern kingdom and left a landscape littered with the battered remains of old prejudices and muddled thinking in her wake'. You can then marvel at the five pages of her listed publications with which that book ends.

Many have also written of Jenny's vibrant, humorous and endlessly interested passion for debate, captured so marvellously by Jamie Reid-Baxter in the *Innes Review*. In Felicity Heal's words, she 'honed a natural pleasure in argument into a passionate commitment to debating, usually carried from the lecture theatre into the bar, where late-night sessions often morphed from discussing history to denouncing the iniquities of Thatcherism'. Her boundless questioning of the historiographical *status quo* will be missed. As Dauvit Broun concluded, 'It is difficult to imagine that there will ever be a brighter light in Scottish history, shining with as much originality, passion and unstoppable intellectual and personal courage.' Republishing the book now gives us the chance to remember and celebrate Jenny at her forthright best, allowing her own inimitable voice to ring again from its pages.

Anna Groundwater

Preface to the 1991 Edition

1987 was a wonderful year for the fans of Mary Queen of Scots. It may seem a little odd to idolize a tragic heroine by celebrating the 400th centenary of her execution – where was the mourning? – but celebrate they did, in lavish style. Indeed, modern and sixteenth-century politics came together in a remarkable fashion when the then Secretary of State for Scotland, Malcolm Rifkind, took time off from the coming general election to involve himself in the general Mariolatry; he went off to Edinburgh Castle on the anniversary of the execution itself, 8 February, to drink 'Mary Queen of Scots champagne' and present a book on Mary's travels to a representative from France, with a speech full of grace, some history and much legend. As it happens, 1987 was the ninth centenary of the death of William the Conqueror, by any standards a far greater ruler with an infinitely more lasting legacy. The Prince of Wales made some very graceful remarks about the relative importance of himself and the Bayeux Tapestry when visiting it with the Princess of Wales. But there was no sign of the English Home Secretary broaching William the Conqueror Calvados in the White Tower. It is, indeed, frankly inconceivable that any centenary of any English ruler would be so swamped with the tours, plays, conferences, exhibitions, books, pamphlets, newspaper articles, radio and television programmes, which were such a prolific feature of the Marian centenary – mainly in Scotland, but, even more extraordinarily, in England as well. From the Mass said in the parish church of Fotheringhay on 7 February right through to the Edinburgh – or perhaps more accurately Marian – Festival and beyond, Marian memorials and Marian games and circuses were so much the order of the day that the writing of this book was done in a state of constant perplexity; sitting, as it were, in the peace of my study, contemplating the reality, while the howls of enthusiasm for the legend thundered outside, was a very puzzling experience.

This is not a book about that legend, which has far less to do with the historical Mary than with the particular tendency of the Scots to follow the lead given by Sir Walter Scott and turn their history into tartan romance, making folk-heroes of failures and thugs, be they Mary Queen of Scots, Rob Roy or Bonnie Prince Charlie. No amount of scholarly history – and at present Scottish history (as opposed to myth) is in a very flourishing state – will ever combat it completely. That is the frustration of being a historian of Scotland, aware that the reality which was the kingdom of Scotland is so much more fascinating than the romantics could ever make it. Mary is not just part of that problem, but compounds it; for it has not been unknown for normally sober historians to lose their scholarly heads when in her presence. It is a baleful legacy. It is fair to add that not every historian who, like myself, is trying to break through the legendary fog which envelops her and reach the historical reality will agree with the interpretation offered here; but the important point is that the effort should be made, and the arguments about her shifted from the bedroom at Holyrood or Dunbar to the world of sixteenth-century politics, which is where she belongs. And if this produces differing views, then the achievement will have been considerable: at last, Mary Queen of Scots will be subject to scholarly scrutiny and debate – just like other historical personalities. My contribution is a book which portrays a monarch of little wit and no judgement, to paraphrase Elizabeth's description of Thomas Seymour, a ruler whose life was marked by irresponsibility and failure on a scale unparalleled in her own day. There is, therefore, virtually no point of contact between the Mary of 1587 and the Mary of 1987, however much fun the latter has given participants in the celebrations. Writing a book about the queen who reigned in Scotland between 1561 and 1567 has not been 'fun'. For while the Mary who died in 1587 was evidently 'dangerous to know', what I have found is someone neither 'bad' nor 'mad', but simply very sad.

The writing of this book was accompanied not just by the distractions of these celebrations, but by the very considerable help given by generous friends and scholars. First, although I did not actually impose the text on them, I owe a real debt to Dr Simon Adams and Dr Norman Macdougall, for general discussions of the subject and for their comments and suggestions on a lecture I gave on Mary which was the genesis of the book. And I hope that Professor Maurice Lee Jr will not object to my saying here how much I have benefitted from his masterly study of James, earl of Moray. Dr Keith Brown, who has himself made a notable contribution to the Marian debate, was the victim of my urgent request for instant reading and advice, and I am extremely grateful for his generous and reassuring response. Dr David Starkey's suggestions about the structure of the book were very valuable. I also thank the members of the extended kin-group who did so much to make the writing of this book possible: Penny Thorne and Jutta Massholder, whose tolerant good humour and delightful ability to keep the family calm, ensured the necessary peace to work; and Angela Galbraith, for her wryly cheerful acceptance of the fact that her historical knowledge and position as family friend has for the third time (and, for my sake, I hope not the last) meant that she has been called on for advice and assistance, once again to my great benefit. It has not, of course, been all a female effort: my sons Tom and Luke may regret that they were old enough to do such things as keeping an exhausted author supplied with tea and coffee, but I do not.

Two final thanks. One is a new debt. I write the preface to the paperback edition of my book with warm appreciation of the person making it possible. I first met Juliet Gardiner when I turned up in the offices of *History Today* when she was its editor. That meeting began a relationship between editor and author which I have always not only valued but also enjoyed; and it is therefore a particular pleasure for me that it is she who is publishing this edition. And above all I thank Patrick Wormald for – as always – the historical and stylistic perceptions which have been so invaluable to me, and for his patience with the particular aspect of the Year of the Queen which intruded itself onto him. Both make it wholly appropriate that I dedicate this book to him.

Jenny Wormald
December 1990

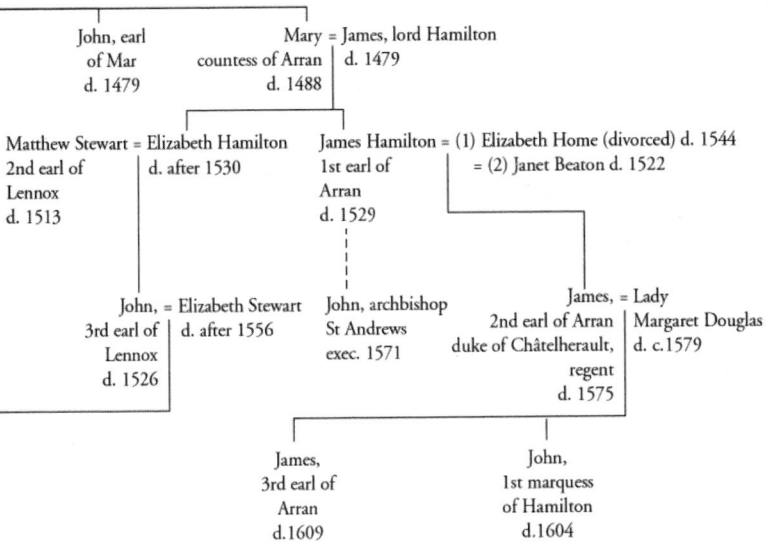

John, earl
of Mar
d. 1479

Mary = James, lord Hamilton
countess of Arran | d. 1479
d. 1488

Matthew Stewart = Elizabeth Hamilton
2nd earl of | d. after 1530
Lennox
d. 1513

James Hamilton = (1) Elizabeth Home (divorced) d. 1544
1st earl of   = (2) Janet Beaton d. 1522
Arran
d. 1529

John, = Elizabeth Stewart
3rd earl of | d. after 1556
Lennox
d. 1526

John, archbishop
St Andrews
exec. 1571

James, = Lady
2nd earl of Arran | Margaret Douglas
duke of Châtelherault, | d. c.1579
regent
d. 1575

James,
3rd earl of
Arran
d.1609

John,
1st marquess
of Hamilton
d.1604

illegitimate descent

exec. executed

xxiii

CHAPTER ONE

Legend or History?
1587–1987

Mary Queen of Scots was born in the palace of Linlithgow on 7 or 8 December 1542. It is perhaps appropriate that even the date of the birth of a personality who still eludes us despite the myriad of books written about her is uncertain. She herself claimed the 8th, the feast of the Immaculate Conception of the Virgin Mary, and in this, if in nothing else, that most powerful of Protestant reformers, John Knox, agreed with her, while one of her staunchest supporters, the Catholic John Leslie, bishop of Ross, believed it was the earlier date. It does not much matter. Far more important was the fact that this baby girl, born two weeks after the defeat of a Scottish army by the English at Solway Moss, and at a time when her remarkable father James V was lying burnt out at the age of thirty in his glorious hunting-lodge at Falkland, was to be within a week of her birth queen of the Scots. James's comment, when the news of her birth was brought to him, that 'it cam wi' a lass and it will gang wi' a lass' (a reference to the way in which the house of Stewart had come to the throne, through the marriage of Walter the Steward to Robert Bruce's daughter Marjorie) may be apocryphal and was, as it turned out, inaccurate; the 'lass' who was to bring Stewart rule to an end was not Queen Mary, but Queen Anne in 1714. But it may still be significant of at least part of contemporary reaction to Mary. For James's saying was first recorded by John Knox, in the version 'The devil go with it! It will end as it began: it came from a woman; and it will end in a woman'. This was in the mid 1560s, when Mary was still in power, so that it reads like Knox's wishful thinking rather than anything else; and it was then recast into the famous phrase by the Protestant chronicler Robert Lindsay of Pitscottie, writing in the 1570s, by which time the representative of the house of Stewart

I

was the child James VI, and the lass had long gone – into English captivity.

Thus the words supposedly uttered by a despairing king, just before he turned his face to the wall to die, are an immediate symbol of the reaction of very many of those on whom Mary Queen of Scots was to make an impact, in her lifetime and thereafter. And there was nothing apocryphal about what her undutiful son was to say, half a century later, in his book *Basilikon Doron*, when he wrote of how his grandfather had been punished by God for his immorality, for his infant sons had predeceased him, and he died 'leaving a double curse behind him to the land, both a Woman of sex, and a new borne babe of age to reign over them'. In the late 1520s and 1530s, Henry VIII had embarked on a spectacular, even murderous matrimonial career in an attempt to save his kingdom from the first part of that curse. For the Scots, Mary embodied both. From the very beginning of her own spectacular career, therefore, even before her own personality could make its distinctive mark, she was a person to create doubts, and even fear.

Four centuries later, doubts have not been dispelled. This is scarcely because she has been neglected. 'Daughter of debate' Elizabeth called her; and mother of a remarkably impassioned series of debates she subsequently became. Did she, or did she not, murder her second husband, Henry Stewart, lord Darnley? Was she the author of the Casket Letters, those letters which totally implicated her in the murder, or were they forgeries? Was she raped by James Hepburn, earl of Bothwell, and forced to marry him, or did she connive at her own abduction? It may seem a little curious that these are the problems which have exercised the minds of so many of the writers on Mary Queen of Scots above all else. They relate to a brief two-year crisis period in her forty-four year life; and although they are by no means irrelevant to her political role, the approach to them has had such a predominantly personal – one might almost say tabloid – quality that the historiographical Mary is immediately marked out from all other historical monarchs, Scottish or otherwise.

Yet these questions have sustained a massive publishing industry, briefly and for good political and confessional reasons in the late sixteenth century, and then almost without interruption from the mid eighteenth. As the subject of historical studies, and the heroine of romantic fiction, Mary Queen of Scots has a massive lead over all other earthly Maries, only the Virgin scoring more heavily – as even the most cursory glance at the British Library Catalogue of Printed Books makes clear. Thus in the 1962 Catalogue, the Virgin Mary has 150 pages devoted to her; Mary Queen of Scots 455 books; the English queen Mary Tudor – 'Bloody Mary' – 73. And that other central figure in a great murder mystery, Richard III, has the pathetic total of 38. Nevertheless, I. B. Cowan could publish a book in 1971 justifiably entitled *The Enigma of Mary Stuart*. For much of what has been written about her does not elucidate; rather, it creates a barrier between us and the historical ruler of mid sixteenth-century Scotland.

The prolific contemporary literature about Mary, which has been extensively and effectively reviewed by J. E. Phillips, *Images of a Queen*, was all understandable enough. For her earlier years, there are the famous Ronsard poems extolling her charm and beauty, along with those in similar vein by the man who was to become her most vicious detractor, the great Scottish scholar George Buchanan – exactly the kind of thing which would naturally be written about an attractive young queen. Her later career, from the time of her marriage to Darnley in the summer of 1565, inevitably gave rise to writing of a very different and much more partisan nature. The heights were to be reached with her execution in 1587, when accusers and defenders rushed into print, producing works with titles like 'An excellent dyttye made as a generall rejoycinge for the cuttinge of the Scottishe queene', or 'Marie Stewarde late Quene of Scotland hath defiled her owne bodie with many adulteries . . .', compared with 'The Martyrdom of the Queen of Scotland . . .' or 'L'Histoire et Martyre de la Royne D'Escosse'. The attackers had far better titles than the supporters; but the scope for emotive, impassioned language was the same for both sides.

One of the most remarkable examples occurs in the set of poems known as *de Jezebelis*, collected and contributed to by an exiled Catholic Scots lawyer and philosopher, Adam Blackwood, one of Mary's earliest and most strenuous defenders. Jezebel, therefore, was Elizabeth of England, that she-wolf, monster of vice and cruelty, sprung of vicious and degenerate stock, for she was born of the incestuous relationship between Henry VIII and Anne Boleyn, who was not only his wife but also his illegitimate daughter. But the Jezebel poems went far beyond vilification of Elizabeth. The majority were written to arouse French opinion, and to push the French king, Henri III, into revenge. One depicts Mary's first husband, Francis II, three times rushing to welcome her in heaven, and three times finding that he can only embrace a headless body, so that he curses his people; whereupon the poet exhorts them to forget their own troubles, and unite to destroy England and send its queen to a dreadful death. France failed to respond. But another European country, Spain, did seek to conquer England, in 1588; and it was encouraged by the dramatic 'Address to the Captains and Men on the Armada', which promised the sailors the aid of the saints of England, John Fisher, Thomas More and Edmund Campion, and above all 'The blessed and innocent Mary queen of Scotland, who, still fresh from her sacrifice, bears copious and abounding witness to the cruelty and impiety of this Elizabeth and directs her shafts against her.' And the future pope Urban VIII could write of Mary as the queen who died without honour due; yet the shadows of night were her funeral robes, the stars her tapers. It was all very stirring.

What is immediately notable, however, is that Mary's own subjects, the Scots – that is, those in Scotland left to deal with the crisis created by her deposition in 1567 and flight to England in 1568, rather than Catholic exiles like Blackwood and the bishop of Ross, on whom there were no restraints – had the good sense to keep as quiet as possible. Initially, of course, those who drove her out had to justify their actions to Elizabeth and prevent the English queen making any serious attempt to restore her sister of Scotland; and they used that scholar of European distinction,

George Buchanan, as their apologist, thus enabling the grave and learned humanist to display a remarkable talent for writing, as it were, copy for the *Sun* in the style of *The Times*, in his sensational *Ane detectioun of the doinges of Marie quene of Scottes*. But generally the arena for attack or defence was in England and Europe. Thus Mary had already passed into legend. But it was legend on a European scale. Her contemporaries were well aware – sometimes all too uncomfortably aware – that she was, in her life and in her death, a figure of European significance. No one in the sixteenth century made the mistake which was to become such a feature of later writings about her, of seeing her crimes or her innocence as a little domestic matter, locking her into a Scottish bedroom debate in which, as far as the outside world was concerned, only Elizabeth had an interest beyond the fleeting and casual.

The move from the international and political to the insular and personal was interrupted by something of a lull in the seventeenth century. The accession of Mary's Protestant son James VI to the English throne naturally cooled anti-Marian passion. James constructed magnificent tombs for the two protagonists, Mary and Elizabeth, in Westminster Abbey; and the more-or-less 'official' account by William Camden in his *Annals* (1615) emphasized Mary's evil fortunes rather than her evil character. Up in the north, there was the occasional extreme Protestant rumble about the evils of that character; but in general, the Britain of the seventeenth century was absorbed by more immediate concerns. Even the hysterical anti-Catholicism stirred up by Titus Oates, inventor of the so-called Popish Plot of 1681, produced only a minor squall. But almost immediately thereafter the basis for modern Mariography was created.

The end of the seventeenth and early eighteenth century saw the publication of Buchanan's works (just after one of them, his treatise on Scottish political theory, *De Iure Regni apud Scotos*, had enjoyed the distinction of being burned, with Hobbes' *Leviathan*, by the University of Oxford in 1683); to begin with, it was works particularly dealing with Mary, the *Detectioun* and the History of Scotland, which were published, and then in 1715 came

Thomas Ruddiman's *Opera Omnia Georgii Buchanani*. There was also the publication of various other sources relating to Mary, such as the *Collections relating to Mary Queen of Scots* by James Anderson (1727–8); and the first critical edition of John Knox's *History of the Reformation in Scotland* (1732). And then in the mid eighteenth century the storm broke, when in 1754 the antiquary and historian William Goodall published *An examination of the letters said to be written by Mary Queen of Scots to James earl of Bothwell; shewing by intrinsick and extrinsick evidence that they are forgeries.*

But the new interest had a significant twist. Violence, sexual scandal and murder had of course been seized on by Mary's sixteenth-century detractors as admirable means of blackening the character of a major political figure – particularly a female political figure. But what in the sixteenth century had been a highly convenient part of a wider whole, a matter of partisanship for immediate political and religious reasons, now took on an objective life of its own. The historical ruler, who might or might not have made disastrous political mistakes, gave way to the woman who might or might not have written the Casket Letters; and scholars plunged into the absorbing task of deciding whether letters whose originals had not been seen since 1584, and whose texts had been translated from French into Scots and then back into French, were forgeries or not.

Scholarly ink, mixed with scholarly gall, was poured forth upon this fascinating and wholly insoluble mystery. Goodall's own *parti pris* title showed clearly where he stood; and he inspired almost immediate counterblasts. Those great figures of the Enlightenment, William Robertson and David Hume, both argued for Mary's guilt of adultery (with Bothwell) and murder (of Darnley), on the grounds that the Casket Letters were genuine, in their histories of Scotland and England respectively which they published in 1759; and they in turn were attacked a year later by William Tytler, in his *Historical and Critical Enquiry into the evidence against Mary Queen of Scots*. The complaint of the contemporary historian David lord Hailes that 'the Marian controversy has already become too angry and too voluminous' was prophetic. The hurricane would never blow itself out; and at its eye was a figure already taking on the lineaments of a familiar enough twentieth-century 'type', the male-dominated, passion-ridden female so well-known to the readers of the novels of Barbara Cartland.

Even in this era of psycho-history, it is impossible to think of any other historical character of note whose public persona has been so submerged, and private morality so relentlessly pursued with such ruthless subjectivity on the part of those who have written about her. Titles like *Mary Stuart, Queen and Woman* by June Meade (pseudonym, 1933), or *A Tribute to the Memory of Mary Queen of Scots: being an attempt to relate simply and truly the history of her life* by J. B. and E. M. Rose (1868), do not obviously suggest serious historical study, but are rather part of a long series of more popular works on Mary, in which Jean Plaidy and Madeleine Bingham are among the most recent exponents; and there is a certain charm about the publication, in 1793, of a work by one J. F. Gaum, *Marie Stuart und Marie Antoinette in der Underwelt. Zwo Koniginnen uber ihre Schicksale in der Oberwelt. Eine Unterredung.* But it was surely more than a matter of stylistic fashion which prompted the Jesuit scholar Fr J. H. Pollen to preface his very useful collection of sources for the Babington Plot of 1586, designed to kill Elizabeth, published in 1922, with statements such as 'The interest attaching to Queen Mary's wonderful personality is so great, that when she is taken away, all else seems to fade into insignificance.'

The personal engagement encapsulated here is not, after all, wholly different from the introduction to that much more objective modern study, the justly acclaimed biography of Mary by Lady Antonia Fraser; for Lady Antonia describes how 'being possessed since childhood by a passion for the subject of Mary Queen of Scots, I wished to test for myself the truth or falsehood of the many legends which surround her'. The legends, of course, are primarily associated with the period from the Darnley marriage to the flight to England, 1565–8; and the next high point of drama came with her involvement in the Babington Plot and her execution in 1587. The balance of Lady Antonia's very long and extremely well-researched book reflects this exactly; she devotes 75 pages to the period of Mary's personal rule from 1561–5, compared to 137 for the years 1565–8 and 81 for 1586–7. In the course of her book, she gives us by far the most detailed and interesting portrait of Mary ever written, free from the excesses of adulation or attack which characterize so much of the writing about her. But as she was writing a personal biography, she inevitably concentrated on Mary at a very personal level, so that her book is rather familiar ground well trod by its author than a foray into new territory.

Lady Antonia's biography is the most substantial example of what may be regarded as the new and sober school of historians of Mary Queen of Scots. Professors Gordon Donaldson and I. B. Cowan have both tried to assess her as a character of history rather than drama, going further than Lady Antonia in considering her political role. Yet the drama and the dramatic personality still insistently break through. The new school is drawn as irresistibly as its predecessors to the great central mystery about Mary, her involvement in the murder of Darnley. That debate – and therefore the debate over the Casket Letters – is still very much alive. The most recent sustained attempt to resolve it, made by a Newcastle doctor, M. H. Armstrong Davison, is also the most recent example of the inexplicable difficulty of avoiding the temptation to become an advocate for the prosecution or defence of Mary Queen of Scots. Dr Armstrong Davison, captivated by the legend like so many others, began on the prosecution side, convinced by what he called the 'orthodox belief that Mary was a wanton and a murderess'. Ten years of study persuaded him that she was no such thing. If he did not go quite so far as Eric Linklater in believing that what Mary was doing down at Kirk o' Field during the last days of Darnley's life in February 1567 was indulging a 'womanly zeal for nursing', he certainly had no doubt of her innocence.

Yet in this book is a sub-theme which immediately raises a highly promising – and unexplored – line of enquiry; for the author remembered that he was a doctor, and added an appendix on Mary's medical history. Like Lady Antonia, he therefore drew attention to a very important fact about Mary. Wanton and murderess she may or may not have been. But hysteric she was, subject to the fatal political weakness of collapsing in time of trouble. The significance of this was not appreciated. So obsessed was he with Mary's charm and the Casket Letters, that it did not occur to him to ask the much more prosaic but crucially important question: what effect did it have on her kingdom, in this age of religious and political upheaval and trauma, to be saddled with a ruler who shut herself off from reality whenever reality became difficult?

There is one honourable exception to the problems of Marian historiography surveyed here. In 1983, Gordon Donaldson published his fascinating *All The Queen's Men*. This prosopo-graphical study of Mary's supporters and opponents certainly 'broke the mould', and indicated a way forward. But there is a long way to go. Professor Cowan rightly commented that

> the enigma (of innocent martyr or adulterous murderess, the dual legend created in the sixteenth century) will persist until histories of the Queen of Scots no longer command attention. Historians will never agree to her character, and in these circumstances, it is perhaps inevitable that the picture of a romantic but ill-fated queen painted by Schiller and Swinburne, amongst others, is the one most likely to engage popular sympathy.

No doubt. But there is an important implication here, which deserves to be explored. Until now, the question of Mary's personal behaviour has been all-important; what has mattered was to establish her guilt or innocence, as if that would be the end of the story. The Marian-centred approach has produced writing which ranges from the absurd and lurid to the scholarly and balanced – about Mary Queen of Scots. Though the last twenty years has seen a major step forward in our understanding of the Scottish Reformation and of Scottish society in the sixteenth century, there is still an extraordinary gulf between the personality and the reign of Mary Queen of Scots. Of course any early modern monarch's personality was of fundamental importance, in

Scotland or elsewhere, and to that extent seeking to understand Mary's personality is an entirely legitimate and necessary exercise. But Cowan's assertion shows all too clearly where the particular problem lies in the case of *this* ruler. Books about Mary the Woman – almost, one feels, Mary the little woman (if only metaphorically, given her physical size); books about her marriages, at the level of personal relationships; books about her Italian secretary Rizzio, Darnley and the Casket Letters; all these make her personality, whether good or evil, an end in itself. It is particularly ironic that a ruler in the age of Machiavelli should have caused such obsession with personal morality, or immorality – not least because her reign produced the first politician in the British Isles, her secretary William Maitland of Lethington, who was described as 'machiavellian'.

What far too few historians have done is to treat this monarch as other monarchs are treated, and to ask what effect her sex and her personal relationships and actions had on her subjects and kingdom. The business of the historian is not to love or to hate Mary Stuart, to judge her as a saint or a criminal, but to ask about the success or failure of her rule. For example: it can be said at once – and briefly – that the probability that she was massively involved in the murder of Darnley is very strong. If she was not, then she must have been almost the only member of Edinburgh political society who managed to know nothing about it – and that in itself would be a comment on her political awareness. If she was, then it is for her God to judge her personal action – and for the historian to wonder whether this was not one of the most sensible political decisions she ever made.

Although the most recent writings on Mary have taken us away from the image of pantomime villainess or fairy queen, created in the sixteenth century and revived with such enthusiasm in the eighteenth and thereafter, and provided us instead with a human being of more believable proportions, nevertheless Mary still remains an infinitely more shadowy figure as queen of Scotland than her Stewart predecessors and successors. We know that she came to grief. We do not yet really know why. But we can be fairly confident, as a starting-point, that Rizzio, Darnley and Bothwell, chief actors in the drama of the last two years of her personal rule, are at best only a part of the explanation. In June 1561, just before the personal rule began, Elizabeth's ambassador Nicholas Throckmorton warned her that 'your realm is in no other case at this day, than all other realms of Christendom are', by which he meant torn by religious controversy and conflict; in the twentieth century, J. H. Elliott was to characterize this period as the decade of revolution, when Scotland was only one of eight countries including France, Spain, the Netherlands and England which experienced upheaval and revolt. That takes us very far away from the little local Scottish drama; and it is in this context that Mary's reign should be understood.

This book therefore is not just 'another on Mary Queen of Scots', in the sense of being another personal biography. Antonia Fraser's admirable book has entirely filled that need. It is about Mary as a mid sixteenth-century monarch. That must mean a new balance. In her forty-four year life, Mary ruled for only six, so that we are faced with another thirty-eight years when she had virtually no role in her kingdom, being a minor and absentee ruler for the first nineteen, and a deposed queen for the second. A study of Mary as queen rather than as a woman of great misfortune and ultimate tragedy necessitates discussion of what was happening when the central figure of the monarch was off-stage, and especially before her debut, when the scene of her rule was set; the problems which her absence created, and the way in which others struggled to resolve them are as relevant as the short period of her personal reign. Moreover, when turning to that short period, the spotlight cannot be focused exclusively on the drama of the last two years. It must be deployed also on the hitherto comparatively neglected first four years of the reign, that brief part of her life which is the only one which can be considered in any way typical for a reigning monarch. In this period alone – the period of normality – do we have the chance to assess her abilities, or lack of them, as queen. Above all, it is essential to regard her not as *sui generis*, but as one of a line of Scottish monarchs.

This brings us to the question central to the understanding of Queen Mary: the nature of Scottish monarchy, and the factors which made the relationship between kings and their subjects successful or unsuccessful. It is a question not answered by the superficial assumptions about the impossible Scottish nobility found in so many of the books about Mary, in stage-plays such as Bolt's *Vivat Regina* and in the celluloid romanticizing of Hollywood and Hal Wallis. This book will not provide a definitive study of the reign of Mary Queen of Scots; such a study lies far in the future, if it can ever be achieved at all. It seeks only to open up the lines of enquiry sketched out here; and it does so in the hope that by bringing them into the debate, it may contribute towards a fuller and more objective assessment of Mary's reign – and Mary's misfortunes.

CHAPTER TWO

The Queen's Inheritance
1424–1542

On 4 April 1558, shortly before her marriage to the French dauphin, Mary Queen of Scots signed away her Scottish kingdom to France, in three secret agreements. First, she made a free gift of Scotland, and her claim to England, to the French king, should she die without issue; second, she put her country in pawn, for the money spent by France in defending it and educating her; and third, she negated in advance any agreement between her and the Scottish Estates which ran counter to her disposal of Scotland in the interests of France. Seven months later, when Mary Tudor died, her father-in-law Henri II had her proclaimed queen of England, Scotland and Ireland, and she began publicly to assume the royal arms of England. Young as she was, these might be considered the most revealing political acts of her life. They stand as a devastating comment on her view of Scotland, the one kingdom which was actually hers to govern. Yet their significance has been consistently played down. It is simply not enough to accept, almost as if it were an understandable and reasonable attitude, that Mary preferred to remain in France, and dream of the English throne, rather than return to Scotland. For much more was at stake than an individual's choice of where she wanted to spend her life. The very year when Mary offered her kingdom to France saw the death of the Holy Roman Emperor Charles V, that colossal and most admired figure of the sixteenth century, who had achieved the impossible by holding together an inheritance which sprawled across Europe. The contrast with Mary Queen of Scots could not be more stark. In an age when personal monarchy was the motivating force of government, and kings were straining every nerve to increase their power and authority, she provides the unique spectacle of an adult reigning monarch who did not want to reign.

As it happened, the death of her husband after a brief period as king of France, and Mary's failure to find a replacement in the royal houses of France or Spain, forced her back to Scotland. Most of the subsequent writing on Mary Queen of Scots has stressed the immense, even intolerable burden placed on the shoulders of this young and carefully nurtured girl, when at the age of eighteen she was driven from the civilized country of France, where she had lived since she was five, to the backward and lawless kingdom of Scotland. In the context of personal biography, this view may be legitimate enough. But it is not the whole story; and it is certainly not the correct starting-point. Reluctance and preconceived distrust of one's subjects, such as Mary showed, are a quite abnormal approach to royal rule, and one which was bound to make its own abnormal impact on her country. The extent to which her attitude violated the traditions of her kingdom is therefore the critical question which underlies all the problems of her reign.

Effective rule of any kingdom necessarily depends on an understanding of its particular characteristics. And here Mary did have an obvious problem; what could she have learned about Scotland? When she did return to her kingdom, what she saw was, inevitably, very small-scale and impoverished compared to what she had known in France. What she undoubtedly failed to see was just how remarkable her Scottish kingdom was, both in its political life and in its perceptions of itself and other nations. This may not appear surprising; it was certainly a serious drawback for Mary as queen that her upbringing had given her only second-hand knowledge of her country.

She was one of two Stewart monarchs who had this experience, the other being James I (1406–37), who was an English prisoner for the first eighteen years of his reign. Both were naturally affected by what happened to them. But it was one thing for James I to have his ideas influenced by Scotland's natural enemy, England. It was quite another for Mary to spend her childhood and adolescence in the most powerful and civilized country in Europe, which was also Scotland's traditional ally, so that she might assume that what she learned there was not the product of hostile bias. And what she seems to have done was to listen too attentively and unquestion-ingly to ideas about Scottish barbarity and backwardness, and, crucially, Scottish lack of respect for their kings. She was not alone, of course, in making the unwarranted assumption that an unruly Scots noble was in some way a fundamentally different and far more dangerous animal than an unruly French, or English, one; generations of historians, up to modern times, have seriously distorted the history of Scotland by taking exactly that view. But what in the case of the academics has simply been misleading, for a reigning queen was to have profound and ultimately disastrous political consequences.

Difficult though it was for her, however, are we entitled to assume that her French upbringing was bound to give her an adverse picture of her Scottish kingdom, and that her view was justified? It was certainly true that, as far as outside observers were concerned, Scotland was unlikely to get a very good press. Apart from any other consideration, this age of travel and commentary was also the age of the emergent nation-state, with all the navel-gazing pride which that engendered. The English, for example, were famed for their assumptions of innate superiority. 'The English are great lovers of themselves, and of everything belonging to them', wrote the Venetian diplomat Andrea Trevisano at the end of the fifteenth century; 'they think that there are no other men than themselves, and no other world but England; and whenever they see a handsome foreigner, they say that he "looks like an Englishman" and that "it is a great pity that he should not be an Englishman"', words echoed exactly in 1521 by the Scottish scholar John Major; while the German knight Nicolas von Popplau, who visited England in 1484, found a people who regarded themselves as the wisest in the world.

The fifteenth-century Germans were themselves building on earlier traditions of *Germania* to create, despite appalling practical difficulties, the idea of the *deutscher Nation*, presided over by the Holy Roman Emperor – *Teutscher Kaiser*, as he was described by the chronicler Hartmann Schedel in 1492. Spain, its two kingdoms brought together by the dual monarchy of the Catholic Kings,

Ferdinand and Isabella, and beginning to benefit from the riches of the New World, was emerging out of its previous isolation and preoccupation with internal affairs to become one of the two dominant powers of Europe. And if national sentiment in the other, France, was initially a response to the threat from England, just as it was in Scotland, there was no doubt of France's position by the end of the fifteenth century; the dazzling army and glittering artillery train which Charles VIII led down through the length of Italy in 1494 – for no good reason other than that a young king, with a well-stuffed treasury, would naturally use his wealth to win military renown – symbolized in the most spectacular manner what this kingdom, so recently weakened by war and internal dissension, had now become.

None of this left much room for openly expressed admiration for other countries, particularly small and peripheral ones. We know what Mary's adopted country thought. Some time before her marriage to the dauphin in November 1558, a memorandum was drawn up describing 'L'Etat et puissance du royaulme d'Escosse'. It was hardly flattering, with its account of the miserable climate – the vehement cold and the winds – and the forbidding landscape, with many rough mountains (for it was to be another two centuries before Rousseau was to alert the attention of Europe to the beauty of mountain scenery). The people were said to be lazy, their manner of living rustic. They were '*assez fins, astutes et inconstans daffection*' [sufficiently subtle, astute and inconstant in affection] – a very unattractive lot, in other words, apart from those courtiers who had been brought up in France. On the face of it, the crown had a very raw deal. Little justice could be done, especially among the nobility, obsessed as they were by family pride and the need to revenge their kin; instead, in order to attract them to his service, the king had to remit the penalty of death. He had no great domain; many of the nobles and churchmen – and especially the latter – were richer and more powerful than he. Nor could he tax: he simply did not have the power to levy impositions like the *taille* and the *gabelle*, as the French king did. The saving grace here was very much played down: that instead of being taxed, every man at his command had to muster armed under his chief. It was the comment by a member of one kind of society on a quite different one, poorer, less directly governed from the centre, and therefore to be despised. It was a subjective, not an objective view; but it happened to be the attitude of a man living in the kingdom which harboured Mary Queen of Scots.

Another way of making the same point about the superior and the inferior societies of France and Scotland came from the pen of the French ecclesiastic Estienne Perlin, who visited England and Scotland in 1551–2. His account showed that French antagonism to England was still very much alive; but of Scotland: 'how happy oughtest thou to esteem thyself, O kingdom of Scotland, to be favoured, fed and maintained, like an infant, on the breast of the most puissant and magnanimous King of France, the greatest lord in the whole world, and future monarch of that round machine, for without him thou wouldst have been laid in ashes, thy country wasted and ruined by the English, utterly accursed by God'. He was to add that the French should also be glad to be allied to the Scots, 'for from Scotland we may repulse the English, and from thence enter easily into their country, which gives no great odds against them, and thus enables us to curb and check them'. There was no doubt who was the junior partner! For Mary Queen of Scots, who, as Lady Antonia Fraser has reminded us, had been conscious all her life that she was a queen regnant, there was therefore a considerable problem. Queen in her own right, yes; but only of that junior partner, while being fêted and ultimately enjoying the pleasures of being queen consort of the senior. It was to be – at best – a confusing experience.

But there is a difference between a confusing experience and an insoluble problem. Mary was indeed brought up in a country far wealthier and more powerful than that which she was to rule. From her point of view, wealthier and more powerful was probably synonymous with easier and more rewarding, though it is questionable whether those who actually had to rule early modern France would have seen it in quite these terms. But the dismissive reactions of the French were by no means the only way in which foreigners described the Scots. For all outsiders, it was common ground that Scotland was indeed small, geographically remote, and impoverished. This only makes it the more significant that contempt and disdain were very far from the whole story of foreign attitudes, and where they were expressed there was normally some particular reason for it. The bias of that early fifteenth-century visitor Aeneas Piccolomini, the future Pope Pius II, for example, was natural enough. Having had a gruesome storm-tossed journey, his first act on landing was to fulfil his vow to travel barefoot to the nearest shrine in thanksgiving for his delivery; the rheumatism which resulted was with him for the rest of his life – as was the sourness with which he regarded Scotland.

It is not surprising either to find that English visitors were hostile; the notable point is that their real venom was unleashed not in the period before 1560, when England and Scotland were nourishing their long-standing enmity, but afterwards, when they were officially allies, and particularly once the unthinkable and shameful had happened, and Scotland had given England a king, in the person of James VI in 1603. Thus it was not until 1598 that an English account – by the scholar, traveller and self-consciously perfect English gentleman, Fynes Morrison – was actually redolent with patronizing contempt, and only in 1617 that there was a complete hatchet job, when Anthony Weldon accompanied James VI and I to Scotland and found the experience utterly abhorrent.

Even in that period, reactions were not always as bad as these; in 1618 the water-poet John Taylor had a wonderful Scottish holiday (having gone there, as a result of a bet with Ben Jonson, without money, so that his account stands as a testimony to the generosity of the Scots). But the general line is understandable enough. There were few English visitors to Scotland in any case. Those who did go before 1560 were writing about a country which the English wanted to conquer. It might be contemptible, but it still had to be worth conquering; and the fifteenth-century verse chronicle by John Hardyng, which demonstrated that Scotland, with its three fair university cities and fruitful countryside, could easily victual incoming English armies, makes the point very well.

By contrast, English anxiety to forget about Scotland – and to persuade their Scottish king to forget about his northern kingdom – produced a much less ambivalent reaction.

But there were also those who were neither ambivalent nor hostile, but impressed – normally to their surprise – by what they saw. For one thing at least the Scots enjoyed a generally high reputation: they were hardy and courageous fighters. Even the English paid grudging tribute to this; those who accompanied Margaret Tudor north in 1503, for her marriage to Mary's grandfather, James IV, were less than gracious about the elaborate and highly expensive entertainment provided by the king, but their contempt was mitigated, for they 'returned into their country giving more praise to the manhood than to the good manner and nurture of Scotland'. That 'manhood' was something which served the fifteenth-century kings of France well, when Scottish aristocrats and soldiers of fortune went to fight in their armies against the English; from their number, Charles VII created the prestigious Scots guard in 1446. And from that centre of chivalry, the Burgundian court, came the nobleman Jacques de Lalain in 1448, to challenge James, brother of William earl of Douglas, 'neither for hatred nor envy nor any evil wish whatsoever, but to do the greatest honour in his power to one who came of such high descent, and was besides of such great renown and courage, that he desired his acquaintance more than that of any lord in the said kingdom of Scotland'. Three Burgundians therefore met three Scots in a tournament at Stirling presided over by James II, which began with all the appropriate pomp and ceremony, and then acquired all the merits of a punch-up, which the Burgundians duly won three-nil. Honour was thereby satisfied. The Scots had lost – but members of the most dazzling court in Europe, the model for the kingdoms of northern Europe, found that they were worth visiting, and they were worth fighting.

Another who seems to have greatly appreciated his visit to Scotland was the Spanish ambassador Don Pedro d'Ayala, who wrote an account of the country at the desire of Ferdinand and Isabella in 1498. Like the French and Burgundians, d'Ayala was aware of the fighting qualities of the Scots; it was indeed, he claimed, because they preferred fighting to work that the country was poor, rather than because of a lack of natural resources. He was highly enthusiastic about the women, whom he compared very favourably with their English counterparts for their courtesy, their ability to manage their households and even their husbands, their grace, and the beauty of their head-dresses. He also lavishly praised the king, James IV, for his learning, love of his religion, humanity and political skill, although he expressed grave and prophetic doubts about the courage which toppled over into foolhardiness in war. What he says about the king's own explanation for his forwardness in battle is one of a number of examples of d'Ayala's perception of the Scottish kingdom: 'He (the king) said to me that his subjects serve him with their persons and goods, in just and unjust quarrels, exactly as he likes, and that therefore he does not think it right to begin any warlike undertaking without being himself the first in danger.' The words are an echo of the great series of Scottish bonds of protection and service – maintenance and manrent – made from the mid fifteenth to the early seventeenth century by the nobles and the lairds; the only difference is that rather than being completely mutual, as these bonds were, the king had the confident assurance that his subjects would serve 'exactly as he likes' – a confidence very far removed from the idea that Scottish kings were in any way at the mercy of their most powerful subjects. But perhaps most interesting of all is d'Ayala's thumb-nail sketch of the Scots:

> the people are handsome. They like foreigners so much that they dispute with one another as to who shall have and treat a foreigner in his house. They are vain and ostentatious by nature. They spend all they have to keep up appearances. They are as well dressed as is possible to be in such a country as that in which they live. They are courageous, strong, quick and agile. They are envious (?jealous) to excess.

It is perhaps a pity that Mary Queen of Scots was not brought up on a diet of d'Ayala. For this passage very accurately and very succinctly encapsulates the characteristics of the Scots of the fifteenth and sixteenth centuries. Those who observed the Scots without the disadvantages of succumbing to rheumatism or feeling the humiliation of having failed to conquer them – or having been brought up in luxury in France – could see beyond the poverty to these characteristics. The Scots were, in fact, an amazing success story; and that success came from their pride, and their enthusiasm for the world outside. The people whom Mary came to rule in Scotland were not simply able to rest on their laurels of size, wealth and power, like the French whom she had ruled as queen consort; nor were they introspective and xenophobic, like the English whom she wanted to rule. It was indeed precisely the combination of as much 'national' pride as was to be found among the greater kingdoms of Europe, with far less material resources on which to base it, which made Scotland so unusual. The Scots had compensated for the lack of indigenous wealth by developing a tradition, over the previous century and a half, of regarding themselves as far more powerful, more important, more interesting than their remote geographic position and comparative poverty actually entitled them to be. In other words, they created a self-image and then sold it to the greater powers of western Europe; and whatever their reaction, be it incredulous, admiring or contemptuous, these powers now found it impossible to ignore the Scots' insistent demands that they should be noticed. It was a remarkable achievement.

It all stemmed from the fact that England had tried for almost a century to conquer Scotland – and failed. That failure owed as much to English inability to sustain their efforts for long enough as to successful Scottish resistance. This was especially so after the death of Edward I in 1307, and in particular when Edward III decided to turn his imperialist ambitions against France. But the hostilities also included the spectacular and almost unique victory of a Scottish army over an English one, at Bannockburn in 1314.

In the 1370s, when the real struggle was over, and the southern Scottish nobility were cheerfully driving the English out of such border territory as they still held, the failure to conquer the Scots produced one of the great literary epics, *The Brus* by John Barbour. This poem extolled the achievements of Robert Bruce and Sir James Douglas – the Good Sir James – and directly appealed to the patriotism of the Scots. Shortly afterwards came the *Chronica Gentis Scottorum* of John of Fordun, again stressing the achievements of the Scots, and the villainy of Edward I. This was followed up in the early fifteenth century by the verse chronicle of Andrew of Wyntoun, prior of Lochleven. The quality of the poetry might have left something to be desired, but not the subject matter. For Wyntoun broadened out the whole context of Scottish history, invoking the model of the fourth-century *World Chronicle* of Eusebius of Caesarea in order to set it, as John MacQueen has written, 'firmly within the framework of the Christian world-picture, and by so doing to demonstrate the links joining the Scottish monarchy and people to the overall providential scheme'. Then came the most popular of the late medieval works, Walter Bower's *Scotichronicon*, written in the mid fifteenth century, heavily dependent on Fordun, and heavily nationalist. Its famous colophon

Non Scotus est, Christe,
Cui liber non placeat iste

has been translated 'he is no good Scot, O Christ, to whom this book is not pleasing', and good Scots duly enjoyed their Bower.

Scottish pride was given a further boost in the 1470s by the second of the great epics about the Wars of Independence, *The Wallace*, written by the poet known as Blind Hary. The image was well established; and it is hardly surprising that when, in 1521, the canny and obsessively fair-minded scholar John Major produced his book entitled *A History of Greater Britain*, in which he argued that better relations with England would make good sense, for political and economic reasons, the plea fell on ears deafened by the awareness that a little nation had fought off a monster by courage and tenacity. It was heady knowledge. And Major himself, an unusually objective Scottish commentator who was not averse to criticizing his fellow-countrymen, is good testimony to the result. 'I am not able to acquit the Scots of this fault (pride)', he wrote; and 'ill est fier comme ung Escossoys' (he is as proud as a Scot) was his record of what the French thought of the matter.

The effects of Scottish resistance were not, however, only confined to literary creation. The hostility between Scotland and England began at the end of the thirteenth century with the Scottish succession crisis caused by the death of Alexander III in 1286 and of his only direct heir, his granddaughter Margaret Maid of Norway, in 1290. This left the throne to be fought over by thirteen competitors and the kingdom vulnerable to the ambitions of Edward I. Wars resulting from territorial ambitions were in no way unusual. But the particular psychological shock involved in this one arose from the fact that for the previous two centuries family ties among the landholding classes of England and Scotland and inter-marriage between the royal families had made relations between the two countries very close. Lingering in the background was the English claim to overlordship of Scotland, occasionally dragged out as a diplomatic counter to Scottish military ambitions on England's northern border; but these neither seriously interrupted the peace between the two countries nor undermined Scotland's status as an independent kingdom.

The Wars of Independence which began in the 1290s and lasted into the late fourteenth century changed that situation radically. Anglo-Scottish trade came virtually to a halt, and did not begin to pick up again until the late sixteenth century. Scottish scholars stopped going to the English universities; the veneer of English influence on Scottish law and judicial practice was torn away. The Scots had not only to reconstruct their self-image, but also to build up contacts with new friends and allies, the main but by no means the only one being France. The result was dramatic. As the south of Britain became hostile territory, the Scots ceased to be north Britons, and became enthusiastic Europeans.

Thus when the two English universities closed their doors, the Scots in the fifteenth century founded three, St Andrews, Glasgow and Aberdeen: an admirable example of the new Scottish combination of pride at home and interest abroad, in that these foundations were to remain largely first-degree colleges. Scottish graduates went on to the major foreign universities, notably to Paris, and to Cologne, Louvain, Bologna and Montpellier. Hector Boece, first principal of Aberdeen, and John Major, teacher of Calvin (though with results which that learned theologian would never have desired), were luminaries of the university of Paris. Boece was the friend of Erasmus; and Erasmus became the tutor of James IV's illegitimate son Alexander, Archbishop of St Andrews, whose death at Flodden he mourned with the most moving grief.

Foreign scholars as well as foreign diplomats found to their surprise that where they had been led to expect barbarity, they found civilization and love of learning; for Giovanni Ferrerio, who settled in the abbey of Kinloss, close to the university of Aberdeen, Girolamo Aleandro, teacher of Greek and Hebrew at Paris, and Girolamo Cardano, physician of Milan, Scottish scholars were welcome members of the academic community of Europe. Scottish merchants grumbled rather more about the new dispensation; they were perfectly willing and able to be Europeans, but any outlet for trade would do, and there were complaints – in 1524, for example – about the Auld Alliance with France, because it affected their opportunities not only in Flanders and Spain, but also in England. But they were hardly doing badly, with their wide area of trading networks operating in Scandinavia, western and also eastern Europe. In general, fifteenth- and sixteenth-century Europe was well accustomed to the appearance of Scottish scholars, merchants and soldiers of fortune, as settlers or visitors; and by the mid sixteenth century, their presence was felt, on both sides of the divide, in the religious revolution. In the words of Luther's great disciple Melanchthon, it was 'a Parisian sophist, a blind Scot', the Catholic Robert Wauchope, who drew up the Tridentine decree on justification, and it was Melanchthon's Scottish friends Alexander Alesius and John McAlpine who, as professors of theology, spread the Protestant gospel at Frankfurt and Copenhagen. Scotland may have been a remote country. But there was nothing remote about the Scots.

We can still get a profound sense of all this today from that astonishing visual image of Scottish self-awareness, the heraldic ceiling of St Machar's cathedral in Aberdeen, constructed by bishop Gavin Dunbar between 1519 and 1522 and, as David McRoberts said in his account of it, 'quite unique in Europe'. For 'it is not just a decorated ceiling; it is a vision of the political situation of Scotland and Christendom'. It displays forty-eight coats of arms, in three lines of sixteen. The central series consists of the arms of the pope, Leo X, the thirteen archbishops and bishops of Scotland, plus the prior of St Andrews, and the university of Aberdeen; on the right are the arms of the king of Scotland, James V, St Margaret, the major nobles, and the royal burgh of Aberdeen; and on the left, the arms of the Holy Roman Emperor, Charles V, the principal European kings and dukes – and the burgh of Old Aberdeen. From locality to Christendom: that was the range of vision of leading Scotsmen, kings, churchmen and nobles – transmitted, we may assume, to all those who sat in St Machar's, their attention on the clergy at the altar distracted by what soared above them.

It was all presided over and to a large extent inspired by a line of kings who personified and embodied the aspirations of this impressive little kingdom. If other powers saw Scotland mainly as France's back door to England, this was certainly not the view taken by the kings of Scotland themselves, who roared for attention, like the most demanding of lusty infants. In the 1450s, James II wrung concessions out of the papacy, offered to arbitrate in a dispute between the king of France and the dauphin, and ran an aggressive foreign policy towards England. In 1469, during the reign of James III, Scotland was first described as an 'Impyre' – sixty-four years before the much better known claim of Henry VIII to the same effect. The king had himself portrayed on the last coinage of his reign, issued c.1485, wearing the closed crown of the emperor, at much the same time as Henry VII introduced the style into England; but James went one better by having himself shown in a realistic three-quarters face portrait, thereby producing what the numismatist Ian Stewart has described as 'probably the earliest Renaissance coin portrait outside Italy'.

He was also to obtain the first formal recognition from the

pope of the right of the crown to nominate holders of major benefices, before the kings of either France or Spain; and he indulged grandiose dreams of annexing continental territories. James IV, most charismatic of the Stewarts, was, like his father, the crucial intermediary in negotiations between France and Denmark. His passionate ambition was to lead a crusade against the Turks, and in so doing to unite Christendom – a vision which anticipated that of Charles V, and a policy which was to be a major preoccupation of both Charles and Philip II throughout the sixteenth century. James was foiled mainly by the determination of the European powers, including the Warrior Pope Julius II, to fight one another instead, and certainly not by any substantial doubt on the part of his subjects that a king from Scotland was overreaching himself; indeed, his popularity was to bring him an enormous Scottish army for the campaign against the English in 1513 which ended in the disaster of Flodden. By contrast, his son James V was the most terrifying of his line; but he was no less successful. His continuing loyalty to the Catholic church was sought, and well rewarded, by the popes Clement VII and Paul III, as Protestantism spread in Europe, and even into England. More generally, he was certainly the most effective in making his mark abroad; he was the most sought-after of them all in the European marriage market, which was both highly profitable and rewarding to morale when this Scottish king succeeded where an English one failed and Mary of Guise became James's second wife, rather than Henry VIII's fourth.

Clearly not all the ambitious schemes of the Stewart kings were successful. James III's idea of soldiering abroad, for example, to win renown and territory in Brittany and the county to the south, Saintonge, and in Gueldres, was blocked by resistance at home; in 1473 parliament tartly pointed out that if renown was what he was after, what he should be doing was 'to travel through his realm and put such justice and policy in his own realm that the brute and the fame of him might pass in other countries'. That was only in part because of good sense. The different reactions to the military adventures of James III and James IV owe much to that most fundamental aspect of rule, the ability to evoke enthusiasm and affection – love, as contemporaries would have said; the former failed to inspire what the latter clearly got in such great measure that the Scots were willing to countenance the idea of a crusade against the Turks, and in 1513 were even prepared to break the habit of more than a century, of avoiding major pitched battles with the English. More important, James IV lived in what J. R. Hale has described as a new age – the age when European wars became more than a matter of 'violent housekeeping'. The date of the change was 1494, the year of Charles VIII's Italian campaign, beginning the destructive French, and therefore Spanish, involvement in Italy which was to be such a dominant theme in European politics and war in the sixteenth century. James III, lacking the French treasury, had had much the same idea – twenty years too soon. His son could capitalize on the mood of the moment, and thereby once again remind his Scottish subjects that they were not mere inhabitants of 'the outpost of mankind', but mainstream, up-to-date Europeans.

That is the crucial point about this amazing monarchy, with its ridiculous assumptions about itself. It consistently indulged in *folies de grandeur* – and somehow it made them believable. The fact that it managed to do so stands out with a clarity so insistent that each individual ruler – including Mary Queen of Scots – must be assessed by the extent to which he or she successfully fostered the self-perception that the Scots were a people who mattered. But we are still left with the problem of just how the Stewart monarchy could achieve what it did.

The answer surely lies in the very curious political situation of early modern Scotland. To begin with, the reality of Scotland's position in Europe meant that she was not vulnerable to attack from countries other than England. Who, after all, was particularly interested in annexing Scotland, other than her powerful neighbour to the south, to whom she was a threat because of her alliance with France? Her kings, in their self-determined role as European monarchs, were therefore in an unusually advantageous position. They were able to take a high line, look impressive, cut a dash –

on the cheap. It cost very little, after all, to demand to be heard, to involve themselves in European negotiations, as all of them did, to capitalize – as James V did with supreme ability – on the problems of popes and European kings. It might look all wrong to the author of 'L'Etat et puissance'; to him, kings who could not tax by definition lacked power as well as wealth. The point he missed was that they did not tax because they did not need to tax; he despised the Scottish crown for its failure to collect the infamous *taille*, but this had, after all, been introduced to France only because of the need to finance military expeditions. And it is, above all, rarity of war and absence of foreign adventuring which is the key to understanding early modern Scotland.

This had a profound effect not just on the monarchy's place in foreign affairs, but on its strength and prestige at home. Scotland was a state which was never burdened by excessive demands, for men or money. This immediately changed the normal rules about the relationship between governor and governed, significantly reducing tension and resentment between them. No early modern king in England or Europe, however wealthy and powerful, actually had the resources to control the localities in his kingdom; all had to persuade, to rely on the cooperation of those with influence in these localities. When, as in Scotland, little was asked, there was little need for strenuous efforts to direct and control local affairs from the centre, little to arouse opposition. The direct result of this was that government institutions, especially the bureaucratic side of government, were comparatively undeveloped; and to those precociously centralized kingdoms, England and France – and therefore, of course, to those who influenced Mary – Scotland appeared backward and less controlled.

It was the inevitable mistake made by those who equate bureaucratic efficiency with political stability. The fact that obligations of kinship and personal lordship, and the justice of the feud, were extremely effective methods of control in the localities of early modern Scotland naturally carried little conviction for societies who prided themselves on having advanced beyond these things; and since a long historiographical tradition has much preferred

28

kings who reduced the powers of their aristocracies, and signed their account books, the Scottish monarchy, whose power rested on quite different things, has not attracted much praise. Nevertheless, an instinct for splendour and the ability to give their kingdom importance were actually still far more fundamental aspects of Renaissance monarchy than the colder, more cautious approach of a Henry VII or Elizabeth, or even a Philip II; and in these terms, the achievement of the Scottish monarchy can indeed be described as remarkable.

There is no doubt of its instinct for splendour; the Stewart kings all had a taste for lavish spending, and the ability to find the money to indulge it. It was not actually the case that the crown *never* taxed. James I did, on the specious excuse of the ransom due to England for his release; James V blackmailed the papacy into allowing him to extort vast amounts of taxation from the church. And they had other ways of raising money. Remissions for crime, given as part of the justice of the feud when the victims of the crime or their kin had been satisfied, were not in fact a sign of weakness on the part of the crown, forced to acquiesce with an aristocracy resistant to justice, as the author of 'L'Etat et puissance' had suggested; they were the crown's part in a highly effective means of controlling crime, dispute and disorder. They were also financially advantageous. So were the compositions demanded for grants and privileges, particularly by James IV and V. In the same period, royal rents were increased as the crown converted its grants of land to feuferme, hereditary tenure for which its tenants paid heavily. And because all this money was not needed for war, it was available, and extensively used, to show its subjects that their monarchy lived in style and elegance.

These kings were, for instance, fully alive to the prestigious military developments of the day, and determined to add to their prestige at home by having them. Guns and ships fascinated the Stewarts. James II's marriage to Mary of Gueldres had the attraction of providing him with a queen who came from the great artillery-making centre of northern Europe. That monstrous bombard Mons Meg was heaved over from the Low Countries to Scotland.

Scarcely ever to be used in war – and as ineffective as so many of these guns were when she was – Mons Meg was nevertheless a source of pride then, and is admired to this day by visitors to Edinburgh Castle. James IV, idealistic and militaristic, 'first and foremost a warrior' as Dr Norman Macdougall has described him, spent at least £100,000 Scots (rather more than three years' income) on artillery and even more on his navy; £30,000 alone went on the building of the huge and spectacular *Great Michael*, a ship so impressive that it was promptly copied by Henry VIII, whose *Henri Grace à Dieu* was built virtually to the same specifications in 1512, a year after the *Michael's* completion. But this was a warrior king who had all the trappings but little of the reality of war. The trappings, the international tournaments which he staged, contributed considerably to his popularity and prestige at home and even his standing abroad. But expensive as these things were for a king of a small country, they were not the crippling drain on his purse that genuine warfare would have been. To that extent – until war eventually came in 1513, and with it his death – James IV undoubtedly had the best of both worlds, the pleasure but not the pain and the expense. It was a very effective balance.

The crown also gave a lead in secular architecture. Every king from James I to James V (though not Mary) built; as with the great guns and the great ships, so they managed to find money for the great buildings. Enough survives today to give a compelling impression of the extent to which the crown supplied visual evidence to its subjects of the splendour of Scottish monarchy; the buildings may be small-scale by comparison with those of wealthier kings, but they are also lovely, and imposing, and above all utterly fashionable. James I began the trend, with a vast and magnificent great hall on the site of the older royal manor of Linlithgow. At Stirling, James IV was to create an even more magnificent hall, of unprecedented size and great beauty; and the same king began the palace of Holyrood in Edinburgh.

But the most lavish and the greatest of the royal builders was James V, and he was also the most consciously French. The court-yard design of Linlithgow was completed under his inspiration;

it was this architectural gem of a palace which so impressed Mary of Guise, whose admiration was by no means merely wifely tact. The royal hunting-lodge of Falkland in Fife was transformed into a Renaissance palace, ornate with pilasters, medallions and allegorical statuary. At Stirling, he created the so-called palace block, with exteriors modelled on French palace architecture like those of Falkland and adorned with statues ranging from dignified sculpture to the grotesque – the latter seen in the splendid representation of the king himself. Inside, the ceiling of the Presence Chamber was decorated with the remarkable collection of oak roundels, the 'Stirling Heads', depicting members of the court, often satirically, and allegorical figures; only on the other side of Europe, in the Wawel palace at Krakow, is there any parallel.

As Dr David Starkey has pointed out, James's palace is today the best example in Britain of that style of royal architecture which had such an effect on the political life of the court. Whereas James I and James IV had built great halls, James V, like the first two Tudor kings, created a series of rooms, in Scotland described as the guard hall, the presence chamber and the bedchamber. The king no longer spent his time in the full company of his court in the hall. He could withdraw – and he could become inaccessible. The change from openness to selective accessibility fundamentally influenced the nature of factional politics at court. For this reason, as we shall see, the architecture of Holyrood palace was to be of crucial political importance in the reign of Mary Queen of Scots.

There were, then, good reasons for the very positive side of the Stewart monarchy. But there was another element in the creation of its unusual nature, one which appears at first sight a source of significant weakness rather than strength. Scotland between 1424 and 1542 was ruled by five kings of great personal power. All of them died leaving a minor to succeed. Royal minorities were things to strike fear; who would control the country in the absence of an adult king? 'Woe unto thee, o land, when thy king is a child.' Scotland's lot was, in these terms, woeful indeed. Yet the actual experience was surprisingly different. First, every king when he came of age had remarkably little difficulty in getting rid of the faction which had been dominant during the minority; Albany Stewarts, Livingstones, Boyds, Douglases, the families who had enjoyed power in the minorities of the fifteenth and early sixteenth centuries, all lost it when the king began his personal rule. It is a spectacle which takes us very far from the idea of lawless Scottish magnates. The evidence is that the magnates infinitely preferred strong royal rule to lack of it; for no king could have ousted powerful ruling cliques without support.

Second, and even more striking, it only took the experience of one minority (strictly speaking, in the case of James I, the absence of the king as an English prisoner) to produce the remarkable expedient of the Act of Revocation, which every king thereafter passed when he came of age. Nothing more clearly shows the power of the crown and the attitude of the aristocracy than this astonishing procedure by which kings revoked all grants made in their names during minority. The agreement certainly included the expectation that the king would regrant what he had revoked. But he did not need to do so; and he could make men pay heavily for the privilege of the regrant, as James V certainly did. If, therefore, minorities created insecurity, in Scotland it was not the crown but the nobility who suffered, making hay, no doubt, while the sun shone, but knowing that in the end the sileage would be the king's.

Moreover, the Stewart kings' lamentable habit of dying young had two consequences, both of which enhanced rather than diminished the strength and prestige of Scottish kingship. One was the absence of faction round an heir to the throne old enough to provide a focal point for political opposition. The only exception came in the last years of James III; in 1488, in the second and final crisis of his reign, his opponents could use his fifteen-year-old son, the future James IV, as their figurehead. The other consequence was that, if Stewart kings did not live and reign until a ripe old age, they had the immeasurable advantage of always having been kings; most were barely aware, some not at all, of any time in their lives when they had not worn the crown. Antonia Fraser's observation about Mary applies, in other words, to most of her Stewart predecessors. In their case, there seems no doubt that it greatly enhanced their belief in the strength of their royalty as kings of Scotland. The question which remains is how far Mary was to follow their example in linking her perception of her royalty to interest in the rule of her kingdom.

Finally, if absence of war created an acceptable balance between royal and local power, so the recurrent minorities created an acceptable level of royal rule. They, and they alone, provided a breathing space from a crown which was always harsh, even if occasionally leavened with the charisma of a James IV. They prevented the development of royal autocracy, even absolutism. For these kings could be frightening men; and kings who can frighten may not be 'nice people', but they will impose their kingship. A host of examples can be cited throughout the period of Stewart rule up to 1542; the fate of the mighty earls of Douglas at the hands of James II in the mid fifteenth century, the case, enshrined in ballad, of the over-confident border reiver Johnnie Armstrong, who suddenly found himself the victim of the utter ruthlessness of James V, tell the same story about how royal power was exercised in Scotland. It was only because it was repeatedly interrupted that it did not become all-pervasive, and ultimately intolerable.

How, then, can we characterize early modern Scottish kingship? It was certainly something which operated on two unusually distinct levels. On the one hand, Edinburgh was far less prevalent and oppressive, in the eyes of the kingdom at large, than Paris or London were already coming to be; great and small in the localities were on the whole left alone to live out their lives. But on the other hand, when the great came into contact with the king, when he held his councils and parliaments, when he decided that a mighty subject had stepped out of line, or had acquired too much power and wealth for himself, as happened to James V's former favourite Sir James Hamilton of Finnart, executed in 1540: *then* there was a high level of direct interventionist rule, very tough and irresistibly powerful. It was precisely that peculiar combination of *laissez-faire* rule over the kingdom at large, but absolute personal involvement with all that went on at the centre, in institutional as well as individual and personal affairs, which is the notable quality of kingship in Scotland and explains the high level of prestige and control which the crown enjoyed. Individuals could and did suffer at the hands of individual kings. But men in Scotland could look to the monarchy as the focal point and representative of their aspirations, not as the frustrator of them.

This, then, was Mary's inheritance: by a combination of political circumstances, luck, strong personalities on the throne and sheer nerve and drive, she was heir to a remarkably stable and remarkably outward-looking society, whose kings commanded a great deal of respect, and exercised a great deal of power. Indeed, the Stewart monarchy can be seen as having an unusually easy time, in comparison with the difficulties faced by others in imposing royal rule elsewhere in the fifteenth and sixteenth centuries. Much has been made of the fact that two fifteenth-century kings, James I and James III, came spectacularly to grief. They did; the first was assassinated in 1437, the second killed in battle in 1488. But comparison with the disasters which afflicted mid fifteenth-century Spain, and most of fifteenth-century England, immediately puts the Scottish experience into context; Scotland was undoubtedly fortunate in being spared the experience of a Henry IV of Castile or Henry VI of England. There was no challenge to the ruling house as such, no Wars of the Roses, no disputes over the legitimacy of heirs. There were no great magnate coalitions, such as the League of the Commonweal which assailed Louis XI of France.

In other words, Scotland had its share of political problems between the crown and its greatest subjects, and here, as elsewhere, these problems were sometimes resolved violently. The difference was that there was no hint whatsoever of any kind of collective or ideological opposition. All that happened was that individual kings and individual magnates or magnate families sometimes came into collision. It was politically very low-key. And the tally of crown successes over its opponents far outnumbers its few failures; Douglases, Crichtons, Livingstones, Erskines, Gordons, Hamiltons and many other members of aristocratic families who lost out to the crown over a huge range of disputes, from the heights of violent conflict to the crown's ability to beat off rival claimants to lands, would have been astonished by the belief of later historians that they were more powerful than the monarchy. In fact, every Stewart king between 1424 and 1542 was able to make his presence felt abroad precisely because he could impose it so effectively at home.

Whatever went wrong in the years of Mary's personal rule, therefore, simply cannot be explained by inherited weakness; her problems have nothing to do with insecure monarchy and overmighty subjects. More specifically, an analysis of Scottish kingship, and of the particular reasons for its strength, enables us to discard the lingering idea that Mary's failure was predetermined by the fact that she was a woman – and worse and more pathetic, a young woman. Youth itself was hardly a disadvantage, in an age when people were ruling kingdoms and leading armies in their teens; the Stewart kings themselves, all but one beginning his personal rule in his teens, two dead at thirty, and only one surviving beyond the age of forty, could hardly have waited for age and experience to bless their undertakings and achievements. To be a woman ruler of course posed problems, severely practical ones. Elizabeth's famous Armada speech – 'I know that I have the body of a weak and feeble woman, but I have the heart of a king and a king of England too' – and Mary's much-quoted desire to live the life of a soldier, wearing a Glasgow buckler and sleeping under the stars, are testimony to one (it is perhaps worth adding that the context for Elizabeth was fighting Spain, for Mary fighting her half-brother). Their different solutions to the question of marriage, neither of which was in any way adequate, are witness to another, even more serious.

Yet there are two reasons why Mary's sex will not explain her failure and downfall. First, the mid sixteenth century saw an astonishing rash of woman rulers: Mary Tudor, Catherine de Medici, Mary of Hungary, Margaret of Parma, Mary's own mother Mary of Guise. With the possible exception of the first, the ability and success of these women are unquestionable, even if they exercised power *faute de mieux*, against the natural order of things. The modern equivalent of Mary Queen of Scots might well be the unsuccessful businesswoman who owes her position to her family, and therefore profoundly irritates women who are achieving success – against the natural order of things.

Second, the problem of female rule was arguably less severe in Scotland than elsewhere. Scotland was still, by contemporary standards, an unusually localized country, in which the government impinged less; and it had two centuries of experience of long periods of royal minorities in which government and political life had to be kept going without the guiding hand of a monarch. For precisely these reasons, there was a well-developed substratum of social and political control at local level in the kingdom at large; and when people are accustomed to running affairs without any monarch at all, then the advent of a female ruler might well not be a substantial cause for concern. Lurking behind all this in Mary's case is, of course, the notion of the gentler sex, with all that entails; if nice men made bad kings, because successful kingship meant toughness and ruthlessness, how could the more emotional, gentler female hope to make a good queen? A string of female rulers, from Boudicca to Margaret Thatcher, gives the lie to that idea. In the end, success or failure was a matter not of sex, but of personality and political intelligence. Rulers who let their hearts rule their heads tended to court disaster, be they male or female; and there have been plenty of examples of both. It is therefore Mary the political animal, not Mary the female of the species, which has to be assessed.

This chapter has been concerned to sketch in the general background to the reign of Mary Queen of Scots, and to clear it of some of the misconceptions about Scottish kingship which have tended to confuse the issues. The advent of the Reformation, which began to influence Scotland from the 1520s, undoubtedly created new problems, and had a significant impact on political life and political relationships. And Mary was to arrive at precisely the time when the reformers were beginning to add a new dimension to Scottish self-perception. God particularly favoured the Scots;

and as it was a Protestant God who did so, the position of a Catholic queen was inevitably made more difficult. But the significance of the political and religious events of the mid sixteenth century, and in particular Mary's part in shaping them, can only be properly understood in the context of the traditional political and social patterns which had created the sixteenth-century Scottish kingdom. For the Scots would hardly have accepted the reformers' belief in God's especial guidance with such assurance had they not been long accustomed to think of themselves with a high level of worldly confidence.

This brings us back, finally, to the question of Mary's own attitude. She was of course aware that she came from a Catholic to a barely Protestant country in a state of intense flux and religious upheaval; her new subjects presented her with a set of pressing confessional and political problems. But behind the imminent business of dealing with the Scotland of the early 1560s lay the even more complex matter of appreciating the nature of her kingdom, and the particular qualities needed for successful royal rule. Had she tried to do so, she would have discovered what her predecessors had known well: that ruling this unusual little kingdom was not an infinitely inferior business to ruling France or England. It does not appear that she did try. For Mary, Scotland was a poor relation of France, which ranked only third in her interests as queen. She seems to have been wholly unaware that she was in fact queen of a kingdom with a justifiably high opinion of itself – so much so that it is actually supremely ironic that Mary, brought up in one of the greatest of European countries, should have found this one, smaller, but passionately European, so much less interesting and appealing than the kingdom of England, not only Scotland's traditional enemy, but already beginning the descent into the isolation which it was to maintain for much of the seventeenth century. Yet such was her view. But the answer to the question posed at the beginning of this chapter, whether her upbringing in France made this inevitable, must be no. Foreign observers were not universally dismissive; and the contact with Scotsmen which she had, particularly in the last year of her life in France, could have told her much, had she cared to listen. It was indifference, even a degree of antagonism, as much as available information, which dictated her approach.

This surely puts into perspective the fundamental problem of Mary Queen of Scots, which was neither a matter of sex nor of religion. It was her perceptions of her kingdom which differed so crucially both from those of earlier kings of Scotland (and, indeed, of her son James VI, who as James I was to infuriate his English subjects by his insistent interest in Scotland, and by his belief that his importance lay not in being king of England but in being a leading European monarch), and from those of her subjects. Because of these perceptions, many of the sources of confidence so completely associated with the monarchy – from its role in European affairs to its architecture – came to an end when Mary reigned; it was left to others to give a lead. The Scottish kingdom's pride in itself had been largely invested in the monarchy. By dissipating this investment she made her first, and her greatest political error.

CHAPTER THREE

The Minority: Mary's First Wooing
1542–50

On 14 December 1542, James V died in his splendid royal bedchamber at Falkland, the beauty he himself had created no longer enough to pierce the malaise of his profound melancholy. His sole surviving child, Mary, succeeded to the throne at the age of a week, and was crowned in the following September when she was nine months old; even by the standards of Scottish minorities, this was spectacularly young. The date of the coronation – an event regarded at the time as a rushed and shabby affair – has inspired comment, for it was the 13th, the thirtieth anniversary of the battle of Flodden. Since we may acquit the Scots of choosing a day of such apparent ill-omen because of their foreboding that Mary represented a new disaster, we have here a good example of their ability to recover self-confidence, and consign catastrophe to the past. They had need of all their self-confidence.

The survival of the Stewart line now hung by the thread of a baby's life, and not surprisingly Mary's health was one of the major worries of the first year of the reign. When the English diplomat Sir Ralph Sadler visited her mother, Mary of Guise, on 22 March 1543, the infant was duly unwrapped, so that her healthy state could be clearly seen, and Sadler could report that 'it is as goodly a child as I have seen of her age, and as like to live, with the grace of God'. For a frightening moment in July, it looked as though God's grace was withdrawn when Mary fell ill with smallpox. She recovered – though the royal nursery in Linlithgow can hardly have been a peaceful place, with its occupant combining convalescence with the more normal infant problem of teething; but she was entirely well by the time Sadler saw her again, in early August.

The question of whether the queen would survive was not the only problem created by James V's early death. There was now another minority, one which would in fact be the longest of them all, lasting for nineteen years. That in itself did not necessarily matter; experience had shown that Scotland could successfully cope with a series of minorities. But Mary's minority was to be very different from any of the earlier ones, for two reasons. The first was her sex. Unlike the infant boys of previous minorities, an infant girl would be a pawn in the marriage market – the traditional female role – but one who took with her to her husband not just a dowry but a kingdom. The choice of her husband was stark and unpalatable. She could be married abroad, in which case there was a danger of her kingdom becoming subordinate to that of her husband; or she could be married into a native aristocratic house, which would inevitably provoke rivalry, jealousy and faction.

That would have been a problem at any time. But the second reason why this minority would be different was wholly new and, as events would prove, would have consequences infinitely more far-reaching and important than the fact that the new ruler was female. For it was not a matter of the life of this particular ruler. Like every other country in western Europe, Scotland had felt the impact of the religious divisions sweeping Europe after 1517. Unlike other countries, she was now without an adult ruler to impose some sort of direction and control. Later examples would show just how serious this could be. Thus the death of Henri II in 1559 left France a prey to young and incompetent heirs and the internecine struggles known as the Wars of Religion; while, if on a less dramatic scale, the six-year minority reign of Edward VI saw less overt religious division but witnessed the fall of Protector Somerset at the hands of a rival faction, and a succession crisis at Edward's death. In Scotland, there would be an unprecedented level of faction fighting at home, and an equally unprecedented degree of intervention from England and France.

Scotland had of course been embroiled in the long-standing hostility between England and France before; but not until the 1540s and 1550s did these powers actually try to determine the government and internal affairs of the kingdom. The fact that they did so makes Mary's minority fall so clearly into two distinct parts. In the first period, up to 1548, Scotland seemed to be moving towards alliance with her traditional enemy, England, by then moving beyond Henry VIII's introspective and idiosyncratic brand of Catholicism to a more Protestant position; in the second, she swung back towards Catholic France. To express it thus is, as will become clear, to oversimplify the religious situation in both countries, and in Scotland. Nevertheless, the fates and fortunes of Catholics and Protestants alike within Scotland would be significantly and, in the end, decisively affected by her shifting relationships with England and France. Never before had events within Scotland been so firmly set on the international stage.

The warning note that it was all going to be very different this time was sounded right at the beginning, with the efforts to establish a minority government. In so far as any rules had been devised in the past, the principle seems to have been to give power to someone close to the throne, and invested therefore with some of the aura of royalty. Immediate adult royal relatives had been embarrassingly scarce; but there was usually a queen mother, who had at least personal legal rights as tutrix of her son. As it happened, the Stewart kings between 1406 and 1542 had married wives of considerable personality and, except in the case of Margaret Tudor, skill; in the power-sharing between Mary of Gueldres, widow of James II, and the then elder statesman, James Kennedy, bishop of St Andrews, during the early years of James III's minority, for example, it was the Queen Mother who pursued a much more intelligent foreign policy towards England than the bishop.

The disadvantage was that they were, inevitably, the greatest prizes in the domestic marriage market – and a target for scandal. When Mary Queen of Scots embarked on her headline-hitting affair with James Hepburn, earl of Bothwell, she not only created an immense drama for herself, but raised echoes of earlier headlines; for two previous queens, Mary of Gueldres and her own mother Mary of Guise were, if rumour could be believed, on the receiving end of the Hepburn family's habit of being 'kind to queens'. Most problematic of all was Margaret Tudor, widow of James IV, whose marital antics were less sensational than those of her brother

Henry VIII only in terms of number: three, rather than six. Her marriage to Archibald earl of Angus – whose name, with unwitting appropriateness, she spelt 'Anguisshe' – and subsequent divorce, combined with her demands for a place in political life, produced on one occasion the agonized response that she might have it if only she would be 'a good Scots women', and created continuing and profoundly irritating headaches for those who were trying to control Scottish affairs.

It is therefore no surprise that in the minority of James V the Scots turned with relief to the fact that this time there actually was a close royal relative, John duke of Albany, son of James III's brother; brought up in France, because of his rebellious father's exile, Albany was invited to Scotland as regent. His problems, as 'the Scot who was a Frenchman', were considerable. So it is worth bearing in mind, when considering the later reign of 'the Scot who was a Frenchwoman', that the story of Albany frantically 'cramming' on Scottish chronicles on the ship which brought him from France is a good pointer to the attitude of a man who managed, with some success, to understand and deal with the domestic problems of Scotland, even while caught in the intolerable welter of shifting relations between France and England, with their rival demands for Scottish support.

Inevitably political faction was a feature of the minorities. In each case, the faction which gained control of the king's person gained control of government. The Livingstones and Crichtons did this in 1439, when they seized James II and then settled down to squabble for the next decade; the Boyds did the same thing with James III; and Angus found time, despite his matrimonial problems with Margaret Tudor, to get possession of James V in 1526 and dominate politics for the last two years of the minority. But the important point about this manoeuvring is how essentially low-key it was. It operated within the limited confines of government at the centre, and in a society as localized as Scotland, did not necessarily have an impact on the domestic affairs of the country as a whole. Nor was it a regular determinant of foreign relations; the faction-fighting between Mary of Gueldres and bishop Kennedy was the exception rather than the rule. Such was the pattern up to and including the minority of James V. With Mary's, it became abundantly clear that the age of limited political struggles was over.

This was seen at the very moment of James V's death. It was entirely unexpected, and its cause a mystery, so much so that poison was inevitably suspected. The late sixteenth-century diplomat James Melville of Halhill wrote of the 'Italian posset' given to the king; the leading churchman, and one of the main contenders for power, David cardinal Beaton, archbishop of St Andrews, was of course the major suspect. But Melville's claim that James was 'vexed by some unkindly medicine' sounds more like a comment on sixteenth-century doctors than poisoners; and his other explanation, that he died 'for displeasure' – presumably some form of extreme nervous exhaustion – is probably as close as we can get to what happened.

Certainly for the king who died, and for the politicians who survived, the last two years of the reign had given few grounds for pleasure, in sharp contrast to the enormous activity and success of the previous decade. His two infant sons had died within a few days of one another in April 1541. In September of that year, he had taken a high line with Henry VIII, letting him trundle up to York only to gaze north at an empty road, for James, probably at the persuasion of his council, failed to keep his appointment with the English king. A year later, the sourness thus created flared into open aggression. The upshot was the appalling rout of the Scottish army by the English at Solway Moss on 24 November 1542. Three days before the battle, James had been with his army. Three weeks after it, he was dead. He left behind him a baby daughter, a huge political and religious crisis, and a power-struggle far more savage than had ever been experienced before, which began literally at the death-bed.

Historians are familiar with the events surrounding the death of Henry VIII in January 1547, and in particular the debate over the authenticity of his will. The situation in Scotland four years earlier was very similar. Four or five days after James's death, Beaton produced what purported to be James's will, nominating four protectors, himself and the earls of Moray, Argyll and Huntly. The notable omission was James Hamilton, earl of Arran, heir presumptive because of his descent from Mary, daughter of James II, who had married his grandfather James lord Hamilton, and Beaton's greatest political rival. The document survives today – in the Hamilton archives at Lennoxlove. It has one very curious feature; it was drawn up by one 'Henry Balfour, priest of Dunkeld diocese, notary public by apostolic authority', who was in fact no notary at all, and this did give ground for doubt. Indeed, John Knox was later to claim that after Beaton had cried into the dying king's ear that there should be four regents, with himself as principal, 'a dead man's hand was made to subscribe a blank'. This story improves on the original version emanating from Arran himself, that the king was almost dead when Beaton took his hand and traced his signature. In such circumstances, clearly the more vilification the better. It is a measure of what, this time, was at stake.

Just as at Henry VIII's death in 1547, what was at stake in 1542 was nothing less than the religious and political future of the kingdom; and that was entirely uncertain. For Scotland, like all other European countries, was now severely affected by the Reformation movement, which not only injected religious confusion and conflict into the church, but profoundly disturbed long-established political traditions, especially in foreign relations. Those who fought for political control after James V's death, therefore, were fighting for far more than personal position. It was no longer a matter of one family or political grouping showing that it was domestically more powerful than any other. Ideological commitments now affected political ambitions. It was a question of which faction would win, that which was at least potentially pro-English and Protestant, or that which wanted to maintain the status quo, pro-French and Catholic.

James's death, in fact, released a great deal which had been held in check during his reign. The king himself had strongly favoured the Auld Alliance with France, particularly as he had been able to use it so much to his advantage, and had certainly upheld the Catholic church. But the idea of closer political ties with England had first been mooted as far back as the late fifteenth century, by James III; and even though it was then an extremely unpopular policy, it was an idea which never again quite went away. The marriage of James's son James IV to Margaret Tudor, from which the Stewart claim to the English throne derived, came about more because of pressure from Henry VII than from any Scottish enthusiasm; and the Treaty of Perpetual Peace which accompanied it would last for no more than eleven years, collapsing because James could not sustain his obligations to both France and England when Henry VIII joined the pope's grotesquely named Holy League against France. It has been suggested that because Flodden was fought to serve French interests, Scottish hearts were hardened against their old ally after the disaster, and indeed there were striking examples of their refusal to fight on France's behalf thereafter, most notably the spectacle of the Scots sitting on the sidelines, as at a football match, while regent Albany's French troops engaged the English at Wark in 1523. But in fact it was Flodden which was a significant break in the pattern of cold rather than hot war with England, and after it the Scots simply reverted to their usual distant hostility.

During James V's personal rule, however, two new factors came into play, which shifted Scottish attitudes further along the road towards friendship with England rather than automatic hostility. One was Archibald, earl of Angus, driven out of Scotland by the king in 1528, and an exile in England until James's death. The other, and much more serious, was the growth of Protestantism. The early stages of the Reformation movement in Scotland have been played down, compared to the sudden rush to success of the Protestant party in 1559–60. But reforming ideas were already circulating from the early 1520s. The fact that the rector of the Aberdeen grammar school, Robert Marshall, was teaching Lutheran ideas from 1521, before having to recant in 1523, shows how quickly they had spread to Scotland; it was only four years earlier in 1517, that the little-known Augustinian monk had first startled Europe by sensationally nailing his ninety-five theses to the door of the castle church of Wittenberg.

In 1525, parliament was sufficiently alarmed by 'the damnable opinions of heresy' of 'the heretic Luther and his disciples' to pass the first of the acts which sought to prevent Lutheran literature being brought into the kingdom. And in 1528, Patrick Hamilton, one of the great martyrs in the eyes of John Knox and John Foxe, was burned for heresy at St Andrews. But the trend went on. In the 1530s, there were pockets of Lutheranism in various parts of the country, notably in Ayrshire, and in eastern Scotland from Lothian to Aberdeenshire; Edinburgh itself witnessed 'a great abjuration of the favourers of Martin Luther' at Holyrood Abbey in 1532, and the burning of five heretics in 1539.

It has been argued that at this stage 'the growth of Protestantism was far from a major problem'; its spread, and the numbers involved, were very limited. Even John Knox found himself somewhat gravelled for lack of matter. The point is, however, that it was there and it was growing; and no ruler in the uncertain world of the 1530s could afford to ignore even limited evidence of its existence within his country. James V certainly moved to meet the threat, with acts like those of 1535 and 1541 against heresy, and, more interestingly, acts designed to safeguard and improve the spiritual standing of the Catholic church: reform, in other words, from within. His 1541 parliament issued a string of acts seeking to underwrite the authority of the pope (despite his own highly cavalier and damaging treatment of the papacy), to insist on greater respect and reverence for the sacraments, for the Virgin and saints, and for statues and images, and to reform 'kirks and kirkmen' so that divine service might be properly held, and churchmen better equipped to hold it. It was the last statement of faith in the church by this most enigmatic and perplexing of kings.

It was not enough. For not only was James trying to hold back a tide, even if a small one, within Scotland. To the south lay a country whose king was trying to establish an English Catholic church, in the teeth not only of the papists but also of those who were much more convinced Protestants. England, therefore, might not be a clearly Protestant kingdom in the 1530s, but for leading Scottish Protestants she offered a better haven than James V's

Scotland. A number of reforming scholars and preachers, men like the highly polemical Alexander Alesius, John McAlpine, Walter Abercromby, Florence Wilson, George Wishart and others went to England to seek protection and the patronage of Thomas Cromwell. After an absence of more than two centuries, the Scots were back in England; and for marginal political reasons but much clearer religious ones, the image of England began to change. England was no longer necessarily the 'old enemy'. Equally, Scotland was no longer inevitably pro-French and Catholic.

This, then, was the situation when Mary succeeded to the throne, and the rival factions lined up. As it turned out, Beaton's efforts, whether nefarious or not, were very quickly nullified. Arran convened his kin and friends, and all the other nobles who would support him, and asked for their backing against the cardinal. At some point in the days following James's death, there was a spectacular public row between Beaton and Arran; Beaton, asserting the advantages of power-sharing in a way which hardly conformed to his natural inclinations, insisted that the Gang of Four Regents was certainly preferable to one, and particularly if that one was a member of the Hamilton family, whom he described as 'cruel murderers, oppressors of innocents, proud, avaricious, double and false'. But the weight of opinion was on the side of the man closest to the throne, murderous and oppressive or not. Arran was proclaimed regent, probably on 3 January 1543. Beaton was initially given a sop; on 10 January he was made chancellor. But by the 26th, he was in ward in Dalkeith, and during the next two months was moved from there to Seton, and then to Blackness and St Andrews before finally being released on 10 April. First blood (metaphorically) had certainly gone to the Arran faction.

Apart from Beaton himself, the major casualty was Mary of Guise. For the first time, the queen mother was not given the chance to show whether she could exercise responsible control or not. As it happened, this queen mother was the most remarkable and able of them all, and it is therefore something of an irony that she had to wait for twelve years, until 1554, and stage a successful coup, before obtaining the place which earlier queen mothers had immediately enjoyed. When that happened, however, there would at least be the compensation that she became the first of them to have her power formally acknowledged with the title of regent. Meanwhile, in 1542–3, her exclusion was by no means the only indication of the profound change taking place in the nature of political life. The other is the way in which Arran had won.

He had done it by convening his kin and friends and other nobles in his support. That may seem in no way remarkable. But it was an action far more deeply rooted in the local and social customs of Scotland than in its political traditions. All Scottish sources of the period are full of descriptions of the actions of great men being taken with their 'kin, friends, allies, partakers, men and servants'; that is, the nobles and greater lairds stood at the head of closely united and sometimes very extensive affinities. These were built primarily round the kin-group, and expanded by the making of bonds of maintenance and manrent, whereby lords and men offered one another protection and support, normally for life, sometimes in perpetuity. When, for example, Alexander Gordon of Strathdon came to Elgin on 5 November 1539 to bind himself in manrent to George earl of Huntly, promising to serve him in peace and war, give him counsel, and protect him against harm, he was only one of many hundreds of men throughout the country during the fifteenth and sixteenth centuries making such an obligation, and thereby creating strong personal relationships based always in theory and normally in reality not just on mutual self-interest but on mutual loyalty and trust.

Because of the localized nature of the kingdom, and the comparative lack of political events and activity, it was for local rather than national purposes that these bonds were made. 'Local purposes' might involve disorder and violence, when heads of kindreds and lords were at feud with one another. But it was these same heads of kindreds and lords who were the major factor in ending feud and in maintaining order within local society; and they were able to do so not as individuals but as men of power with powerful backing.

What had been very much less a feature of Scottish society were bonds made for immediate political needs and opportunism, rather than to create lifelong and general obligations. Bonds of this type were not entirely unprecedented; in 1466, for example, during the minority of James III, the Boyds had used them to create support for their seizure of the young king, and then dropped their allies once they had achieved their end. In the 1460s, that was an outrage to accepted norms, and it had much to do with their downfall two years later. But such bonds were rare. In the minority of Mary, this – like so much else – was to change dramatically. The language of the local bonds of maintenance and manrent was used in the bonds that politicians, including Mary of Guise, made during the 1540s and 1550s; indeed, if anything they were even loftier in their talk of mutual support. But their purpose was very different, short-term and political rather than long-term and social; and that was no longer an outrage. In other words, political faction as a regular and fundamental fact of Scottish political life burst fully into life after the death of James V, affecting not just those involved with the immediate concerns of central government but the kingdom as a whole.

The change is strikingly illustrated by the number of surviving political bonds. For the century before 1542, there was a total of seven. In Mary's reign, between 1542 and 1574, when the civil war which followed her deposition was finally over, there were twenty-five large-scale bonds involving groups of people, five of which were made in the first six years of the minority, as well as the thirty-six individual bonds made mainly for political purposes by Arran and Mary of Guise, and the two by Beaton which, in view of the comment by John Knox about the extensive number of his bonds, can only be a small proportion of the total.

The minority, in particular the 1540s, also produced a concentration of the more 'normal' bonds by the magnates, hitherto made for local purposes but now reflecting the need for support in a major political crisis. Political faction had become far more pervasive because the Reformation raised the temperature of Scottish politics, which now took on a focused European dimension, and because once the strong rule of James V had gone, men without the aura of royalty had to struggle with religious and political problems that they had never experienced before. Yet at least in the first two decades of this major shift in political life, faction was based on commitments other than the purely personal. It was in the brief period of Mary's adult rule, as we shall see, that the pattern shifted once again. The great political bonds which – for all the associated chicanery – did articulate political groupings and attitudes based on considerations of foreign policy and religious belief, gave way to bonds motivated by reactions to the personal behaviour of the monarch.

The aristocracy of this period has been castigated for its naked self-interest and expediency. True, Scottish nobles happily accepted bribes from the kings of England and France, as well as the two regents, Arran and Mary of Guise, without necessarily doing much in return. Understandably, much has been made of Henry VIII's offer of a pension of £1,000 to the pro-English and Protestant earl of Glencairn in 1544 and of the money to be sent from France for Mary to distribute to Arran, Beaton and others in 1545. And then there were Henri II's handouts to various Scottish nobles, including Glencairn, who accompanied Mary of Guise on her begging expedition to France in the winter of 1550–1. Moreover, the most impressive and unusual feature of Scottish bonding, the loyalty to a single lord which had done so much to make lordship so stabilizing a factor, was inevitably diminished. Men now changed sides under the pressures of shifts in the political situation and inducements. Thus Mary of Guise and cardinal Beaton fought for the support of lord Gray and lord Ruthven; Beaton won the first, though in 1548 he came over to Mary; two years after the cardinal's death, Mary won the second. Patrick earl of Bothwell made two bonds of manrent, one to Mary in August 1543 for a yearly pension of £1,000, the other to her great rival regent Arran in January 1546, not for the normal term of his life, but for as long as Arran remained governor. Small wonder, then, that the Scotsman Sir George Douglas burst out, as the English ambassador Sir Ralph Sadler reported to Henry VIII on 13 October 1543, that 'the world is so full of falsehood, that he knew not whom he might trust!'

The English ambassador – and the English king – no doubt found the spectacle of what was going on in Scotland rather less surprising than Sir George Douglas. The whirling kaleidoscope of factional politics, the patronage which now included financial inducements, the intensity of concern and confusion about foreign policy, were a new experience for the Scots; it was familiar enough territory in other kingdoms of early modern Europe. This no doubt explains why historians writing about Scotland in Mary's minority have tended to sound more shocked about the activities of the Scottish nobility than historians of other contemporary societies, and find it harder to reconcile the idea of ideological commitment with changes of the political and even religious heart produced by additions to the pocket. But there is another way of looking at it. The Scots had never been parochial in their cultural self-perceptions. Now, as Scotland's religious and political position came to be a matter of major concern to France and England, they fully grabbed the chance to enter the world of European politics, and to behave like those who already inhabited it. Naturally they took what was on offer, and no doubt thoroughly enjoyed the experience – just as a later Scottish politician, James VI, did when he collected £58,000 in pensions from the notoriously parsimonious Elizabeth, without feeling any need to deviate from the path which suited him and his kingdom, and without being regarded as particularly unprincipled. Equally naturally, in Scotland as elsewhere, there were few in this age of profound uncertainty who maintained an unchanging stance throughout.

This is the context in which the immensely complex events of the minority were played out. Yet in the early months of 1543, it almost looked as though the complexities might be avoided by a pre-emptive strike by the English which would immediately and radically resolve Scotland's position. They seized the chance offered by the dominance of Arran's party, while the pro-French Beaton was in ward and Mary of Guise had not yet established a major political role. Henry VIII began cautiously enough. A group of

Scots taken prisoner at Solway Moss, the earls of Glencairn and Cassillis, lords Fleming, Maxwell, Somerville and others, obtained their release and were sent back to Scotland when they signed a request to Henry that he should take Mary into his care, with the intention of marrying her to his son, the future Edward VI; their offer that they would help to bring him to power in Scotland, should Mary die, was kept entirely secret. And Henry also sent north those men who had fallen foul of James V and been in exile in England during his personal rule, Archibald earl of Angus, his brother Sir George Douglas, and Patrick earl of Bothwell. France rushed to counter this move by sending back her own notable exiles, Matthew earl of Lennox, and John Hamilton, abbot of Paisley, bastard half-brother of Arran and no supporter of Protestant reform. For the moment, her effort was ineffective.

Instead, it almost looked as though the English would succeed. On 13 March, parliament met. It was, by Scottish standards, a comparatively large body: seventy people. Some, like Archibald earl of Argyll and Bothwell, initially stayed away; but Bothwell at least turned up on 15 March, to promise the support of himself and his kin and friends to Arran, for which his estates in Liddesdale were restored. Parliament trumpeted – somewhat repetitively – Arran's position, as 'second person of this realm and nearest to succeed to the crown' if Mary failed to have heirs of her body, and therefore 'tutor lawfull to the queen's grace and governor of this realm'. Such an assertion must have come as a considerable relief to Arran. His place as governor was publicly recognized. So was his position as heir presumptive, a necessary acknowledgement in order to remove any doubt created by the fact that he was the son of a divorced father and his second wife. This doubt allowed the possibility of a claim by his rival, Matthew Stewart, earl of Lennox, even though by the rules of primogeniture Arran had the stronger case; for he was descended from the son of James II's daughter Mary, whereas Lennox was descended from her daughter. Now, the Lennox claim was formally set aside.

Parliament then took two critical decisions. First, it agreed that negotiations with Henry VIII for the marriage of Mary and Edward should begin. Second, despite the instant protest by Gavin, archbishop of Glasgow, on behalf of the clergy, it authorized the reading of scripture in the vernacular. It looked as though the repressive policy of James V had died with him, and that Scotland, presided over by Arran and the powerful Hamilton faction, was now moving with almost unbelievable ease towards alliance with England and some measure of Protestant reform. Knox, when he wrote his *History of the Reformation* in the 1560s, looked back to the time when 'all men esteemed the Governor to have been the most fervent Protestant that there was in all Europe', so that although 'The Papists raged against the Governor', his fame 'was spread in divers countries'.

It was not, of course, as simple as that. Arran was giving an impression of strength and direction wholly at odds with his personality. This was the man whom Mary of Guise described to Sadler as 'a simple and the most inconstant man in the world; for whatsoever he determineth today, he changeth tomorrow'; and there were plenty of people in Scotland to help him to change from his position of March 1543. In sharp contrast, there was no doubt about the determination and constancy of Henry VIII. The English king was, and remained, stubbornly deaf to the point crucial to the Scots: that the marriage of Mary and Edward should not in any way endanger Scottish independence. The point was made by the very parliament which supported the marriage. Memories of what had happened in the 1290s, when John Balliol was a vassal king and Edward I intervened all too directly in Scottish affairs, produced a careful spelling-out of the Scottish position. Thus, at no time in the future should any Scot be summoned to court or parliament outside Scotland – a direct reminder of Edward I's particular offence.

More immediately, while realism dictated that Mary would go to England when she married, Henry was told very bluntly that she must not go sooner: such a demand would be 'a right high and right great inconvenience to the realm of Scotland', and parliament trusted to the English king's 'high wisdom', and assumed that he would not insist. Henry's wisdom was not high enough.

Despite the outspoken warning by the Scottish parliament, and the reiteration of it by his own envoy, Sadler, he continued to demand that Mary be given into his keeping immediately. It was the main reason why the marriage was never to take place.

For the moment, however, negotiations went ahead, and seemed to go well. They culminated in the treaties of peace and marriage, agreed to by both sides at Greenwich on 1 July 1543. Scottish fears of absorption by England seemed to have been allayed. Her status as a separate kingdom was guaranteed; and if there were no heirs of the marriage, succession to the respective thrones would diverge, leaving Mary's Scottish heir to inherit her crown. Mary would remain in Scotland until she was ten, when she would be married by proxy and go to England. Yet the English king was not satisfied. He found it necessary to try to offset any lingering Scottish doubts by suggesting his daughter Elizabeth as a bride for Arran's son, and, more to the point, offering 5,000 men to aid Arran in defeating any opposition. It was a deeply tactless idea. What Arran wanted was £5,000; what he saw clearly enough was that the support of 5,000 Englishmen would lose him four times that number of Scots. But Henry's indifference to the realities of the Scottish situation came out most clearly in this third, amazing, offer: if resistance to the marriage was successful, he would respond by making Arran king of Scotland north of the Forth by force. The Scots did not initially resist; they ratified the Treaty of Greenwich, at Holyrood Abbey on 25 August. It was the English who failed to do so within the agreed period of two months. But already the whole scheme was looking increasingly doubtful.

It is from this period that the first two political bonds of the mid sixteenth century come. One, undated, but clearly made while the negotiations were taking place, bound the earls of Angus, Argyll, Crawford, Marischal, Cassillis and Glencairn and ten others to fulfil the council decision that pledges should be sent to England as surety for the accomplishing of the marriage – that is, human pledges. The council meeting took place on 6 or 8 June. It was clearly not an easy one; and the small group who made the bond designed to shore up its decision pales into insignificance when set against the numbers involved in the second bond. This was made on 24 July, between cardinal Beaton, the earls of Huntly, Argyll, Lennox, Bothwell, Sutherland and Menteith, the bishops of Moray, Whithorn, Dunblane and Orkney, and thirty-six prominent lords and lairds. Its justification was the lack of policy in the country since the death of James V; it attacked the desire for private profit of those who governed, and the threat of the subjugation of Scotland by the old enemy, England; and it asserted the signatories' zeal for justice, and the liberty and honour of the realm. It was made at Linlithgow, where the infant queen and her mother were then living. Mary of Guise's name nowhere appears, but she must surely have been involved. Two days later, on 26 July, the dowager and the queen left Linlithgow for the greater safety of Stirling, presumably an indication that, with the making of this bond, the relatively straightforward period of the first half of 1543 was over.

It is stretching cynicism too far to doubt that these men meant what they said, even though other less obviously praiseworthy intentions crept in. Beaton was visibly trying to regain power. Bothwell, sent back from English exile with the Douglases by Henry VIII, and present – perhaps reluctantly – at the March parliament, was no longer even a wavering supporter of the English king and the governor. The arch-ditherer Argyll, signatory of the first bond, now subscribed the second. Lennox, despite his anti-English position, would find it intolerable to be a member of the Beaton faction; within a few weeks, he would go over to the pro-English party, his hopes of his marriage to Margaret, daughter of Angus and Margaret Tudor, and of English recognition of him as heir-presumptive, should Arran break with England, weighing more with him than the desire for liberty and honour expressed in the July bond. Nevertheless, the bond is not just a conglomeration of individual ambitions and fears. It is a collective expression of extensive opposition to – even outrage at – the attempt by Henry VIII and Arran to stampede the Scots, the moment the opportunity appeared to present itself, into a complete denial of their long tradition of independence fought for and achieved in the teeth of English aggression.

The opportunity was there, of course, because everything centred round the life of a baby girl, and therefore the politics of the minority were inevitably a matter of potential marriage alliances. That a sufficient number of influential Scots initially entertained the idea of Mary's marriage to Henry VIII's son shows immediate awareness of the problem, and the preferred solution: marriage into a foreign royal house rather than into a Scottish aristocratic family. It may be that long experience of minorities encouraged them to feel that they could cope better with an absentee ruler than one who upset the balance of power at home. Their attempts to impose conditions on a man like Henry VIII only show how far, in the initial stages, they were turning a blind eye to the implications of their policy.

They did not remain blind for long. What sprang the trap in which they found themselves was not so much any actions of theirs, but the intense pressure which Henry applied. The English king was being offered what English kings had so long desired. He reacted by behaving in a way which rammed home to the Scots memories of Edward I. The events of 1543 took on a sinister familiarity; for Edward's attempted annexation of Scotland had also begun with a proposed marriage, between the infant Margaret, Maid of Norway, who succeeded Alexander III in 1286, and Edward's son, the future Edward II. Now, even while the treaties were being negotiated, Henry was seizing Scottish shipping, demanding the queen's person, trying to bully Arran into handing over the Scottish castles south of the Forth into English hands, considering setting up Arran as a client king. What Henry wanted was control of Scotland, no matter whether by marriage treaty or by force. Indeed, his actions, and his refusal to listen to advisors telling him to proceed gently, made a negotiated settlement look almost irrelevant.

The result was predictable. Arran gave way to the persuasions of his half-brother, the abbot of Paisley, and to the ascendant Beaton faction. On 28 August, he ratified the Greenwich treaties. At the beginning of September, he slipped out of Holyrood and went to Falkirk. There on 4 September he met Beaton, and they 'agreed very well'. That night, they went to Stirling, to join with Huntly, Argyll and Bothwell, and made plans for Mary's coronation. Arran's capitulation was remarkable. He agreed to hand over 'the castles, holds and fortresses of Scotland to the cardinal and the said earls, to cause them to be kept by such as they thought meet'. He confessed to Beaton all that he had done at the behest of the English king, including 'the suppression of sundry abbeys and friaries'. For this, he incurred the sentence of excommunication, from which he was promptly absolved by the cardinal after public penance; he then heard mass and received the sacrament, while 'the earls of Argyll and Bothwell held the towel over his head'. The wonder of Protestant Europe, the ally of Henry VIII, the ruler of Scotland, had, said Sadler, 'forsaken both God and man'.

The English policy was in ruins. Yet despite Arran's defection, the pro-English party was not; it survived, and was indeed strengthened by the addition of Lennox. For the next few months, foreign and domestic policies were in stalemate. In December 1543, parliament declared the treaty with England to have expired, renewed the Auld Alliance with France, recorded Beaton's acceptance of the chancellorship, and renewed the laws against heresy. During the winter, the pro-English party continued to negotiate with Henry VIII, to no great effect for either side. And then on 10 April 1544 came Henry's chilling order to his brother-in-law Edward, earl of Hertford, to

> put all to fire and sword, burn Edinburgh town, so razed and defaced when you have sacked and gotten what ye can of it, as there may remain forever a perpetual memory of the vengeance of God lightened upon [them] for their falsehood and disloyalty . . . and as many towns and villages about Edinburgh as ye may conveniently, sack Leith and burn and subvert it and all the rest, putting man, woman and child to fire and sword, without exception where any resistance shall be made against you; and this done, pass over to the Fifeland and extend like extremities and destructions in all towns and villages whereunto ye may reach conveniently, not forgetting among all the rest so to spoil and turn

> upside down the Cardinal's town of St Andrews, as the upper
> stone may be the nether, and not one stick stand by another,
> sparing no creature alive within the same . . . And after this sort
> spending one month there.

The English king was certainly identifying himself with God, and
with a vengeance. In 1547, after the English victory over the Scots
at Pinkie, Huntly was to say 'I hold well with the marriage, but
I like not this wooing'. That gave a name to the war; in May 1544,
the Rough Wooing had begun.

It happened because Henry had no options left. He desperately
needed at least a neutral, if not a friendly neighbour to the north.
His own break with Rome in the 1530s had led to strenuous efforts
to persuade his nephew James V to do likewise, and to desert
France for England. These had failed. Not surprisingly, therefore,
a man never noted for the quality of patience had rushed bull-
headed on the opportunity offered by the accession of Mary.
Force and diplomacy went hand in hand in 1543. But more than
impatience was involved. The basis for his Scottish policy was his
conviction that English safety lay in separating France and Scotland,
and that conviction reached fever pitch in 1543. In February, he
had entered into alliance with Charles V against France; by June,
he was sending English soldiers to the Netherlands in response to
a French attack. In 1544 there was a full-scale onslaught on France,
in which the English took Boulogne. So whereas he had treated
with the pro-English party in Scotland in the first half of 1543, in
1544 it was the pro-French faction which was uppermost in his
mind. Hertford's first expedition to Scotland was Henry's way of
eliminating the Scots, potential allies of France.

The campaign against the Scots was operated with ruthless
efficiency, and was violent and vengeful in the extreme. The years
1544 and 1545 were to see a number of English invasions, of which
those of May 1544 and the autumn of 1545 – timed for the
destruction of the harvest – were by far the worst. Hertford took
his instructions seriously, devastating Lothian and Edinburgh and
laying waste the great border abbeys, as well as destroying numerous

small towns and villages. His detailed reports to his master are a hideous record of fire and bloodshed, chronicled in the most factual and laconic manner. It was easy to burn Haddington, a substantial town east of Edinburgh (and birthplace of John Knox); at Dunbar, the inhabitants were trapped inside the town and burned with it. And so on. It was not entirely one-sided. Its impact drove the strongly pro-English Angus into the Arran-Beaton camp; his lands lay in the path of oncoming English armies, and the Scottish government could capitalize on this, by appealing to his position as the great man and protector of his locality, reinforcing such sentiments with a pension. And Angus had the pleasure – rare for a Scot in any century – of defeating an English army at Ancrum in February 1545. But this was no more than a temporary reversal in the most savage onslaught from England which the Scots had ever experienced.

Yet for all the expense, the effort, the bloodshed, Henry achieved only one obvious success, and that had nothing to do with Hertford's armies. His support of plots against Beaton in 1544 and 1545 came to fruition in May 1546, when a group of Fifeshire lairds headed by Norman Leslie, son of the earl of Rothes, broke into the episcopal castle at St Andrews, murdered the cardinal and slung his body over the castle walls; the murderers, henceforth known as the Castilians, barricaded themselves inside the castle, which they held as a Protestant stronghold. John Knox joined them in April 1547. Yet even this was not a long-lasting achievement. The earl of Hertford had emerged supreme from the power-struggle which surrounded the death of Henry VIII in January 1547. Although this ardent Protestant was now protector (and duke of Somerset), his government did nothing to help the Protestant Castilians. It was the hostile French who turned up. They arrived in July 1547 and took the castle, after a brief siege featuring a spectacular air-battle in which the outer walls were battered by artillery hoisted on to the church steeple of St Salvator's College and the abbey walls; the lairds disappeared into prison in France, and Knox and others went to the galleys.

The failure of the English to intervene at St Andrews, however, brought no general relief to the Scots. The Rough Wooing was to continue, not this time as a series of devastating raids, but by seizing and garrisoning Scottish fortresses as the basis for English control, and by Somerset's own comprehensive victory over the Scots at Pinkie in September 1547. It may be that Somerset was as much in the grip of the obsession to unite England and Scotland as ever Edward I or Henry VIII had been, while like them asserting English power in France; for he continued Henry's policy of war on two fronts, at enormous financial expense, and ultimately at the cost of his own position in England. Indeed, as C. S. L. Davies has suggested, the arrogance with which he treated his fellow-councillors in the two years before his fall in October 1549 may owe a lot to his outstanding success at Pinkie, when he may have believed that he was about to achieve what some of the greatest of English kings had failed to do.

Yet he had no more chance than they did. He did manage to establish the English in a ring of garrisons in southern Scotland, but – like Edward I before him – he found that he could not extend his grip in any effective way into northern Scotland beyond the Tay; and his southern castles could be recaptured. The geography of Scotland, in the sixteenth as in the thirteenth century, allowed temporary successes directed from London, whether taking castles or winning battles. But it utterly prevented permanent victory. What it did make possible was stalemate; and that was what happened in the 1540s. The Scots could not rid themselves of the English. The English could not make that final spurt, establish dominance and impose their demands for the marriage.

One way out for the Scots was to contemplate a different marriage for their queen. Formal negotiations for the English match might have been dead by the end of 1543; discussions about the queen's marriage were not. The collapse of the English plan had opened the way for the possibility of marriage within Scotland, to Arran's son. On 11 July 1546, at a council meeting at which Mary of Guise was present, the idea was rejected. Arran had to promise to destroy the 'contract and bond' made to him concerning the queen's marriage, and discharge all noblemen who had consented to it – a considerable number, according to the letter written to the dowager by John, son of Lord Somerville, in October 1545. Mary responded by cancelling all bonds made against the Arran agreement. And generally the making of bonds was now prohibited. This was, of course, a dead letter; no council ordinance was going to dissuade Mary of Guise or Arran from the useful practice of making bonds with their potential allies. Nor did Arran obey the injunction to destroy all his bonds; one, made by Hugh, master of Eglinton in 1545, still exists in the Hamilton archives. Its stated intention was that Mary should not marry any foreign prince; she must marry a prince born of this realm – and Arran's son was the most suitable candidate. The problem for the Hamiltons was that there was an obvious alternative.

The idea of marriage into the royal house of France had been openly raised at least as early as September 1543, and presumably had been in the mind of Mary of Guise long before that. Arran himself had joined Beaton and the dowager at the end of 1544, when they 'promised and made bond to the French ambassador, that the French king shall have the young queen, to marry where he list . . . and also that they shall at the spring of the year, send both the young queen and the old (Mary of Guise) into France'. Nothing came of it in 1545, though in June French troops arrived to give the Scots temporary assistance against the English. But the stunning defeat at Pinkie in September 1547 changed wavering into decision. Mary herself was moved to the island stronghold of Inchmahome, west of Stirling, for her safety during the Pinkie campaign. Her visit produced a flowering of names associated with her on the little island, like Queen Mary's Bower and Tree, and stories grew up that the five-year-old child began to learn Latin, Greek, Italian and other subjects there, including the art of embroidery for which she was later famous, while taking time off for gardening. As she seems to have stayed on the island for only three weeks, however, being moved back to Stirling when the English army left Scotland at the end of September, we can only conclude that these are testimony not to Mary as an infant prodigy, but to her fascination as a source of romance and legend.

But fears for her were real enough. The need to enlist French help, with the awareness that it would come on French terms, was agreed by the council which met at Stirling on 2 November 1547. In January 1548 Arran, in return for the promise of a French duchy, made a formal contract with Henri II of France. He agreed to summon the Scottish parliament, that it should consent to Mary's marriage with the dauphin Francis and to her departure for France, and that Scottish castles should be handed over to the French – as indeed Dunbar and Blackness were. The queen was taken to the west-coast town of Dumbarton in February. In June, French troops arrived at Leith, and the French and Scots settled down to besiege Haddington. Parliament met at the nunnery outside the English-occupied town, and on 7 July agreed with the French commander and envoy, the seigneur d'Essé, that 'the ancient bond, confederation and amity standing between the realm of France and this country' was the best chance against 'the mortal wars, cruelties, depredations and intolerable injuries done by our old enemies of England'. The French king would offer Scotland protection. Mary would marry the dauphin. Meanwhile, the Scots who had refused to allow her to be brought up in England sent her, at the beginning of August, to France. The Treaty of Haddington – unlike the Treaty of Greenwich – was to last.

The pay-off came fairly quickly. Already Arran's son had gone to France, in pursuit of the bride offered by Henri II, the eldest daughter of the duke of Montpensier. In reality, he was a hostage; the marriage never took place. But Arran did get his duchy of Châtelherault, worth 12,000 livres (£1,000 sterling) per annum, in February 1549; and in June or July of that year, his half-brother John abbot of Paisley was finally recognized as Beaton's successor in the archbishopric of St Andrews, to which he had been provided in November 1547. More important, the Franco-Scottish armies succeeded where the Scottish ones had not. The years 1548–9 were years of English reversal, as the fortresses they held were recovered. By September 1549, when Haddington fell, it was virtually all over. Meanwhile, the French were mounting a major attack on Boulogne. The combination was impossible. The deeply unpopular Somerset was overthrown in October, and power passed to those who had opposed the war; his successor, John Dudley, earl of Warwick, was only recognizing the inevitable when he gave up Boulogne at the same time as peace was made with Scotland in March 1550, when the last stronghold held by the English, Lauder, capitulated.

In April, the French and the Scots embarked on a polite exchange of congratulatory diplomatic compliments, with the French claiming that they had attacked Boulogne only for the sake of the Scots. The Auld Alliance looked very strong; English hopes in Scotland seemed to be annihilated. But as in 1543, when the English appeared to be completely in the ascendant, it was not a straightforward matter.

It had been a decade of bloodshed and confusion: English bloodshed and Scottish confusion. The most notable thing about the Rough Wooing is not that in the end the savagery of the English attack drove the Scots away from the new idea of friendship with England and back into the arms of their natural and ancient allies, the French. That was only part of the story. What was really remarkable was that although people did change their ground as a result of English pressure, Henry VIII and Somerset never actually dispelled all their support in Scotland. Throughout the period of the Rough Wooing, there existed in Scotland men known as the 'assured Scots', those who formally contracted with and were often paid by the English – in other words collaborators. These were not the great nobles. They were lesser men, lairds, burgesses and others, mainly from southern Scotland – the area of the English 'pale' – but not exclusively so; it was 'assured Scots' from the Highlands, bound to and paid by Henry VIII, who ravaged parts of Argyllshire in 1545. So there were many others besides the great earls like Lennox or Glencairn who saw advantages in supporting England. Undoubtedly many collaborated out of fear, or under pressure. But there were positive as well as negative reasons which influenced Scotsmen in the 1540s.

So it was not only English hopes which were dashed in 1550. The great difference between the events of the 1540s and earlier periods of hostility between England and Scotland was that this episode was far more than a particularly dramatic example of the eternal political and military triangle of England, Scotland and France, or even just the revival by Henry VIII and Somerset of that old English dream, the unification of England and Scotland. For this time there were others who shared in that dream, at least to the extent of wanting friendship between England and Scotland. In 1542, Henry received a long and rambling letter from a crank, one John Elder, clerk of the diocese of Caithness, and therefore claiming to speak for the Highlanders. Elder assured Henry that, with Highland support, he could achieve what the Scots themselves wanted: freedom from France, the establishment of the Protestant faith, and union with England. This claim very much fitted with Henry's own ideas about what the Scots should be wanting. But he could justify this because there were other Scots besides Elder, drawn from the ranks of the leading politicians, who gave him the same message.

The king's initial statement on the matter, *A Declaration, conteyning the iust causes and consyderations, of this present warre with the Scottis, wherin alsoo appereth the trewe & right title, that the kinges most royall maiesty hath to the souerayntie of Scotland'*, produced in 1542 during the Anglo-Scottish war, was a singularly tactless trumpeting of the old claim of English overlordship. It could be conveniently set aside in the changed circumstances after James V's death, when the real issue became clear. It has been called the 'British Problem', brought into being by a combination of renewed English ambition and, for the first time, a new attitude among at least some of the Scots to their southern neighbour. It was to last throughout the 1540s, and then go into abeyance, lying dormant – despite Mary Queen of Scots' burning awareness of her position as Elizabeth's heir presumptive – until it had to be faced again, when James VI succeeded to the English throne in 1603. It was given expression not only in the letter by Elder and the *Declaration* by Henry VIII, but in an intensive burst of propaganda in 1547–8.

In that year, the Scots were assailed by no less than five tracts extolling the benefits of union, including one by Somerset himself, the *Epistle or exhortacion to uniti & peace to the inhabitauntes of Scotland*. Not all were as moderate as Somerset's, with its stress on equality; the title of one of the others, Nicholas Bodrugan's *Epitome of the title that the Kynges Maiestie of Englande hath to the souereigntie of Scotland*, shows how willing the English were to assume that the Scots could be persuaded to accept a union of unequal partners. And indeed some were. Among these tracts were two written by a Scotsman, James Harryson or Henderson, merchant of Edinburgh, who had joined Somerset in 1544 and been an English pensioner since 1546: *An Exhortion to the Scottes* (1547) and *The Godly and Golden Booke for Concorde of England and Scotland* (1548), which remained unprinted because, ironically enough, the Scot was continuing the propaganda battle on behalf of England after the English had withdrawn from it.

These works produced only two Scottish replies arguing against the English case, *The Complaynt of Scotland*, and the recently discovered *Ane Resonying of ane Scottis and Inglis merchand betuix Rowand (Rouen) and Lionis (Lyons)* by the royal councillor and administrator William Lamb, an imagined discourse between two merchants travelling in France, in which the Scottish merchant utterly refuted, point by point, the claims of Henry VIII set out in his 1542 *Declaration*. But there was no wholesale Scottish rejection. So we are faced with the amazing fact that neither the insistence on English superiority nor a savage level of English military aggression was enough to produce widespread, let alone total, resistance by a people who for well over two centuries had determinedly and successfully resisted both. There is, of course, no single explanation for this. But over and above other factors such as the growing disenchantment, after long experience, with the Auld Alliance, and the beginning of awareness that living at peace with the English might be better than suffering the massive destruction inflicted during the Rough Wooing, there was one compelling new element: Protestantism.

Whatever the brutality of their methods, or the tactlessness of their secular claims, there is no doubt that both Henry VIII and Somerset were also motivated by religious considerations, seeing themselves as releasing Scottish Protestants from Catholic bondage; old claims had a dramatic new dimension. The Scots themselves provided sufficient evidence that the English mission was to be welcomed. In 1543, Knox joyfully recorded the effect of allowing the reading of scripture in the vernacular: 'Then might have been seen the Bible lying upon almost every gentleman's table. The New Testament was born about in many men's hands.' Ralph Sadler wrote of the thirst for the vernacular scriptures and other works, 'marvellously desired now of all the people in Scotland', and of Arran's particular request for guidance in his reading. It is a measure of the enthusiasm which he observed that, when Sadler duly provided a reading-list – tactfully headed with the 'King's Book', an episcopal compilation in which Henry VIII had had a hand – he felt it necessary to advise caution; religious works circulating too freely had their own dangers, as Henry had recognized, when he passed an act in that year forbidding the reading of them by unfit groups, women, artificers and labourers.

Somerset seems to have felt less restraint. Certainly he saw the Pinkie campaign not only as a military endeavour, but as something in the nature of a religious crusade; Scotland would be snatched not just from alliance with France, but from the yoke of Rome. It was not the most obvious way to proselytize. But it was followed by slightly more peaceful methods. In February 1548 the English captain, Thomas Wharton, sent a bible to Dumfries, at the request of the citizens – while leading an English force in a border raid. The English government followed this up by sending them the preacher John Rughe, and by giving pensions to some Scottish preachers. Not all of the English government's assured men were Protestants; not all Scottish Protestants assured. Nevertheless, it was now possible for men to decide their political allegiance for religious reasons; England could be identified with the Protestant cause. In March 1544, before the Rough Wooing began, Lennox had been warned against being one of those who 'favoured the case of England or their new opinions' – a warning which he did not heed. In June 1548, when the Scots had suffered it for four years, lord Methven reported to Mary of Guise the results of his inquiries as to why the Englishmen were favoured. Methven gave four reasons. Three were fear, desire for profit, and the assumption that there might be more quietness and better justice under the English than under Arran's rule. But the first reason was religious: 'part of the leiges has taken new opinions of the scripture, and has done against the law and ordinance of holy kirk'.

So Protestant opinions had not been silenced by Arran's change of heart after the initial heady days of 1543; and the Rough Wooing had not broken the link between the English and the hopes of Scottish Protestants. In 1544 and 1545, one of the most attractive of the leading Scottish reformers – and a man certainly working on behalf of England – George Wishart, was preaching openly, with remarkably little difficulty; only in the spring of 1546 was he finally apprehended by Beaton, and burned for heresy. This act led, with Henry VIII's blessing, to Beaton's murder two months later; and it was while he was with the Castilians in St Andrews that Knox first went far further than any earlier reformer in Scotland. In a sensational sermon in the parish church of St Andrews at Easter 1547 he articulated his radical view of the papacy as Antichrist. Individual popes therefore could not be reformed. The whole must be torn out by the roots. And even after that high point of drama and inspiration had passed, and the French had launched their successful attacks on the Castilians, Protestantism survived in pockets throughout the kingdom. It was a fallow period, but that might well in itself prepare the ground for more spectacular growth.

Nevertheless, there may be a danger here in looking at the events of the late 1540s from the vantage point of the apparent Protestant triumph of 1560. When the Scottish government turned to France for aid in 1547–8, it was undoubtedly doing so because it recognized that the level of English aggression was both intolerable and irresistible without foreign help. It could and did then turn on the assured men – but primarily as collaborators rather than as religious dissidents. The very existence of a Protestant party makes it impossible, however, to see this simply as a re-run of the older style international politics whereby Scotland turned naturally to

France when menaced by England. The invocation of French help was certainly not a general affirmation of enthusiasm for the Auld Alliance, nor did it signify total alienation from England nor a concerted drive to eradicate Protestantism. On the other hand, it can hardly be doubted that the policy of Henry VIII and Somerset had disastrously misfired. Scotland was now diplomatically further removed from England than she had been at the beginning of Mary's minority, and the Protestants were denied the backing of allies who could have advanced their cause had they not so dramatically overplayed their hand. The Scots might remain divided, on religious as well as political grounds; and it is oversimplistic to equate pro-English with Protestantism, pro-French with Catholicism. But the great paradox of English policy was that its beneficiaries could only be those who sought not to overthrow but to maintain and, indeed, strengthen the Catholic church.

It is important, however, to put this into context. This was not a seismic change. Scotland had never been other than a Catholic country. So all that really happened was that the position of those who sought to challenge the *status quo* was weakened. But if the respective strengths and weaknesses of the rival religious groupings in Scotland depended primarily not on the internal state of the kingdom but on the fluctuations of its foreign relations, then the whole concept of Protestant advance or Catholic triumph begins to look very shaky. And indeed one only has to compare Scotland with England to see where the real problem lay. The 'official' religious position of England never encompassed all English men and women, once Henry VIII had shattered the unity of the church. Nor did it have a consistent history in the sixteenth century. But it did relate to – and therefore change with – the monarch on the throne. At no time did England lack a government which could give direction to religious affairs, whether that of Henry VIII, Mary and Elizabeth, or the minority government of Edward VI, presided over by the exceedingly tough Somerset and Northumberland. There was no such government in Scotland during Mary's minority. Arran was far too weak to pursue a consistent policy. Mary of Guise had infinitely more ability and determination, but for the first twelve years of the minority she had no official role in government, and throughout the whole period her main interest lay in achieving a French marriage for her daughter, even if that meant doing little about the existence of Protestantism. There was therefore no authority powerful or concerned enough to encourage or root out any of the religious persuasions in Scotland. The events of the 1540s led not to decision, but to increased floundering, and a rush for cover.

What happened in 1548 was that the ruling party came to terms with France, in order to find quick relief for only one of their difficulties. In the circumstances, they had little choice. But in so doing, they did not resolve an existing problem, the emergence of a Protestant challenge to the Catholic church. And they unwittingly created a new one, for the price they paid for the French troops who solved the English military problem was a monarch who was taught to be both French and Catholic. This was by no means unacceptable in 1548. But it would be a very different matter when that monarch returned to her country thirteen years later, when both these things clashed with the prevailing balance of power in Scotland. On 7 August 1548, Mary Queen of Scots sailed for France. 'Everything', as Mary of Guise rejoiced, 'was put into the hands of the French.' Her jubilation was understandable. But for John Knox, 'so she was sold to go to France, to that end that in her youth she should drink of that liquor (the Catholic faith) that should remain with her all her lifetime, for a plague to this realm and for her final destruction'. These wholly conflicting statements beautifully encapsulate the rival positions whose balance had been altered, but no more than that, by the swing from England to France. But they also had one significant thing in common. Both Mary and Knox were thinking about the kingdom of Scotland. For Mary Queen of Scotland, it was a very different matter. She was embarking on what she would always regard as the pleasantest years of her life.

CHAPTER FOUR

The Minority: The Auld Alliance Rampant
1548–60

It was undoubtedly unusual – and normally disadvantageous – for any ruler brought up in one country to rule over another, very different, one. As a Fleming, Charles V was never loved by the Spaniards; as a Spaniard, his son Philip II was alienated from the Flemings. Both were at home in their country of origin, and had to struggle to establish viable contacts and understanding with their subjects elsewhere. It was far from ideal, in an age which put such a premium on the identification of the ruler with his kingdom; Elizabeth's boast of being 'mere English', James VI and I's difficulty with his English subjects because he was a Scot, make the point very well. But it was a rather different matter in Mary's case. The cultural difference between Spain and the Spanish king's northern dominions was considerably greater than that between France and Scotland; Scotland managed to resist becoming a permanent part of the French political hegemony, but she had long been an enthusiastic member of the cultural one. The swing towards England in the 1540s had not eradicated the outward-looking tradition built up throughout the later Middle Ages. A queen brought up in France was therefore geographically remote, but she was certainly not alien. French architectural styles at home, the desirability of French education for Scots abroad, military and economic ties, all combined to produce the feeling that even if a French upbringing for their monarch was only to be countenanced because of the extreme dangers created by the Rough Wooing, it was not unnatural in the way that an English upbringing would have been. A French accent in Scotland was a good deal less unacceptable than a Scottish one in England. In 1548, therefore, there was no reason for the Scots to fear the alienation of their queen. As in the earlier case of David II, sent as a child to France in 1334 in exactly the same circumstances, when the English were menacing southern Scotland, the presumption was that she could grow up in safety, until she could return as an adult to rule her kingdom. In the event, Mary of Guise's optimism would turn out to be misplaced, Knox's stricture correct. But this was not simply because Mary was sent to France. The reasons are more complex than that.

There was of course the complicating factor that this time it was 'Mary', not 'David'. From the moment of her arrival in France, her royalty was fully acknowledged. Henri II insisted that, as a reigning monarch, she must take precedence over his daughters. But her value in his eyes was that she was his son's future bride, through whom he would control Scotland; he did not envisage her doing so herself as an individual monarch, and the secret agreements she made just before her marriage show how far she agreed with him. Indeed, his view of this independent sovereign as purely a pawn in the French political game was never more clearly seen than in 1556, when he contemplated marrying her to the English nobleman Edward lord Courtenay, in response to the threat that Philip of Spain, then married to Mary Tudor, would give her sister Elizabeth as a bride to Ferdinand of Austria. Such a match, compared to that with the dauphin, would have been distinctly disparaging for Mary. For Henri, the desire for French control of Scotland had for the moment given way to Valois need to counter an extension of Hapsburg power; and Mary was as useful for the one as for the other.

For most of the time, however, it was as their future queen that this undoubtedly attractive child – Henri II's 'most perfect child' – was to enchant everyone in France, apart from Catherine de Medici. For ten years, from the time she arrived in France – after a journey in which she showed considerable enthusiasm for the new life to which she was going, and very little sign of regret about leaving her country, let alone her 'dearest mother' (in contrast to Mary of Guise's grief) – until her marriage, she was the fêted darling of the French court. Money was poured out in an endless, and, as far as she was concerned, inexhaustible stream for her clothes and entertainment. Her wardrobe was, of course, immediately refurbished when she arrived, and continually added to, though on occasion she did wear 'Scottish dress', to the patronizing admiration of the French.

As far as possible, her Scottish attendants were removed and replaced with French ones. Her famous 'four Maries' – Beaton, Seton, Fleming and Livingstone – who had accompanied her to France, remained there with her, to join the new friends in France, the king's daughters Elisabeth and Claude, the dauphin Francis, and the other royal children. But her other Scottish attendants were quickly despatched home; only at the insistence of Mary of Guise was her daughter's governess, Lady Fleming, allowed to remain – until 1551, when a brief affair with the French king ensured her disgrace and expulsion. Mary was regularly on the move, from one spectacular French château to another; as well as the royal palaces, Saint-Germain-en-Laye, Fontainebleau, Meudon and Blois, there was also Anet, magnificent home of Henri's mistress, Diane de Poitiers. Antonia Fraser has aptly described the dream-like quality of these years. It was an enchanting and heady experience, and one which could hardly be other than irresistible: a delightful upbringing for the future queen consort of France, but not one which at first sight looks like adequate preparation for the future queen regnant of Scotland.

But Mary was not actually being singled out for special treatment or favour, except in so far as her own attractiveness and charm marked her out. On the contrary, she was given an upbringing just like that of the dauphin, heir to one of the two most powerful monarchies in Europe; and that was certainly designed to train a king. Her education was heavily concentrated on languages, Latin, Spanish and Italian, even probably some Greek; among her formal Latin letters, written as exercises, one stands out with ironic interest, for it was addressed to John Calvin. It was less demanding than the similar education given to Elizabeth or Lady Jane Grey, and Mary was undoubtedly of far less intellectual a cast of mind. This did not particularly matter. She was not a scholar but a queen, to be trained for the needs of diplomacy, and also as the centrepiece of a Renaissance court; and she was certainly skilled in the courtly arts, music and dancing. She was, therefore, simply being treated in the way in which the French thought royal children should be brought up.

It may be, therefore, that the dream-like quality of growing up in one of the most cultured courts in Europe had its own dangers for any who experienced it. In other words, a French upbringing for the future queen of Scots was not in principle a matter for concern; but the particular nature of French royal upbringing in the mid sixteenth century may have been. After all, none of Henri II's three sons, all of whom sat on the French throne, and all of whom were products of the same education as Mary, was in any way an impressive or successful ruler. Admittedly, dealing with a woman as dominating as Catherine de Medici and a family as powerful as the Guises, which all three had to do, would have put strains on personalities far stronger than Francis II, Charles IX and Henri III; but the fact remains that while, unlike Mary, they did not show indifference to their kingdom, they were exactly like her in failing to assert their control of it. What we are surely witnessing is the effect on these people of the 'divinity which doth hedge a king', which may be translated more prosaically as the persistent flattery and adulation with which kings were treated – and in France, it seems, not only kings, but their children.

Monarchs themselves encouraged such attitudes with spectacular ceremonial, from coronation to funeral. One only has to look at the woodcuts of Henri II's entry into Rouen in 1550 – which Mary very probably witnessed – to get a breath-taking impression of the splendour of royal pageantry, with the king himself riding on a chariot of immense size and grandeur, accompanied by heavily caparisoned elephants. Henri II and, perhaps to an even greater extent, Catherine de Medici, were notable exponents of the art; so were Henry VIII, though in a less dramatic way, and his daughter Elizabeth. The monstrous arrogance of a Henry VIII, the pathological need for flattery of an Elizabeth, may suggest that this was a side of kingship which was in danger of taking monarchs out of touch with reality, as they wound themselves into a cocoon of adulation. Indeed, given the high claims monarchs made for themselves, and the excesses of adoration with which they were treated – and by the time of Mary Queen of Scots, this had reached a very high level indeed – we may wonder that so many of them retained any sense of balance at all. But the great monarchs of the sixteenth century knew very well how to use that adulation to enhance their power. The cult of monarchy which they so strenuously and even sometimes grotesquely encouraged made very good political sense; it was a visual demonstration of monarchy as in theory envisaged, and therefore a substantial basis for monarchy as in practice exercised.

Thus such monarchs were in fact profoundly in touch with reality. But it took a hard head to be so. Arguably the necessary detachment was more likely to be found in people who had not had the kind of upbringing so thoroughly enjoyed by Mary Queen of Scots. The extreme contrast is with her cousin Elizabeth, declared bastard before she was three, enduring four stepmothers thereafter, and brought up mainly away from court circles. Their different reactions to political pressures when both were aged fifteen are therefore instructive. Mary was signing away her kingdom, at the behest of Henri II. Elizabeth was preserving her reputation, and the possibility of one day ruling her country, in the face of irresponsible sexual scandal about her created by one step-uncle, Thomas Seymour, her supposed lover, and of implacable hostility from the other, Edward duke of Somerset and protector of England.

Moreover, despite Elizabeth's personal danger during the Seymour affair, she added to the risks to herself by strenuously protecting her governess, Catherine Ashley; loyalty to those who had given loyalty was the mark of the true ruler. At the same age, Mary's understanding of the nature and exercise of royal power found its most direct and deeply-felt expression not in awareness of the great political and religious crises of her day, but in quarrels with *her* governess, Madame de Parois, which were the subject of her most impassioned, 'near hysterical' letters to her mother, her regent in Scotland, in 1556–7. Elizabeth's upbringing was certainly at the other end of the spectrum from Mary's. But it does indicate the extent to which Mary's cushioned childhood created not only a cocoon of adulation, but a cocoon of immaturity which she seemed remarkably reluctant to pierce.

But this was not the whole story; for there were people all too anxious to pierce that cocoon. One, a strong influence on her while she was in France, was her maternal grandmother, Antoinette duchess of Guise, a woman of formidable personality who seems to have regarded membership of the house of Guise as a distinctly higher form of life than membership of the French royal family. Antoinette would therefore have hardly rated queenship of Scotland as a matter of much importance. But for her, Mary was a Guise; and a Guise was not a court butterfly. She was the daughter of the woman controlling Scotland, and niece of both the leading churchman and the leading secular politician in France, Charles cardinal of Lorraine, and Francis duke of Guise. And where Antoinette laid down guidelines – just as she had done when she advised her own daughter on Scottish affairs when Mary of Guise first went to Scotland – her son, the cardinal, filled in the details.

In January 1554, at increased expense for the Scots, he had Mary established in her own household. From that time, he was to direct her education, and to try to instil in her an awareness of statecraft and of the political circumstances and problems not only of her adopted country but of her kingdom. So one of the great figures of mid sixteenth-century France was emphatically reminding Mary of her position as the crucial link between Scotland and France; for that was where her importance would really lie even if she spent most of her life in France, and knowledge of Scotland therefore mattered greatly. Mary had the chance to learn her trade as something much more than a queen consort from a politician of great skill and finesse. She listened very dutifully. She related the cardinal's opinions to her mother. But as events were to show, the cardinal was unable to transmit the finesse.

If it was being pointed out to her that she had been born to a life of political responsibility and not simply pleasure by one member of the powerful and able house of Guise in France, the message was being reinforced from Scotland by another: her mother,

Mary of Guise. From 1538, Mary, widow of Francis of Orleans, duke of Longueville, and then aged twenty-three, spent her life first as the wife of James V, when she fulfilled her function as queen by producing two sons, only to see both of them die, and then as queen dowager fighting to maintain her daughter's interests. This kept her in Scotland cut off from the son of her first marriage and the daughter of the second in France, both of whom she clearly loved. It is one of the greatest examples of the age of a woman who had stern awareness that high birth was indeed a matter of high responsibility. She was not simply stern. She enjoyed the pleasures of court life as much as her daughter; and the woman who rejected Henry VIII's proposal by saying that although she was a tall woman she had a little neck, showed that she did not lack wit.

But when events forced her on to the centre of the political stage, she took her role very seriously indeed. Her letters to her daughter were a constant reminder of the affairs of her kingdom – and of the fact that regents could only do so much. Mary herself had to sign her act of revocation in 1555, and that was not the only matter for which the queen's signature was necessary. This was practical detail rather than high policy; and to deal with it, Mary sent over blank sheets signed 'Marie'. Nevertheless, it was not unimportant. Yet as far as we know, these pinpricks to the memory that she was queen of Scots did not seriously upset her ready assumption that her mother would do the job for her. Mary did refer to Scottish affairs in her letters, but under the influence of the cardinal, and in a manner which visibly lacked the vigorous interest shown in her determination to get rid of her governess. Meanwhile her mother did get on with the job. Despite her exclusion from formal power after James V's death, sheer personality had made her a force in political life in the 1540s. In the 1550s, she was the dominating force.

By 1550, the Scots could stop to draw breath. Whatever lay ahead, it must have seemed that the worst was over. The English had withdrawn. The young queen was safe. Mary of Guise had got what she wanted, in terms of policy. Arran had got what he wanted: international recognition of his importance, in the form of a French duchy, which might enhance his failing prestige at home. The dowager did her best to satisfy the nobility by trailing a number of them off to France, and getting pensions for them – even if some, like the master of Ruthven, complained about the shabbiness of the pay-off. With England discredited, the Protestants were in a much weaker position; from Mary of Guise's point of view, there was now no particular reason to suppose that they would upset the old order.

Indeed, there were those taking steps to ensure that they would not. Scotland was remarkable in having a counter-Reformation before the Reformation engulfed her. In 1549, two years after the close of the first session of the Council of Trent – the Council whose stupendous achievements encompassed the comprehensive definition of Catholic doctrine and the unchallengeable assertion of papal power, and which has been described as the creator of the modern Catholic church – John Hamilton, archbishop of St Andrews since 1547, held the first of his own reforming councils. The second, in 1552, saw the publication of Hamilton's *Catechism*, a vernacular work setting out the basic tenets of Catholic belief. It was also able to claim, with confidence, 'how many frightful heresies have, within the last few years, run riot in many divers parts of the realm, but have now at last been checked by the providence of the all-good and Almighty God, the singular goodwill of princes, and the vigilance and zeal of the prelates for the Catholic faith, and seem almost extinguished'. The situation was rather more fluid than this suggested; 'almost' might have been better expressed as 'not sufficiently'. But it was events during the 1550s, rather than the situation at the beginning of the decade, which were to determine that.

Meanwhile, with the queen now in France, and in view of the relative skills of dowager and regent, it was only a matter of time before Arran was eased out of office. The moment arrived in 1554. The dowager declared that, on the advice of the *parlement* of Paris, her daughter, being now in her twelfth year, had reached 'her perfect age'. Legally this entitled her to choose her own curators

– which in this case meant her regent. Arran accepted the inevitable, and made way for Mary of Guise, in return for various financial inducements for himself and his family, and a discharge securing him from any actions against him for anything he had done during the period of his regency. Parliament, in April 1554, formalized the transfer of the regency, though carefully asserting the Scottish position, as opposed to the French: Arran was demitting the regency *before* the queen reached her perfect age.

The new regent was given the opportunity to determine a much more clear-cut policy than that of the 1540s. In 1553, the Protestant Edward VI had died. The attempt by the power behind his throne, Warwick – now duke of Northumberland – to secure the succession for his strongly Protestant daughter-in-law Lady Jane Grey was a dismal failure; and England was now ruled by the Catholic Mary Tudor, then in her late thirties, married to Philip of Spain, and therefore potentially capable of establishing a Catholic dynasty which would make Henry VIII, Somerset and Northumberland look like a temporary aberration. There was now no obvious ally to whom Scottish Protestants could look. Isolated, they could be treated as virtually impotent, and therefore tolerated. But the moderation shown to the Protestants was not matched in the regent's determinedly pro-French policy. Throughout its history, the Auld Alliance had worked best when French and Scots did not try to live together, and particularly when the French kept out of Scotland. As early as the 1380s, and as recently as the 1520s, the presence of French troops in Scotland had produced hostility rather than amity. Now, the French were all too present. Not only were there French troops, but Frenchmen were infiltrated into the royal household, and even into the higher levels of government. Bartholomew de Villemore was plucked from Mary's household to become comptroller in 1555; and if the highest secular office, the chancellorship, was held by a Scottish magnate, Huntly, the vice-chancellor, de Rubay, was a Frenchman – and the man closer to the regent.

It was not only the pervasive presence of the French which roused alarm. As the final item of business in the parliament of 1555, the queen's advocate got up to present her act of revocation to the regent and the three estates, signed with Mary's own hand and sealed with her privy seal at Fontainebleau on 25 April. He then requested that it be registered in the books of parliament; to which regent and parliament obligingly consented. Mary was then twelve years old. No previous Scottish king had ever tried to claim that this was the age when his minority ended. And indeed, the habit had grown up of issuing acts of revocation well after the minorities were in practice over, at the age of twenty-five; James V was so scrupulous on this point that his was announced in Rouen, where he was on his twenty-fifth birthday. At less than half that age, Mary declared, in her act, 'the full administration and ruling to be in our own hands'.

Looking back, it is a ludicrous spectacle. Aged twelve, living in France and betrothed to the dauphin, Mary was asserting her position as the adult reigning monarch of Scotland. In 1555 it was not ludicrous; it was horrifying. Nothing could have been better designed to ram home to the Scots that monarchy as they understood it was a thing of the past. The present was a figurehead in France, and at home, a ruthlessly pro-French government headed by her mother. Mary of Guise had apparently managed to do, in one year, what Henry VIII and Somerset had failed to do in seven. The problem for the Scots this time, whatever their varying political and religious persuasions, was that there was no-one to whom they could turn as a counter-weight. They were, for the moment, hamstrung.

Lack of viable opposition enabled the regent to resolve her financial problems by resorting to a radical solution. She had inherited the substantial deficit of £30,000 Scots (£7,500 sterling) from Arran. She used her own French pension of 20,000 livres (c. £1,700 sterling) to pay for her daughter in France, but in addition the Scots had to provide 25,000 livres (£2,085 sterling). She had to pay her French troops. Her first effort to raise money echoed that of her dead husband. She turned to the pope; and although she was in a less strong bargaining position than James V, now that there was no Protestant threat from England, she was given a certain amount of clerical taxation in 1556 and 1557. But in 1556 she instituted a devastating new scheme, a perpetual tax. Her own country, France, had been accustomed to regular taxation since the fourteenth century; but if she was seeking to invoke this model, she might have remembered that there the nobles were exempt from taxation. Her new taxes – which included £60,000 Scots (£15,000 sterling) for her daughter's marriage – were collected in the teeth of considerable hostility. The principle was profoundly unpopular. The practice looked all too much like an effort to make the Scots pay for the French, and for French interests.

There is no doubt about Mary of Guise's political ability. She had played a waiting game with great skill in the 1540s. It therefore looks as though a decade in which her political nerves had always been stretched was succeeded by a dangerous level of confidence when the situation became apparently so much safer; she was no longer walking a tightrope, and she now walked too boldly on the ground. Whether she realized that the French alliance of 1548 was exceedingly fragile, entered into *faute de mieux*, or whether she assumed that it had a solidity which almost three centuries might have been expected to give it, is not clear. Either way, the effect was the same: she pushed her policy with immense and undue vigour. But it is important to remember what that policy was. She was a Guise, and a politician of European stature and vision. She was not simply trying to turn Scotland into a satellite state. She was trying to forge permanent links between France and Scotland because only then could the house of Valois survive against the monstrous growth of Hapsburg power, centred on Spain and the Empire, controlling the Netherlands and, in the very year she became regent, clutching England into its maw with the marriage of Philip and Mary. But for the Scots, it served to show that the unprecedented level of strenuous intervention from France in the 1550s might be as unpalatable as the similar experience in the 1540s from England.

There were some signs of reaction. Scottish resentment can be seen in the half-heartedness of the act of 1555 concerning the spreading of seditious slanders. An earlier act of 1424, repeated in

1540, had made the penalty death. In 1555, it was punishable only 'according to the quality of the fault in their bodies and goods at the Queen's Grace's pleasure' – that is, there was now an element of doubt expressed about the exaction of the extreme penalty. But then earlier laws had been concerned with tales about the monarchy, where this one related to the regent and the French. And there was another act which surely reflects Mary's fears about disorder. The banning of popular plays is normally associated with the hard-line Calvinist reformers. But the first parliament of Mary's regency anticipated this, for reasons which were purely political rather than moral, when it utterly banned 'Robert Hood nor Little John Abbot of Unreason [and] Queens of May' in both town and countryside. Robin Hood plays had been performed in the burghs at least since 1492, and the stories were certainly known in Scotland by the early fifteenth century. Now, in order that the French presence in her daughter's kingdom should not be threatened, not just by English intervention, but by any occasion such as a burgh play when Scottish mobs might get out of hand, Mary of Guise put a stop to a source of enjoyment and fun. As the act said, even 'women or others about summer trees singing' were to be viewed with concern, because they might 'make perturbation'.

Two years later the regent came up against more visible opposition. In the summer of 1557, Mary Tudor, under the influence of her husband Philip of Spain, brought England into the war between Spain and France. Scotland, France's ally, dutifully declared war on England. Mary of Guise and the highly influential French ambassador in Scotland, Henri, sieur d'Oysel, collected an army of French and Scottish troops, and got it to the borders. The French managed to move the artillery across the river Tweed, being – as even the hostile Knox admitted – 'in such facts expert'. The Scots stopped short, went to d'Oysel and told him 'that in no wise would they invade England'. This was not, of course, just a Protestant response, although it benefited the Protestants that the great Catholic powers of France and Spain should tear one another apart; their temporary truce in 1556 had been regarded as a significant reversal to the cause of reform, and when the war was renewed one of the leading English preachers, Christopher Goodman, was to urge the English not to fight for Spain, just as Knox urged the Scots not to fight for France. More generally, it was the first clear rejection by the Scots of French demands in the 1550s. But such refusals to fight had happened before, in the 1520s. It was an irritant, no more – especially as Mary of Guise was now moving towards the culmination of her policy, the French marriage.

On 14 December 1557, parliament agreed to send commissioners to France to negotiate the marriage, while making a sideways nod to Châtelherault's shrill demand that this should not prejudice his right as heir presumptive. Of the nine appointed, three were Protestant; Gilbert earl of Cassillis, lord James Stewart, bastard half-brother of the queen, and John Erskine of Dun. Their place in a group dominated by the Catholics no doubt reflected the regent's desire for consent from Catholic and Protestant alike; and as yet she saw little reason to fear the Protestants, who must still have seemed to her far less of a threat than the strong Huguenot party in France. The negotiations were successful. On 24 April 1558 Mary married the dauphin.

The ceremony at Notre-Dame was one of the great royal spectacles of the sixteenth century. Paris was packed for the occasion. The wedding procession was of enormous size and enormous splendour, the largesse scattered lavish, the banquet which followed 'Lucullan'. The festivities went on for days. With vast pomp and vaster cost, Scotland was officially linked by a marriage alliance to France; indeed, in terms of Mary's secret agreement, it became part of it. Not only the glittering figure at the centre of it all, but also her mother and the king of France had, it seemed, every cause for jubilation as well, no doubt, as relief. What the blustering and bullying of Henry VIII had failed to do in the 1540s, the gentler approach of Henri II had now achieved triumphantly; the Scots had given the French king what they had refused to the English one, control of their queen and, it seemed, control of their country. In November 1558 they appeared to offer even more, when parliament agreed that the dauphin should be given the crown matrimonial. It was, above all, a tribute to the formidable political ability of Mary of Guise. But besides ability, the other essential element in political success is luck; and at the precise moment of ultimate achievement, her luck deserted her, and the hollowness of the victory was revealed. For in November 1558, the Catholic Mary Tudor died, to be succeeded by Elizabeth; and whatever Elizabeth was, she was not a Catholic.

While Mary Tudor lived, the Protestants in Scotland had never actually given up, but as long as England as well as France and Spain was Catholic, all they could hope for was survival; and there was no point in preferring an English alliance to a French one. No wonder, then, that Mary of Guise could deal tolerantly with them; for they had no grounds for opposing her. In a revealing little episode in May 1556, she quashed the trial of John Knox, summoned by the Catholic hierarchy on a charge of heresy. This future leader of the Scottish Reformation was actually at that stage far more interested in England, where he had found a haven under the Protestant Edward VI. He had fled abroad when Mary Tudor succeeded, and had passed the time writing letters of consolation to English Protestants, and, in 1554, a savage attack on the English government, the *Admonition to England*. His return to Scotland late in 1555 was reluctant, and seems to have been less concerned with the Protestant cause than a personal one; in Edinburgh he could be reunited with Elizabeth Bowes and her daughter Marjory, whom he had met while a preacher at Berwick, and marry Marjory. But he did inveigh against those Protestant nobles who placated the regent by going to mass, and he preached, mainly in the Protestant strongholds of Angus and Ayrshire. Mary of Guise had the sense not to make him a *cause célèbre*. Her reward, in the summer of 1556, was a lengthy letter from Knox, encouraging her to embrace the Protestant faith. He seems to have thought it conciliatory. By his standards, no doubt it was. To Mary, reading that if she did not do so, 'this pre-eminence wherein ye are placed shall be your dejection to torment and pain everlasting', it looked more like the kind of bullying to which, on his own account, he would later subject her daughter. Her response was pithy and to the point. 'Please you, my lord', she said to James

Beaton, archbishop of Glasgow, handing him the letter, 'to read a pasquil' (lampoon).

Knox's attitude turned to bitter hostility. In 1558, he worked up his letter into a second edition, three times as long as the first, which he certainly wrote as an outright attack; and his portrayal of the dowager in his *History of Scotland* is one of hacking savagery. Meanwhile, the Protestants remained in their position of impotence. There seemed little alternative, with a woman whose reaction to them was to tolerate – and to laugh. In the summer of 1557, some of them tried to break the stalemate. Knox was invited to return; but when he reached Dieppe, he found messages telling him that the time was not ripe. The blow was enormous, not least because Knox had been once again reluctant to leave Geneva for Scotland, and had done so only after consultation with his English congregation there, and with John Calvin. He settled down to compose his *First Blast of the Trumpet against the Monstrous Regiment of Women*, a long diatribe against rule by women, written in a screeching style far removed from his usual mastery of prose. He would have done better to have let his temper cool.

Neither Mary Tudor nor Mary of Guise was much affected. But the Protestant Elizabeth, the queen whom he thought he was flattering by likening her to Deborah (the prophetess who, with the help of the Lord, saved Israel from the Canaanites), was never to forgive him, and this ensured that his role in the years of success for the Scottish Protestants after 1560 was less than it might otherwise have been. Meanwhile in 1558 he wrote the *Appellation to the Nobility and Estates of Scotland*, a work which, taken in conjunction with his *Letter addressed to the Commonalty of Scotland*, shows how far his mind was moving towards a positive theory of the rights of resistance in God's cause. For that cause, the nobles could resist the crown; if they failed, then it was the duty of the common people to resist them. It was a far-reaching and radical attack on the powers of the legitimately established authority, not only of those who ruled kingdoms but also of those who ruled localities. But these were not men who could afford such single-minded commitment.

Yet some did take a step of great courage. The widespread practice of making local, individual and personal bonds had, as we have seen, been taken over into the world of factional politics in the 1540s. Now, it was invoked for a religious purpose. In Edinburgh, on 3 December 1557, the earls of Argyll, Glencairn and Morton, Argyll's son lord Lorne and John Erskine of Dun made a bond whose text dramatically threw down the gauntlet. These five people promised 'before the Majesty of God and his congregation to . . . maintain, set forward and establish the most blessed word of God and his Congregation . . . and forsake and renounce the congregation of Satan, with all the superstitions, abominations and idolatry thereof'. This 'First Band of the Lords of the Congregation of Christ' was followed up by four other such bonds between then and 1562, charting not only the growth of the Protestant movement but also the increasing resistance to the regent and the French, which by late 1559 would reach heights undreamed of at the end of 1557. The First Band itself may have seemed of small significance at the time compared to parliament's apparently much more crucial decision one week after it was signed to go ahead with the marriage negotiations. Yet the very fact of taking action was undoubtedly a source of inspiration. Even Archibald earl of Argyll, nearing the end of a long life noted mainly for a remarkable inability to make decisions, now found 'boldness' in him; he 'reformed many things', we are told, and, despite the strictures of archbishop Hamilton, he maintained the Protestant preacher John Douglas in his household. And others did likewise. Knox's account of the bond and its aftermath compellingly conjures up the new spirit released by that small group in December 1557. The political situation still gave them no alternative to the regent's French policy. But 3 December 1557 does mark the move from mere existence to the beginnings of Protestant action within Scotland.

The next action, however, was taken not by the Protestants but by the Catholics; and a very puzzling one it was. On 28 April 1558, only four days after Mary's marriage, an old man called Walter Myln was burned for heresy at St Andrews. Myln was a former priest, who had abjured in the early 1540s. Why he was dragged out in 1558 and transformed from an obscure apostate into one of the very few great martyrs of the Scottish Reformation, remains a mystery. Despite Knox's fulminations against 'that cruel tyrant and unmerciful hypocrite', the archbishop of St Andrews, and the 'woman born to dissemble and deceive', Mary of Guise, it was in fact an act quite out of character of both archbishop and regent, neither of whom showed any taste for persecution. It may be that, even if the final stages of bringing the marriage about had temporarily overshadowed the making of the First Band, the Protestant threat thus created had sufficiently alarmed Mary of Guise and Hamilton into reacting with swift and exemplary violence once Mary was safely married. It was a very great mistake.

Of course the burning of one old man cannot be described as persecution; it was in no way a parallel to the persecution in England which gave an instinctively kindly woman the name of Bloody Mary. But knowledge of the English burnings was widespread, and Scottish Protestants could not be sure that something similar might not now happen to them. It must have been at the very time of the proceedings against Myln that the archbishop of St Andrews received the earl of Argyll's answers to his letter of admonition of 31 March 1558, in which he warned the earl of the dangers of his support for Protestantism. Argyll's reply included a counter-warning against listening to the counsel of those who would persuade him to 'blood-letting and burning of poor men, to make your Lordship serve their wicked appetites'. That shows clearly enough what the Scottish Protestants feared. And it was to take only one Scottish burning to achieve what some 275 burnings did in England: not only fear, but a Protestant backlash, 'a new fervency amongst the whole people; yea, even in the town of St Andrews began the people plainly to damn such unjust cruelty'. Knox recounts how they piled up a great heap of stones at the place of martyrdom, and no matter that the priests had them removed, and threatened excommunication, they were always replaced, until one night the papists found the permanent solution, taking them away to build into walls. True, Knox might exaggerate the effect, just as Foxe no doubt inflated the consequences of the English persecution in that Elizabethan best-seller, his *Book of Martyrs*. But exaggeration is not invention.

And indeed, where little had happened in the years before December 1557, there was an alarming upsurge of Protestant activity in 1558. In Dundee, in the spring of that year, the Protestant preachers John Willock and Paul Methven were having considerable success, in effect establishing a public Protestant church in the burgh. Methven was later to create an embarrassing scandal among the godly, when he was publicly deposed for adultery in 1562 – a sin which did not prevent him finding a niche among the ministry of the Church of England – but in 1558 he was a major asset to the Protestants, preaching not only in Dundee but, during the summer months, in other parts of Angus and in Fife. Over in the west, Ayr had a Protestant minister, Robert Leggat, under the protection of the burgh council, from May 1558. The same area saw a direct reversal for the bishops in July, when they had to withdraw their summons to the reforming preachers in the face of strenuous opposition from the local Protestant gentry who complained directly to Mary of Guise; the regent promptly denied knowledge of the summons and proclaimed the doctrine of love of God and neighbour to the Protestants, while instructing the bishops to leave them alone. In anticipation of the feast of St Giles, patron saint of Edinburgh, the statue of the saint was dumped into the Nor' Loch in the town, and then taken out, presumably dried off, and burnt. The attempt to hold the annual procession on the feast-day itself, 1 September, with a substitute statue borrowed for the occasion from the Greyfriars, produced a riot; 'the Grey Friars gaped, the Black Friars blew, the priests panted and fled' – and the Greyfriars lost their statue, its head shattered on an Edinburgh causeway.

But even so, there was not what could be described as an irrevocable Protestant march towards Reformation; the new activity of 1558 took place in a Scotland which was still largely Catholic. The real point about the events of 1558 is that it was a missed opportunity for the Catholics, missed because Mary of Guise still temporized, still would not put the weight of the 'state' behind that of the church. In terms of her own policy, she had little choice; she needed the support of leading Protestants as well as leading Catholics to complete the link with France. To the Protestants, according to Knox, she complained about opposition to her policy from the Catholics and Châtelherault; only if the crown matrimonial was granted would she have sufficient authority, and 'then devise ye what ye please in matters of religion and they shall be granted'. To the bishops, she explained that she needed Protestant support to get the crown matrimonial for the dauphin; then would she be in a position to combat heresy.

She might well have done so; it was, after all, a Catholic Scotland which was to be so closely allied with France. And as things stood in 1558, she could still afford to wait; for the Protestants, whatever their renewed fervour within Scotland, still had no support from outside, and without such support their chances of success remained remote. What she could not know was that by refusing to deal with the Protestant threat until the crown matrimonial had been obtained, she would throw away the strongest card in her anti-Protestant hand before having a chance to play it. For on 17 November 1558 – in the same month as the Scottish parliament did grant the crown matrimonial – Mary Tudor died. The situation changed radically. There was no longer a Catholic country to the south.

What did lie to the south was not immediately apparent. For English and Scottish Protestants, Mary Tudor was a disaster, inexplicably visited by God on her kingdom. Her younger sister and successor Elizabeth was much more of an unknown quantity. The Protestants could hope but by no means be certain of what she would do, though they could take comfort from her dramatic gesture on Christmas Day 1558, when she ordered the bishop celebrating Mass in her chapel not to elevate the host, walking out when he refused, and her even more spectacular gesture on 25 January 1559 when, at the opening of parliament, she told the abbot and monks of Westminster, processing with tapers burning, 'Away with these torches! We can see well enough'. But she had also issued a proclamation forbidding all preaching and teaching. And although the Marian exiles were hurrying back to England, there was no evidence that she was in sympathy with their Calvinist brand of Protestantism. Moreover, foreign policy dictated caution; with France and Scotland in alliance, she could not immediately break with Spain, and for the first four months of her reign the watching world was asked to believe in her willingness to contemplate marriage with her late sister's husband, Philip II. Nevertheless, where there had been four interlinked Catholic countries before November 1558, France, Spain, England and Scotland, there were now three; the possibility of advancing the Protestant cause in Scotland with help from England, dead for five years, was once again open.

The Scottish Protestants had their own dramatic gesture to make within a few weeks of Mary Tudor's death. On 1 January 1559, the 'Beggars' Summons' was nailed to the doors of the Scottish friaries, demanding in the name of the 'Blind, Crooked, Bedridden, Widows, Orphans and all other poor, so visited by the hand of God as may not work', that the friars should give up their patrimony by Whitsun. But it was a defiant rather than a triumphant gesture. Mary Tudor's death had given them hope, but that was far from certain victory. And even before she died, there were already signs of a new threat, when in October 1558 a truce was made between France and Spain. The threat turned into reality in April 1559, when Spain and France brought their long struggle in the Italian peninsula to an end by the Treaty of Cateau-Cambrésis. The peace which they made included England and Scotland – and menaced the Protestants in both. For by freeing themselves from war, the great Catholic powers were freeing themselves to attack the heretics, and attack they did. In Spain, what Henry Kamen has called the 'series of *autos-da-fé* which burnt out Protestantism' began at Valladolid in May 1559, while in France, at exactly the same time, persecution of the Calvinists so much increased that Calvin's greatest follower, Théodore Beza, began to question Calvin's insistence on non-resistance to authority. If England feared Spain, for the Scottish Protestants Henri II became a very present menace; for through his daughter-in-law Mary he might turn his attention to the Calvinists in Scotland as well as those in France.

They were right to fear. On 29 June 1559, Henri wrote to the pope, that notorious bombast Paul IV, about 'the incredible disaster which has since befallen the realm of Scotland to our extreme regret, disgust and displeasure'; the letter stated his 'confidence in God who is so signally offended at this wretched plague of ruffians', but God was to be given worldly assistance in the shape of 'a large and sufficient force of French soldiers, infantry and cavalry'. Divine favour was not, however, visibly given to the French king and his enterprise. Death overtook events only one day after the writing of this letter, when on 30 June the king took part in a joust, that 'peaceful' demonstration of the military arts which was in fact potentially lethal. Flaunting to the last the colours of his mistress Diane de Poitiers, while self-avowedly riding in honour of his queen Catherine de Medici, he was pierced in the eye and throat when the lance of his opponent, Jacques count of Montgomery, splintered on impact with his helm; and on 10 July, in great pain, he died.

An ineffective teenager and his charming teenage wife now occupied the throne of France. Youth was not a fundamental problem, but lack of ability was; and it drove the focal point of French politics away from the king to the dominant and rival forces of the Guises and the queen mother Catherine. Yet it was to be under the new regime, for all the difficulties of the power-struggle at home, rather than under the strong rule of Henri II, that the French were to come in force to the aid of Mary of Guise against the Scottish heretics; for the effective rulers of the two countries were now, after all, the two Guise brothers in France and their sister the regent in Scotland.

These heretics had not, however, waited upon events. On 2 May, Knox had arrived in Scotland. For the third time this greatest of Scottish Protestant heroes, whose name has lived for four centuries as the architect of Scottish religious life (not to say the strict bleakness of that life), whose statue in Edinburgh gazed balefully down on the meeting between pope and moderator of the General Assembly of the Kirk in 1982, and whose inordinately lofty statue in the Glasgow Necropolis lours at patients in the upper stories of the Royal Infirmary, made a strenuous effort not to return to his native country at all. Only when, in April, Elizabeth made it clear that he was the one Marian exile who would not be welcomed back to England did he accept the inevitable and come to Scotland. It is indeed a nice irony that two of the most famous characters in Scottish history, Mary and Knox, were united in their preference for countries other than Scotland, and that it was Elizabeth's eventual, reluctant decision to have Mary executed, and her earlier unrelenting hostility to Knox, which catapulted them both into the realm of Scottish fascination and Scottish legend.

In any event, unlike the autumn of 1557, the time was now certainly ripe for the peculiar inspiration of John Knox, the man who, in the words of the English diplomat Randolph, 'is able in one hour to put more life into us than five hundred trumpets continually blustering in our ears', and who would later be described by the same diplomat in 1561, a week after Mary's return to Scotland, as the preacher who 'thundereth out of the pulpit . . . he ruleth the roast, and of him all men stand in fear'. On 11 May 1559 Knox preached his great and wholly inflammatory sermon in St John's Kirk in Perth, producing mob riot not only in the church itself but also in the Black and Grey Friars and the Carthusian monastery, all of which were sacked. Knox, like Luther before him, recoiled in horror from low-born violence; the godly commonalty to whom he had appealed in 1558 now became the 'rascal multitude'. But his political theory, unlike Luther's, was radical in the extreme, and proved highly dangerous, when combined with his amazing powers of oratory, in the tense and excitable days of 1559 when, as Kirkcaldy of Grange wrote to Sir Henry Percy on 1 July, 'the manner of our Reformation is this: pulling down friaries, and using the prayer book of the godly King Edward (Edward VI)'.

In these circumstances, the regent had no choice but to act. She had summoned the Protestant preachers to come to Stirling on

10 May, and outlawed them when they refused. Two weeks later, she responded to the Lords of the Congregation's threat to fight in defence of reform, and summoned her forces to Stirling. The first act of the leaders of what were now rival armies, at Perth and Stirling, was to arrange a truce, on 29 May; almost as quickly, Mary of Guise broke its terms, by having the Mass restored in Perth. It was an action which drove the earl of Argyll and lord James Stewart firmly into opposition. Civil war – even if very low-key civil war – had begun, and would last until July 1560, by which time the regent herself would be dead. Initially the advantage lay with the Lords of the Congregation; by the end of June, they had driven the regent's troops out of Fife, had regained Perth and moved in on Edinburgh, where, on 7 July, Knox was appointed minister. But in July Mary of Guise was able to fight back more successfully, and at the end of the month the two sides made another truce, by which Edinburgh was to be free to choose its religion, and Catholic observance was not to be reinstated where it had been suppressed. With their agreement to meet in Stirling on 10 September, the Lords of the Congregation, in military terms at least, appeared quiescent; the first stage of the war was over.

But in the summer of 1559, something potentially much more radical was happening. One obvious problem about the regent's earlier policy of marrying her daughter to the dauphin is why leading Scottish Protestants like lord James Stewart and John Erskine of Dun had not only accepted this symbolic and political consolidation of the alliance with Catholic France, but had given it positive support, being among those who negotiated it. The most likely explanation is that they saw it as a way to keep the Catholic-educated Mary out of Scotland, while maintaining their formal loyalty to her, thereby maximizing their opportunity to advance the Protestant cause while minimizing the need to clash directly with their sovereign; there was, after all, no sign that Mary was particularly interested in the internal affairs of her kingdom, and although it was a gamble, and a risky one, leaving her to continue to enjoy life in France appeared to be the best chance they had.

Now, there are hints that they were moving beyond that position. A series of very guarded letters written in July and August 1559 between them and Elizabeth's leading minister, William Cecil, shows that they were contemplating at the very least an outright challenge to the regent's authority – a bold enough but not actually unprecedented step – but possibly something more, and infinitely more sensational, the deposition of the queen herself; and at the same time they were proposing a dramatic reversal of foreign relations, in which Scottish friendship would certainly be switched from her traditional ally France to her traditional enemy England, and that even closer ties between Scotland and England might be envisaged.

The hand of that great radical political theorist, John Knox, can certainly be detected in this – literally, for it was he who penned the letters. But Knox could always afford to be a great deal more cavalier about the dangers of rebellion against established authority than those who, being themselves great lords who ruled over men, knew very well the chaos which could result if the bonds of obedience and loyalty were violently broken. So what was it that pushed them into a far more extreme position towards Mary than that of 1558? The initial reason must have been Protestant fears of what Henri II, using his daughter-in-law, might do after the treaty of Cateau-Cambrésis; the public Protestant call to arms and the private and tentative contact with England were part of the same desperate reaction to a situation which left the Protestants no more time to move slowly, and forced them into overt action against the regent – the representative of legitimate authority – and, perhaps, a covert move against her daughter – the legitimate authority. Henri's unexpected death changed the political circumstances, but left the need to act unaltered; for the accession of Francis and Mary opened the way for the dominance of Mary's uncles of Guise: the duke, and the cardinal who had already tried to teach Mary a statecraft which left no room for indifference to Scotland.

The letters themselves began with a private approach to Cecil by William Kirkcaldy of Grange; then came one from five Scottish

Protestants, Argyll, lord James and others, written on 19 July, and remarkable for its spelling, its rhetorical power, and its refusal to state positively what was wanted. Both were cautious in the extreme. Those who composed them were certainly prepared to assert their intention to advance Protestantism, their desire for 'perpetual amity' with England, and their hostility to France. But they raised the question of authority only in the most ambiguous terms: 'we have yet made no mention of change in authority nor has it even entered our hearts, but seeing that France and the Queen Regent here, her priests, etc., intend nothing but suppressing Christ's evangel . . . we are fully purposed to seek the next remedy and withstand their tyranny'. And so they asked for English counsel and 'furtherance'.

Cecil's response, which they received on 6 August, was an expression of sympathy – and equally cautious. As Argyll and lord James said, in their reply of the 13th in which they openly declared it to be the role of the nobles and council 'to provide that the ancient liberties of the realm be freed from tyranny of strangers [and] to abolish (God assisting us) all manifest idolatry and maintainers', he had not been 'so full and plain as we expected'. What prompted blunter speaking we do not know, but there was to be no lack of plainness in the English memorandum drawn up on the 31st. This recommended at least perpetual peace between England and Scotland, and even a single monarchy. The French were to be excluded from offices in Scotland – and Scottish noblemen must reject French pensions. Châtelherault and the Hamiltons, as heirs to the queen, must have regard to Anglo-Scottish friendship. And if the queen would not agree to all this, 'as is likely', for the 'greedy and tyrannous affection of France, then it is apparent that Almighty God is pleased to transfer from her the rule of the kingdom for the weale of it'. The Rough Wooing, when the tyrannous strangers had been the English, was forgotten; what was resurrected from the 1540s was the idea of a united, Protestant Britain. And if necessary, the Francophile queen would go.

What are we to make of all this? Surely confusion in the minds of the leading Protestants, pushed down strange paths by the increasing pressure of religious and political tensions, rather than a determination to rush upon revolution. At most, they had hinted only obliquely at the removal of Mary herself; the phrase 'to seek the next remedy' in the letter of 19 July could not be more guarded. Indeed, the measure of the difficulty they were in can be seen in their own statement of 6 August in defence of their lack of achievement, made on the very day they had been disappointed by Cecil's letter; for Knox was inscribing a letter from Argyll and lord James to Sir James Croft, captain of Berwick, saying that they were 'sorry to be judged slow, negligent and cold in our proceedings. . . . You know, sir, how difficult it is to persuade a multitude to revolt of established authority'.

It is the eternal message of men of vision, pushing against the dead weight of conservatism. And it was of no help to the Scottish Protestants that on 8 August, in the instructions given to that experienced diplomat of the 1540s, Sir Ralph Sadler, now sent north to make a comeback in the Scottish political scene, the English were encouraging the idea of being anti-French and anticipating their outspoken memorandum of the 31st by warbling about the need for government by someone of the blood of Scotland. Indeed, the casual indifference of this earlier document makes it quite clear what the English were after; France, as the later memorandum said, must not make Scotland a 'footstool' to look over England, and whether that be resolved, as the memorial of the 8th put it, by Mary's heir Châtelherault or by her bastard half-brother lord James, should he have designs on the crown, really did not matter. It was not so easy for the Scottish Protestants.

Their problem was that, for all the clarity of their insistence that God was on their side, their world was a complex, not a simple place. It was they who were the defenders, not the aggressors, the men pushed by fear of extermination into acts which they knew came dangerously close to that disturbance of the social order which was almost as much to be feared. They were well aware that the natural secular order of things was rule by the monarch. But for them, events had been dictated by the regent's French policy,

French officials and, during the fighting in 1559, French troops. Meanwhile, what could they look for from their monarch? On 17 July 1559, the answer was a scolding letter from her husband the king of France to lord James, marvelling that he, who 'has the honour to be so near the Queen's Grace, my wife . . . should be so forgetful as to make yourself the head . . . of the tumults and seditions'; only six days later did the queen get round to sending a similarly plaintive message herself.

There could hardly be a better reminder of what they were up against: a regent in Scotland with whom they were now at war, but whose political skills they recognized, and whom they regarded with respect, acting for their sovereign in France who so far failed to rule that she got a foreign monarch to tell them off. Unlike them, Mary Queen of Scots did not see complexities in the situation; like her grandson Charles I after her, she assumed that the expression of the royal will from a distance was enough to make problems go away. And the Protestants' only hope of redressing the imbalance of power created by the French lay in turning to the English, even though they well knew that protestations of Anglo-Scottish friendship and desire for union in no way wiped out the instinctive hostility between Scots and English which ran so deep that half a century later it would still cause grievous problems for the first king of Britain. Certainly it made nonsense of their appeal for support within Scotland on the grounds of freeing the kingdom from the tyranny of strangers.

Nor was that their only headache. Whatever ideas of deposing Mary were tentatively circulating in the summer of 1559, it would have been an immensely dangerous step to take. There were, of course, grounds for taking it; they could well argue the impossibility of continuing to give their loyalty and service to a monarch who was creating a totally new situation by failing in her fundamental duty of ruling her people. And getting rid of an unwelcome ruler would not actually be novel; it had happened twice in the fifteenth century, to James I and James III. But this time there would be a complete novelty, and one that would have given the most strongly anti-Marian pause. For whereas two individual kings had been removed, it had been the experience of their personal rule which had provoked men into lethal opposition. But the royal house of Stewart itself had not been threatened; in both cases, the king's son had succeeded. There is no doubt about the strength and prestige of the house of Stewart, and the profound unwillingness of the Scots to challenge it. In this case, therefore, the problem was horribly compounded by the fact that the queen was as yet childless; and the heir who would succeed was James duke of Châtelherault, head of the unpopular house of Hamilton and discredited former regent.

In May 1559, Mary of Guise had hurled at her opponents the accusation that they 'meant no religion, but a plain rebellion'. The first claim was certainly wrong, and hence the second far too stark. So long as France and Scotland were run by three members of the mighty Guise family, the cardinal and the duke in France and their sister Mary in Scotland, then the only way for the Lords of the Congregation to achieve their religious ends, and prevent Scotland from sinking into provincial status, was to resist the regent. Only the most cynical of historians can attempt to challenge the religious sincerity of men like Glencairn and Argyll and their associates. They were not simply rebels. But anything other than acquiescence with the regent could only tie them into political and ideological knots of Gordian proportions.

We do not know how close they came to attempting to depose Mary. We do know that, if it had been an idea seriously mooted, they drew back. This left them in the ludicrous position of having to claim that, out of loyalty to their sovereign lady, they were embattled against their sovereign lady's mother. In the propaganda warfare of this period which both they and Mary of Guise plunged into with alacrity, Mary certainly had the stronger case. The Lords of the Congregation could rightly assert the duty and responsibility of the nobility to act for the good of the commonweal, and indeed experience of minorities over two centuries had in practice underwritten the theoretical position to an unusual extent. But so long as Mary of Guise's position was upheld by her daughter, no amount of rhetoric could conceal the fact that in attacking the regent they were attacking the queen, and religious sincerity did not get them off the hook of treason; thus, for example, when they seized the coining-irons of the mint in Edinburgh in July, it was an intelligent enough political and military act, but their efforts to justify it on the grounds that they were serving their country by stopping the regent's debasement of the coinage rang all too hollow. And underneath the lofty claims that they were fulfilling the will of God and freeing the kingdom from oppression and tyranny, and the open attacks on the regent's actions, there were still hints of the desire to come to terms, which reflect their awareness of how shaky the basis of their self-defence was.

These hints had their final expression in an astonishing personal letter written by Knox to Mary on 26 October 1559, claiming that 'if it be the office of a very friend to give true and faithful counsel to them whom he sees run to destruction for lack of the same, I could not be proven enemy to your Grace but rather a friend unfeigned' – even if moderation was never Knox's strong suit and so, unable to keep up the quiet tone of the letter, he felt impelled to throw in a postscript: 'God move your heart yet in time to consider that ye fight not against man, but against the eternal God, and against his Son Jesus Christ, the only Prince of the kings of the earth.'

The most remarkable thing about this letter was that Knox thought it worthwhile making his appeal even although five days earlier the Lords of the Congregation had taken decisive action. On 21 October a Convention summoned to the Tolbooth in Edinburgh accused Mary of Guise of the fundamental failure to take counsel from the nobility of the realm, something which touched on a very sensitive aristocratic nerve, and with reason. And so in ludicrous language, 'with one consent and common vote . . . In name and authority of our Sovereign Lord and Lady (Francis and Mary), [the Convention] suspends the said commission granted by our said Sovereigns to the said Queen Dowager'. So Francis and Mary deposed the regent. The principal catalyst behind this act was the fact that in September the wavering Châtelherault had come to a decision as a result of Cecil's help in arranging the escape of his son Arran from France, and finally agreed to join the Lords of the Congregation, thus ending the uneasy situation in which the Hamiltons had dithered between two opposing forces. The significance of the act is that it shows how much further the Lords of the Congregation were now prepared to go. Its lack of significance is that it made no real difference to the political situation, except for putting the burgh of Edinburgh through a rapid change of councils and giving it the burden of housing the army of the Congregation. By early November, the Protestant lords had been forced to slip out of Edinburgh, leaving the Catholics in the ascendant and the Mass restored. The queen dowager might no longer be regent, in Protestant eyes, but she still had her French troops and stalemate continued.

It was to last for some months yet. But while Francis and Mary fussed about the situation in Edinburgh, setting up an enquiry into what had happened to the burgh council, in February 1560 the Protestant lords did something ideologically much less courageous than their deposition of the regent, but in practical terms infinitely more crucial: they made the Treaty of Berwick with England, and were assured of English help. At an informal level, they had not wholly lacked it before; £3,000 had been sent to them in August 1559, and in January the English admiral Winter had appeared in the Forth, officially searching for pirates but actually cutting the French troops' line of communication between their strongholds in Fife and Leith. But help was now guaranteed, by a treaty which was the triumph of Cecil's clear policy over Elizabeth's instinctive desire to obfuscate and temporize. The English queen, like the Scottish Protestants, was caught in an intolerable ideological trap. English political interests on balance dictated help for the Protestants, even though that in itself meant the risk of stirring up reaction from France and perhaps even Spain. But for the first time, and not the last, Elizabeth had to agree to support Scottish rebels against their rightful queen; it was a nightmare created in 1559 which was not to end until Mary's death in 1587.

English troops arrived in Scotland at the end of March. By July, it was all over. It was not only English intervention which brought this about, for although this undoubtedly tipped the balance, Mary of Guise held Edinburgh castle, and the French appeared almost impregnable in Leith. But there were two other factors. In France, a conspiracy of Calvinists and 'political' Huguenots against the Guises, which ended with the 'Tumult of Amboise' in mid March with its hideous reprisals, left the Guises victorious, but it deflected their attention away from Scotland at a critical moment. They could no longer pour in troops. Instead, in April and May, they sent Jean, bishop of Valence and Charles de La Rochefoucauld, sieur de Randan, by way of London, to treat with the Lords of the Congregation. Then came the crowning blow for France and for the Catholics in Scotland. On 11 June, Mary of Guise died of dropsy.

The jubilant Knox wrote about her death in terms which make it clear why charity has not been thought a notable feature of Scottish Calvinism. In fact, at the death-bed there was an astonishing display of Protestant respect for the regent who had fought so hard for the French alliance and the survival of the Catholic faith. For with her when she died were those leading Calvinists lord James Stewart and Archibald earl of Argyll. It is a remarkable demonstration of the attitude of the Scottish aristocracy to authority – no matter the existence of political hostility and religious division – when that authority was effectively exercised. Mary of Guise was brought up in the charmed circles of the greatest French aristocracy. She was not brought up to be a major figure in political life, let alone a ruler. She was pitchforked into it by the early death of her husband James V. But this woman from France made sure that she learned about the country she would control. She did things which were deeply unpopular to a large section of the political community which she was striving to hold together. But she shared one crucial thing with the whole of that community, friends and enemies: awareness that the struggle was not just a Scottish matter, but something fought out on the international stage. Moreover, she had shown that, even if she was only regent and not queen, let alone king, she was, like the Stewart kings themselves, a formidable personality, all too able to impose her policies.

CHAPTER FIVE

The Reluctant Ruler
1560–5

Mary of Guise died on 11 June 1560. Mary Queen of Scots returned to Scotland on 19 August 1561. It is highly symbolic that Mary's personal rule should begin with a vacuum, which lasted for fourteen months; not only was she absent, but throughout that period, as lord James Stewart pointed out to her, she left her kingdom without any legally constituted government at all. If it is puzzling enough that a ruler should behave in this way, what makes it all the more remarkable is that she simply sat back and allowed the Protestant rebels of 1559–60, who had illegally deposed her regent and set themselves up as 'the Great Council of the Realm', to control the affairs of her country. It can hardly be overstated just how remarkable this was. Even inept monarchs usually attempt to exercise control; their problem arises from the ineffectiveness with which they do it. In Mary's case, we have the unique spectacle of a monarch who made no attempt at all to impose her rule. Instead, the men who in 1560 rebelled against legitimate authority were enabled to exercise power by that legitimate authority, so that it was the Protestant lords who dictated the events of one of the most momentous years of Scottish history. After the tensions and drama of the summer of 1560, the queen's absence for a further twelve months must almost have seemed liked anti-climax, though one to be welcomed profoundly by the Protestants. No doubt, when they remembered the determined activity of another Catholic queen close to home, Mary Tudor, or contemplated the problems of the Huguenots across the channel and the ruthless eradication of heretics in Spain by Philip II and the Spanish Inquisition, they were also considerably surprised. Mary Tudor; Catherine de Medici, now, after the death of Henry II, the French equivalent of Mary of Guise; Philip II.

These were rulers who behaved as rulers were expected to do; and one only has to consider their ability to achieve their ends, even in the case of France, torn by religious and factional strife, or – a much more attractive proposition for the Scottish Protestants – Elizabeth's successful reversal of her sister's policy in England, to see what could have happened in Scotland. But in Scotland, an absentee Catholic queen sat back and allowed the Protestants to build on their success of 1560. And while they did so, that queen lingered on in France, trying to determine her personal affairs.

The only direct part she played in the resolution of the conflict between French, English and Scots, which took place less than a month after the death of Mary of Guise, was on the matter of her use of the English arms, which she had promptly assumed on the death of Mary Tudor, thus publicly asserting that Elizabeth, illegitimate in Catholic eyes, had no valid title to the English throne. On 6 July 1560, the French envoys, acting in the name of Mary and Francis, concluded the Treaty of Edinburgh with the Scottish and English commissioners. The bargaining was hard. But in the end the Scottish Protestants emerged victorious; both the English and the French were to leave Scotland. The English gained from the removal of the French, for that meant the hope of Protestant success in Scotland and, with it, closer links with the country. The French lost entirely the position they had had since 1548. Mary, apparently indifferent to the fact that the policy maintained for so long by her mother and by her adopted country was now in ruins, refused to ratify the treaty solely on the grounds that the French had agreed to the English demand that she should no longer use their arms on her armorial bearings; for her, political reality waited upon empty gesture.

Much has been made of the fact that the treaty said nothing about religion. It did not need to. It was accompanied by a list of 'Concessions' drawn up on behalf of Francis and Mary by the French commissioners. These included the agreement that a parliament should meet. It was announced for 20 July, but 'continued' (prorogued) until 1 August. It was to be one of the most dramatic and profoundly important of all Scottish parliaments; for this was the Reformation parliament. Its proceedings were short. The English Reformation parliament lasted for seven years, the Scottish one less than three weeks. It passed only three acts. It abolished the power of the pope within the realm; it forbade the saying of Mass; and it annulled all acts from the time of James I 'not agreeing with God's holy word' – that is, those acts protecting the old church. That was all that was needed to dismantle the base of the pre-Reformation church.

Small in number, challenging every conservative instinct, and with a deal of luck as well as English help (though luck is not how they would have seen it) the Protestants had won a considerable victory. But it was not a conclusive one. It was lack of effective response from their Catholic queen which ensured that their luck continued to hold. This was an act of defiance infinitely greater even than the events of the past year; and Mary was understandably – and noisily – indignant. As with the Treaty of Edinburgh, she refused to ratify the acts. As with the treaty, her refusal made no difference whatsoever. The Protestants could therefore, for the moment, draw breath. But there could be no assurance that they would be left alone indefinitely; Mary's own inactivity did not necessarily mean that France might not renew her interventionist policy, trying to work through the volatile Châtelherault. And indeed, for a very different reason, their breathing space did seem to be short. On 5 December, in unspeakable agony, and possibly refused adequate medical treatment, Francis II died. Mary, now junior queen dowager, drew back to let the senior, Catherine de Medici, pass out of the death-chamber first. She was no longer queen of France. What she might become was anyone's guess.

What probably no-one could have guessed was what actually happened: that Mary would still do all in her power not to rule Scotland. As Knox later said, 'in whose default, we pray you, was the queen absent from this realm?' The answer was the queen. She emerged from the forty days limbo of court mourning not to plan her future as the inheritor of the Stewart throne, but to use her position in the marriage market to acquire another continental husband. At this stage, she rejected the Hamiltons' frantic proposal that if Elizabeth would not agree to the idea of marriage with Châtelherault's son, James earl of Arran, she should; it was a suggestion deeply disliked by almost everyone in Scotland, and one without any appeal to the queen. But her Scottish subjects could only wait and watch as hints were made about her possible marriage to Francis's brother and heir, Charles IX – which would keep her in France – and as negotiations began for her marriage to Don Carlos, the terrifying and lunatic heir of Philip II – which would presumably move her further away, to Spain. In the end, neither materialized, largely because of the opposition of Catherine de Medici, whose outward show of friendship to her daughter-in-law disguised the absence of either affection or respect. The French match was probably always a non-starter; and Catherine had no intention of enhancing the power of the Guise faction by allowing Mary to make what was politically, if not personally, the best match in Europe, and turn up in Madrid as a potential rival to her own daughter Elisabeth, wife of Philip II himself.

Antonia Fraser has made the best possible defence of Mary in the period after Francis's death, rightly pointing out that her position naturally made her the target for 'almost any currently unmarried male of roughly suitable age' who would benefit her 'either by establishing her own throne of Scotland, or by strengthening her claim to the throne of England, or even by re-establishing her on the throne of France'. And she reminds us that, whatever their later reputations, at this time the modest Mary, 'anxious to do her best as a ruler by taking wise advice', was rated higher than the 'headstrong, extravagant and stubborn' Elizabeth. Thus the English diplomat Nicholas Throckmorton clearly found Mary a soothing and delightful change from his own difficult mistress when he first met her on 31 December 1560; in an obvious side-swipe at Elizabeth, then keeping her ministers in a state of constant fear that she would marry her favourite, Robert Dudley, he praised her because not only was she prepared to listen, but 'she more esteemeth the continuation of her honour and to marry one that may uphold her to be great than she passeth to please her fancy'.

Yet this is not in the end convincing, for two reasons. First, we are left with the undeniable fact that Mary was very good about thinking about her marriage and her honour, but totally indifferent to the real source of that honour. She had no need to marry to establish 'her own throne of Scotland'. That was hers, if only she would occupy it; and her determined preference for someone else's, be it in France or Spain, was a denial, unparalleled in her day, of the position to which she had been born, and of the tradition, reputation and achievements of her Stewart predecessors. Second, marriage had nothing to do with her claim to the English throne; that depended solely on English willingness to recognize that the heir of Margaret Tudor, elder of Henry VIII's two sisters, could succeed, despite Henry's will which had cut the Scottish descendants of Margaret and James IV out of the English succession, on the grounds that they were aliens. In any event, it was surely premature to put her claim to the English throne before her position as queen of Scotland when it was still perfectly possible that Elizabeth would herself marry and have children; for as yet only she knew the extent of her determined virginity.

In the sixteenth century, royal marriages involved three things: honour, political and religious advantage, and the provision of an heir for the kingdom. With luck, they might also involve affection and personal pleasure. But even Mary Tudor, tragically besotted by her husband Philip of Spain, but nevertheless marrying him to help her restore England to Roman Catholicism and to provide a Catholic heir for her kingdom in place of Elizabeth, shows that the marriage of rulers was never a matter of purely personal consideration. Uniquely – whether one is considering the 'normal' male rulers of sixteenth-century Europe, or the 'abnormal' and undoubtedly more difficult female ones – Mary put marriage before monarchy. She had a very high sense of what was due to her as queen. What was apparently lacking was the recognition that there was something fundamental due from her. At a personal level, we may sympathize; to return to Scotland meant facing problems of truly formidable proportions. But the question is whether they were worse than those faced by her contemporary rulers. In June 1561,

Throckmorton told her bluntly that they were not: 'Madam, your realm is in no other case at this day, than all the other realms of Christendom are; the proof whereof you see verified in this realm (France).' And as we are dealing not just with a personality, however attractive, but with a queen regnant reluctant to rule, we should reserve some sympathy for her subjects.

By March 1561, the future was closing in on both queen and subjects, as it became increasingly clear that her hopes of continuing to sit charmingly on a consort's rather than effectively on a sovereign's throne were not going to be realized. Whatever her own inclinations, her role, as seen by the royal houses of France and Spain, was that of a Catholic queen who could advance the Counter-Reformation in her own kingdom. In these circumstances, she transmitted a message of remarkable tactlessness to her Scottish council. For it was treated to a harangue by M. de L'isle on behalf of the new French king, Charles IX, in which he began by offering Charles's condolences with the Scots on the death of his brother Francis II, which also meant the dissolution of the firm Franco-Scottish alliance created by his marriage to Mary. He then assured them that their queen wished to bury her memories of all their past offences and show them her sincere love, 'for which he desires them to render in return their perfect obedience to her, so that they may not make her regret having been so benign'. And he told them of the French king's offer to Mary to continue the old alliance and friendship, and of the assurances of the queen mother, Catherine, that she would do all in her power to assist its continuation.

Her councillors – who included the leading Protestants whose policies she had done nothing to counteract since the previous summer, and who were now once again under threat from the French – replied with considerable dignity. They said that they were indeed much grieved at the death of Francis; for they were sure that, had he lived, he would have punished those of his French ministers who had been the cause of the recent troubles in Scotland. They would welcome perfect friendship between Charles and their queen, and thanked the queen mother for her expression of goodwill. And 'as for his offer of reconciling them with the Queen, they are no otherwise affectioned towards her than becomes good and obedient subjects, and are willing to recognize the Queen's goodness with all submission and humble service. They beg that the king will be pleased to consider that there are no subjects in Europe more ready to serve their Sovereign than they are their Queen.' This was not just window-dressing; the history of crown-magnate relations in Scotland gives credence to their claim.

This exchange therefore encapsulates beautifully the attitudes of both sides, and the almost intolerable nature of the problem. The queen who did not want to be in Scotland at all was again using a king of France, as she had done in July 1559, to tell off those trying to control events like naughty children. The naughty children might privately have wished otherwise; but in the last resort they were prepared to welcome the heir of the Stewart kings back to Scotland and make the best of a bad job – if only she would turn up and do the job.

Whether Mary had been indulging her own loftily one-sided view of royalty or, as Throckmorton suggested, acting on ill-conceived advice, the recriminations and the pushing of the Auld Alliance were as empty as the refusal to ratify the acts of the Reformation parliament had been. Mary's desire to remain in France as queen after the regent died, and then to remain abroad after her husband died, had given the Protestants time to advance their position. Both options were now lost to her; she had to come back to Scotland. But she had a third desire: the English throne. That determined her reactions to the envoys sent to her by the rival religious and political forces in Scotland, in anticipation of her return. The Catholic John Leslie, future bishop of Ross, suggested something which would have undoubtedly satisfied her Catholic friends in France, not to say the Spaniards and the pope as well. As a Catholic monarch Mary should initiate the Counter-Reformation in her kingdom by arriving not in the capital, Edinburgh, but in the important northern burgh of Aberdeen; there she could immediately invoke the backing of the most powerful Catholics in the kingdom, the group of northern earls.

This included one of the most influential nobles in Scotland, George Gordon, earl of Huntly, who had temporarily swung towards the Lords of the Congregation because of antagonism to French control, but who remained Catholic and would certainly support the queen in Scotland. Leslie was turned down flat.

The reception given to the other envoy, Mary's half-brother lord James, who spent five days with her in April 1561, was very different. She concealed from him the fact that her Spanish ambitions were still alive, and declared that if she were to come to Scotland, she would come under the pro-English and Protestant banner. She would accept his assurance that she herself could hear Mass in her private chapel in Holyrood, while leaving everyone else bound by the act of the Reformation parliament abolishing the Mass – the act which she had refused to ratify. If Leslie is correct, she even agreed to lord James's request to be given the earldom of Moray – the earldom controlled by the earl of Huntly, her greatest Catholic supporter. Only one explanation seems possible: lord James and his political associates could offer her what she could not hope for if she fulfilled the expectations of the Catholics in Europe and Scotland: support for her claim to be recognized as Elizabeth's heir.

One may question the political intelligence of someone who determined her policy towards her own kingdom simply in order to be acknowledged as heir to a young woman of child-bearing age. One may also wonder at her apparent lack of religious commitment as a ruler, as opposed to as a private person. To the Protestant party, of course, exceptional as her attitude was, it came as a huge relief. A combination of John Knox and hindsight has created a wholly misleading impression of the inevitability of Protestant triumph in 1560. And on the political and diplomatic front, modern students of Scottish history may intone with the equal certainty of hindsight that the Auld Alliance between Scotland and France, created in 1295, had now come to an end. But in 1560 that was by no means so certain. The summer of 1560 was certainly a high point for the Protestant, pro-English party. Catholic hopes had been rapidly and dramatically extinguished. It was the Protestants who seemed to have the better claim to the providence of Almighty God. The Reformation parliament itself was a statement of great confidence by those who, only a few months earlier, had been fighting for very survival. Its composition was quite illegal. The hundred or so small lairds who poured into Edinburgh to take part in it had no constitutional justification for their presence. They invoked the dead-letter statute of 1428 which had in fact enacted that from their number shire representatives should be elected. But their *de facto* justification of their right to have a voice in the affairs of the realm was not challenged, and indeed in view of the claims of the greater nobility during the preceding year this is hardly surprising.

It was a time of wild excitement for the Protestants, with a flood of ministers and superintendents being appointed, with Knox giving public sermons on the prophet Haggai, who had adjured his people that the time had come to build the house of the Lord, who would 'shake the heavens and the earth . . . and will overthrow the throne of kingdoms, and destroy the strength of the kingdom of the heathen'. In such an atmosphere, there was only a handful of dissident voices to oppose the acts of the parliament. Above all Protestant doctrine was articulated when, on 17 August, parliament ratified the Confession of Faith, a most moving statement of Protestant belief, uncluttered by anti-papist diatribes, clear and forceful in its language, visionary in its portrayal of the little new Scottish church as part of the great community of Christian believers, visible and invisible. It is a document which stands as an incontrovertible reminder that whatever the perplexities and squalid political struggles which had led to this point, and would go on thereafter, what happened in the summer of 1560 was not just political 'revolution'. It was the culmination of the desire of the great laymen as well as the great religious leaders like John Knox and John Willock 'to set forward the Reformation of Religion, according to God's word'.

But there success ended, and the problems began. In the first place, there was still a large number of Catholics in Scotland. Secondly, although the Mass and the power of the pope had been abolished, the structure of the old church remained untouched. This was indeed the most amazing aspect of the Scottish Reformation. Unlike their English counterparts, the monasteries were not suppressed, but left to wither away. The Catholic clergy, from bishop to parish priest, continued to enjoy their revenues; financially that may not have meant much in the case of the desperately impoverished vicars in the parishes, but it was certainly significant where the higher clergy were concerned.

The reason for this astonishing, even ludicrous, situation was not just that the Protestants lacked sufficient muscle to wipe out the pre-Reformation church. Much more important was the extent to which the intensely felt personal bonds of kinship and of lordship still survived. If the leading Protestant nobles were there to give comfort to their greatest enemy, Mary of Guise, on her death-bed, they were hardly likely to turn with savage determination on their kinsmen and friends who held the benefices of the old church. And as with the clergy, so with the laity: in their roles as head of kindreds and as great lords, they did not distinguish between their Catholic and Protestant kinsmen and followers when called upon to fulfil their traditional secular obligations. Thus, for example, the Catholic earl of Eglinton and the Protestant lord Boyd made a bond of friendship in 1563, in the time-honoured way in which heads of kindreds acknowledged that a feud between their houses was over and amity restored. Ideologically, men like Argyll, Glencairn and lord James were totally committed Protestants. But they would never join Knox in allowing their religious stance alone to dictate their attitude to political and social associates and friends who happened to be Catholic.

The unity of the secular and religious leaders of the Protestant party, born of the fight against France and the Catholic church, was therefore bound to show cracks once the immediate crisis was over. Indeed, they were becoming evident even in the Reformation parliament itself. In April 1560, the Great Council of the Realm had commissioned a work setting out the needs of the new kirk. The result – the First Book of Discipline, drawn up by Knox, Willock and four other ministers – was deeply impressive; its vision of universal education, for example, reflects the approach which produced five Scottish universities by 1600, compared with England's two, and which in the nineteenth century still ensured that far more Scottish children were educated than their English counterparts. By integrating church, family and school, it saw the way to create the godly community on earth. The snag was that this was going to need money; and when the laity were asked to hand over the church's patrimony to enable it to educate, to heal the sick and to care for the poor, they baulked. The Book of Discipline was not ratified by the Reformation parliament. The struggle to endow the church had begun.

This was not just a problem of lay greed. The demands made in the First Book were sweeping and unrealistic, showing total disregard for the hideous complexities of disentangling ecclesiastical and lay revenues in a country where the churchlands had been extensively secularized by the end of James V's reign. Nor was the problem only one of finance. From its beginnings the new kirk was making claims which could only be seen as dangerously threatening to the authority of the leading Protestant laity. The difficulty began with the absence of a 'godly prince', for in no sense could Mary fulfil that role. That pushed the kirk into an unusually radical stance, which revived the great medieval struggle between the spiritual and temporal powers, the former claiming superiority over the latter. Thus, although the kirk insisted on the essential importance of the godly magistracy – the Protestant nobility – it also insisted on its role in dictating to and disciplining that magistracy. The courts of the new church, from the highest and national – the General Assembly, which came into being in December 1560 – to the lowest and most local, the kirk sessions, would now assume the right to control the moral behaviour of the greatest laymen, openly criticizing not only the Catholic Mary, but Calvinist aristocrats and even, when they did at last get a godly prince in the person of James VI, a Calvinist king. In so doing, they posed an intolerable challenge to the secular powers.

Thus two areas of considerable weakness lay under the veneer of Protestant success. First, as an institution, with its clergy, its buildings and its abbeys, the old church remained largely intact, so that Catholic revival would involve reactivating what was already there rather than creating anew. Second, social, financial and ideological pressures inevitably wrenched the Protestant clergy and the Protestant laity apart, for the single-mindedness of the former could never be matched by the latter. When Mary returned to Scotland, therefore, the position was very fluid indeed; the question of Protestant consolidation or Catholic restoration was entirely open, and thus the role of the monarch, once she was back in Scotland, was potentially crucial. Since the monarch in question was a Catholic, in theory at least it was the Catholics who could begin to hope again, while the Protestants could only take what comfort they could from what they already knew of Mary.

Finally, there remained the uncertain political situation; for linked to the possibility of Catholic revival was the concurrent possibility of the restoration of the alliance with France. The cultural, political and trading links of the past three centuries were not in any case going to be broken overnight; and without the advantage of hindsight, it is readily understandable that both the English and Scottish Protestants were deeply fearful of France. In the last months of 1560, there had seemed two ways in which the policy of the French and Mary might be circumvented. One was to persuade Elizabeth to marry Châtelherault's heir, James earl of Arran, thus certainly consolidating the Protestant Anglo-Scottish alliance, and potentially leading to an Anglo-Scottish monarchy, if Mary died without heirs of her body. The second, undoubtedly linked to the first in the minds of those who wanted the Arran match, was that Mary herself, whose health had periodically been a cause for grave concern, might die. But reality had turned out to be very different. By 8 December 1560, Elizabeth had finally refused the Arran marriage. And it was Francis who died; Mary survived, to confuse and complicate the situation in the first few months after Francis's death. Then, in her discussions with lord James in April 1561, she took up a position which offered the Protestants as much as they could have hoped for, in both religious and political terms. There was absolutely no guarantee that she would stick to it. That was the intolerable dilemma created by Mary's refusal to return to her kingdom which underlay the Protestant successes of 1560–61. Now she was coming back. The unnatural limbo was over; and those who had gained from it were well aware how fragile their gains had been.

Mary at last returned to Scotland on 19 August 1561. The events leading up to her journey home are well known. Her refusal to ratify the Treaty of Edinburgh provoked Elizabeth into refusing her a safe-conduct, but neither gesture, redolent on both sides of spitting cats, mattered; the English ships which intercepted hers merely saluted her, and the only real misfortune was that the warden of Tynemouth impounded her horses for a month, thus enabling her charm and beauty to triumph over her shabbily mounted entrance into Edinburgh. She left France on 14 August in misty weather, gazing at the French coastline until it was out of sight, and repeating over and over again *'Adieu France, adieu France, adieu donc ma chère France'*. She landed in thick fog. There is no record of what she said when she had her first sight of her native country, but John Knox certainly made the most of the opportunity offered by the appalling weather: 'the very face of heaven . . . did manifestly speak what comfort was brought unto this country with her, to wit, sorrow, dolour, darkness and impiety. For, in the memory of man, that day of year was never seen a more dolorous face of the heaven than was at her arrival. . . . The sun was not seen to shine two days before, nor two days after. That fore-warning gave God unto us; but alas, the most part were blind.'

By now, in the eyes of the dedicated Knox, 'the most part' seemed to include the Protestant politicians. Their point of view was, however, naturally more complex than his. Whatever personal doubts their experience of Mary might have given them, her arrival had the merit of restoring the natural order of things, an adult monarch present in the kingdom; and even if the religious situation inevitably made this 'coming of age' a more tense business than earlier ones, the arrangement she had made with lord James offered the possibility of a *modus vivendi*. One aspect of his agreement was instantly kept. It is a very familiar part of the story of Mary Queen of Scots that the general enthusiastic rejoicing at her return gave way to an ugly explosion of violence only five days later, on Sunday 24 August, when lord James had to bar the door against a group of Protestant hotheads trying to burst into her private chapel at Holyrood and disrupt her Mass. Preaching against the Holyrood Mass, Knox claimed, with a deal of hysteria and a total lack of logic, that the hearing of one Mass was 'more fearful to him' than an army of 10,000 arriving in the realm to suppress 'the whole religion'. More prosaically, a proclamation was rushed out on 25 August forbidding any alteration in the state of religion as the queen had found it 'publicly and universally standing at her majesty's arrival', until the Estates could resolve the matter. The episode immediately revealed the complexity of a problem which would not go away so long as Mary reigned.

This was not the only manifestation of the religious dilemma in the early weeks after her return. Her state entry into Edinburgh on 2 September was seized as an occasion for Protestant symbolism and anti-Catholic pageantry. In the course of it a child appeared from out of a cloud to give her a bible and a book of psalms; with understandable pique, and some style, she promptly handed them to the nearest notorious Catholic. More serious was her clash with the Edinburgh town council. The capital had inevitably been a major centre of disturbance in 1559–60, and the composition of the council a battleground between Mary of Guise and the Lords of the Congregation. When the former was in control, the Catholic and unpopular George lord Seton was provost; when the latter, the council was headed by the Protestant Archibald Douglas of Kilspindie. It was thus changed three times between the elections of October 1559, when the regent had imposed her council, and April 1560, when the Protestants were finally restored. The elections of October 1560 took place, unlike those of the previous year, 'by normal and due process'; and a Protestant council was returned. But in 1561, the presence of the Catholic queen seems to have heightened Protestant determination and fear. The state entry itself has been described by Michael Lynch, in his study of Edinburgh and the Reformation, as part of an 'organized campaign', leading up to the municipal election.

The Protestants were again returned. On 4 October they threw down the gauntlet by re-issuing anti-Catholic ordinances passed in June 1560 and March 1561. On the 5th, the queen picked it up; the council was told to sack the provost, Kilspindie, and the four bailies. They did so; for all their reluctance, they were not yet prepared to resist a direct royal command – although they were able to sidestep the inexperienced Mary's suggestion of Seton's return.

This contretemps certainly does not suggest that any attempt by the queen to restore Catholicism, should she have wanted to make it, would have been doomed to failure. Mary was able to replace a Protestant with a Catholic provost. Edinburgh itself was far from solidly Protestant, despite the council elections, the demonstrations and the thunderous sermons of its minister John Knox. The Lords of the Congregation had failed to establish Protestantism in the burgh in the autumn of 1559. Dr Lynch has convincingly argued that religion was not the main motivating force in the two serious craftsmen's riots which disturbed the town in November 1560 and March 1561. And there is the splendid case of the Catholic schoolmaster of the grammar school, William Robertson, who had been appointed in 1547 and who in the 1560s simply resisted all the council's attempts to oust him; powerful support within the burgh helped to keep him in his post, and his final victory came as late as 1569, when he raised an action against the council in the highest civil court, the Court of Session, and won. Moreover, the events of these first few weeks of Mary's reign may be compared to the experience of that totally dedicated Catholic monarch, Mary Tudor. She faced exactly the same paradox of enthusiastic welcome and anti-Catholic demonstrations in London, yet went ahead, with determination and considerable success, with her policy of wrenching her kingdom away from the extreme Protestantism imposed in the reign of her brother Edward VI, and turning it firmly back towards Catholicism. That Mary Queen of Scots might do the same was a very real possibility.

For the moment, however, there was another pressing problem:

the establishment of the queen's government. On 6 September 1561, she nominated her privy council. Sixteen were chosen; ten earls, lord James and John lord Erskine, and four officers of state. We do not know the composition of Mary of Guise's council, for there is a gap in the records from 22 January 1554 until September 1561. We do know, however, that Mary Queen of Scots' council was dominated by the leading Protestants of 1559–60, Argyll, Glencairn, lord James and others. Of the sixteen, only four were Catholics: Huntly, his junior partner in the north, Erroll, another northern earl, Atholl, and the earl of Montrose. We also know that she simply retained those who already held the offices of state, the brilliant secretary William Maitland of Lethington, the treasurer Robert Richardson, the clerk-register James Makgill of Nether Rankeillour and the justice clerk John Bellenden of Auchnoul.

This was all very remarkable, and not just because it must have been very comforting for the Protestants. The sixteenth century has been characterized as the age of the council, and of the secretary. In the kingdoms of Europe, monarchs were turning, as far as possible, away from Estates and representative assemblies, and from councils in which their 'natural counsellors', the magnates, had a dominant part, and ruling through increasingly professional bodies – indeed, in the vast kingdom of France and the vaster Spanish hegemony, through a series of them. This development was accompanied by a rise in the importance of the secretary, both in his new title – by the mid sixteenth century, secretary of state – and in his political role as the man who formed the link between king and council, and was therefore very close to the king. Gonzalo Perez and his son and successor Antonio in Spain, Nicolas de Neufville, seigneur de Villeroy in France, Thomas Cromwell, Burleigh and his son Sir Robert Cecil in England, William Maitland of Lethington and his younger brother John Maitland of Thirlestane in Scotland all stand as towering examples of the power of the secretary, and also of the importance of the office; families sought to retain it within their ranks, for through it power was accrued. For the monarch, therefore, his or her choice of secretary and council was a matter of the most critical importance, over which he had to retain control despite pressures from vested interests.

This underlies just how dismal Mary's record was. She can hardly be said to have made any choice at all. The heavily aristocratic composition of her council is not the issue. The gradual process had begun whereby increasing lay literacy, and with it rising aspirations among the lairds, would bring to Scotland something equivalent to a *noblesse de robe*, (that is, an aristocracy which acquired its titles from service in royal government) in the later sixteenth century; in 1561, however, after a long minority when the absence of a ruler flung the immense problems of foreign policy and religious conflict on to the shoulders of the aristocracy, there was nothing sinister about a council still drawn mainly from the landed nobility. But the heavily Protestant composition of the council is another matter. The idea that the queen was treading carefully – even perhaps had no alternative but to tread carefully – simply will not do.

To get some idea of the difference between a monarch who means to be master (or mistress) of the kingdom and one who does not, it is only necessary to compare Mary in 1561 with her son James when he became king of England in 1603 – a very tense moment for the king, and one in which he might certainly have felt it expedient to tread warily. James had to face exactly the same problem as his mother, in that he too had a powerful party which wanted to 'run' him; his equivalent to the Protestant leaders of 1561 was the Cecil faction which had dominated English politics as Elizabeth's political finesse and grip began to slacken in the 1590s. Yet even before he arrived in London he was asserting his authority by appointing new councillors who would bring a wider range of political and religious opinions, and indeed a wider geographical base, to the narrow circle of the late-Elizabethan, 'Cecilian' council. The option of creating a similarly balanced council, representing a range of views, was certainly open to Mary in 1561. But a one-sided, Protestant and pro-English council was what she was happy to settle for. In religious terms the reason for this is not clear; for the queen who maintained a Protestant-dominated council still refused to ratify the religious decisions made by the Protestants in 1560. Once again, we are brought back to her obsession with the English succession. If this is the explanation, then she was still brushing aside, as much as she had ever done, the internal problems of her own kingdom in the interests of someone else's throne.

As in general, so in particular. If it is hard to think of another adult ruler who showed such indifference to domestic political matters as she did over the nomination of the council as a whole, it becomes impossible to find a parallel where the officers of state – and in particular the secretary – were concerned. These were the crown's key political servants, who would speak for it and advance its policies, in council and in parliament. It was therefore axiomatic that the crown would use its right of appointment to create a group of men on whom it could rely. It is certainly the case that William Maitland of Lethington, the secretary she inherited, originally appointed by her mother in 1558 and a member of the Protestant party since 1559, was a man of great skill; and in her terms – the English succession – he would serve her well. But that was a matter of luck and gun-barrel vision; it was not the independent judgement of a ruler making her own well-thought-out political decisions. And the measure of her failure to concentrate on Scottish politics, whatever the non-Scottish future might hold, was to appear all too clearly in 1567, when the officers of state, on whom monarchs could primarily rely, were solidly ranged among those who brought her down.

But the problem goes even deeper than the election of the council in 1561. The sederunt (attendance) lists show three things. First, the regular attenders were the Protestants. Of the Catholics, only the name of the earl of Atholl appears frequently; certainly he clung tenaciously to his faith, but in political terms he was not a threat to the Protestants, for although he had been one of the few dissenting voices in the Reformation parliament, he had made it clear that he would not join Huntly in a move to restore the old church. Otherwise, while many of the attendance records were patchy, Morton, lord James, Marischal (until the end of 1562),

James V, 1512–1542, father of Mary, Queen of Scots, by unknown artist
(Scottish National Portrait Gallery)

Mary of Guise, 1515–1560, mother of
Mary, Queen of Scots, by Corneille de Lyon
(Scottish National Portrait Gallery)

Catherine de Medici, 1519–1589, queen of France, and Mary's first mother-in-law
(© Victoria and Albert Museum, London)

Palace of Fontainebleau, typical of the palaces in which
Mary stayed during her early life in France
(© PlusONE/Shutterstock.com)

Portrait of Mary as a young woman aged 16 in 1558,
while still in the court in France

(Royal Collection Trust / © Her Majesty Queen Elizabeth II 2017)

Mary in white mourning after the death of Francis,
unknown artist, after Francois Clouet

1563

Henry, lord Darnley, second husband of Mary, and his brother
Charles Stewart, 1563, by Hans Eworth

James Hepburn, 4th Earl of Bothwell, c. 1535–1578,
third husband of Mary, Queen of Scots, by unknown artist
(Scottish National Portrait Gallery)

James Stewart, c. 1532–1570, earl of Moray, half-brother of Mary, and regent 1567–70
(© National Galleries of Scotland)

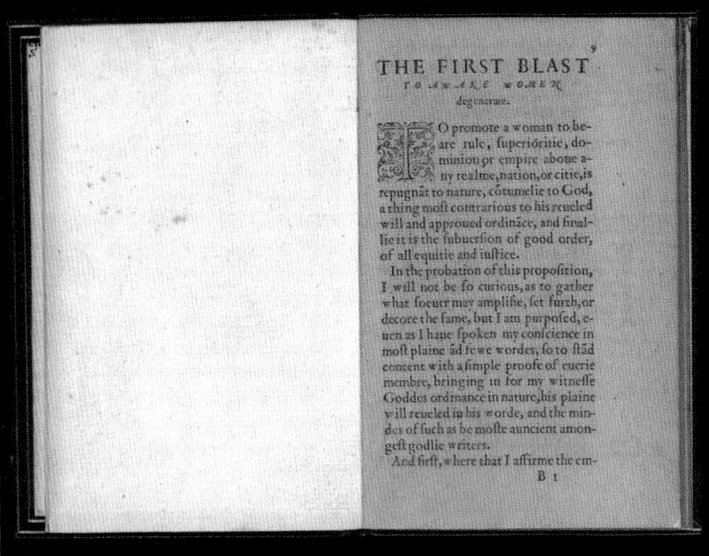

First page of John Knox's *First Blast of the Trumpet against
the Monstrous Regiment of Women*, Geneva 1558

Engraving of Linlithgow Palace from John Slezer,
Theatrum Scotiae, London, 1693

The Palace of Holyrood and burgh of the Cannongate,
sketch by unknown artist during the Rough Wooing, 1544
(© Edinburgh City Libraries)

Stirling Castle, engraving from Slezer, *Theatrum Scotiae*, London, 1693
(Reproduced by permission of the National Library of Scotland)

Edinburgh Castle, the
room where James I and VI
was born, 19 June 1566
(© Crown Copyright HES)

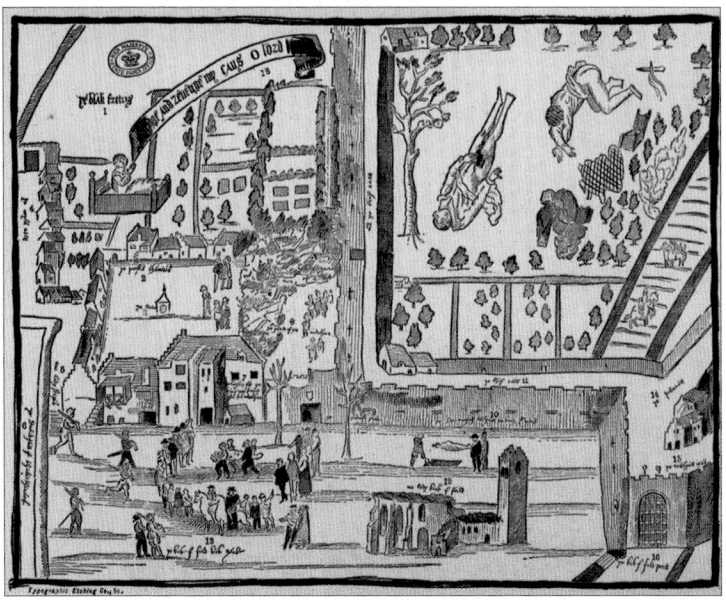

Contemporary sketch of the murder of Darnley,
10 February 1567, sent to William lord Cecil
(© National Museums Scotland)

Two embroidery panels from the Marian hanging, now at Oxburgh Hall,
Norfolk, produced when Mary was in the care of the 6th earl of Shrewsbury.
The top panel bears Mary's cipher and is regarded as her work.

Sketch of Mary and her son James, from John Leslie,
bishop of Ross, *Historie of Scotland*, 1578

Elizabeth I: the Ditchley portrait, c. 1592, by Marcus Gheeraerts the younger
(National Portrait Gallery, London)

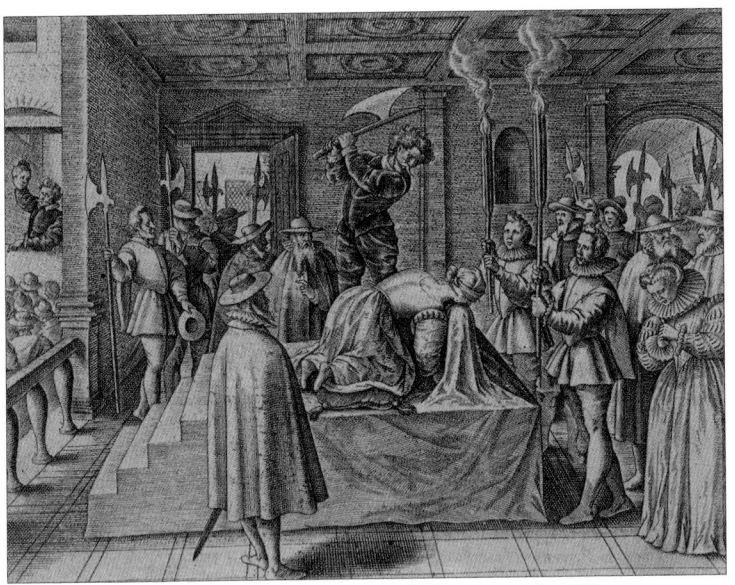

Contemporary drawing of the execution of Mary, from Richard Verstegan,
Theatrum crudelitatem haereticorum nostri temporis, Antwerp 1587
(Reproduced by permission of the National Library of Scotland)

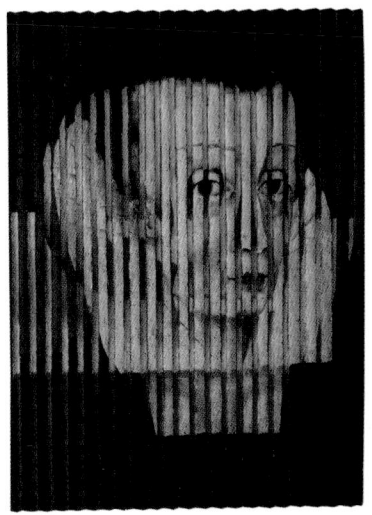 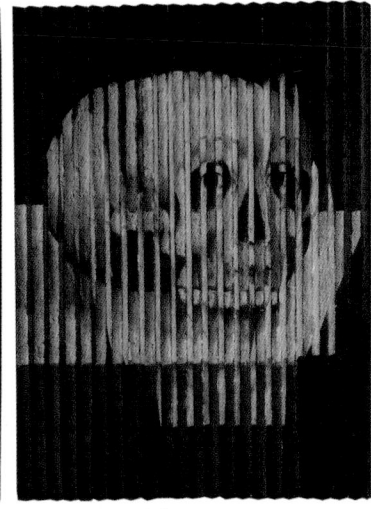

'Memento Mori': Anamorphosis, called
Mary, Queen of Scots, 1542–1587, by unknown artist
(Scottish National Portrait Gallery)

ABOVE.
Tomb of Elizabeth I, Westminster Abbey
(Copyright: Dean and Chapter of Westminster)

LEFT.
Tomb of Mary, Queen of Scots,
Westminster Abbey
(Copyright: Dean and Chapter of Westminster)

lord Erskine and, rather more intermittently, Argyll, were the ones who turned up to sit with the officers of state, the backbone of the council. Second, further proof against the idea that Mary was cautious at the beginning of her reign, but intended gradually to establish her own authority, is that for most of her personal rule her council remained remarkably static. There is no evidence that until late 1565 she ever tried to expand its ranks, and bring on to this supremely important body those who were close to her and who knew her mind about anything other than the pro-English policy. There was only one significant addition to the Marian council: the strongly Protestant Patrick lord Ruthven, who sat with immense regularity from December 1563, the man whom, as Mary said all too revealingly, 'I cannot love . . . and yet is he made one of my Privy Council'. Third and most important of all, the attendance record of the queen herself was abysmal.

This would not be a matter for comment in the case of, for example, the English monarchy by the later sixteenth century. But Scottish monarchy remained less institutionalized, more intimately personal; and rulers therefore still took a direct part in meetings of council. Again, comparison between Mary and her son James VI puts Mary's behaviour into sharp relief. In the single year 1596, for example, out of forty-seven recorded sederunts the king appeared on all but ten, and most of his absences occurred between 3 June and 12 August, no doubt while he was away indulging his passion for hunting. Between September 1585 and February 1603 James turned up on 384 occasions, a level of attendance beaten only by the most committed and hardworking of the officers of state, like Maitland of Thirlestane 314 times (1585–95) and Thomas Hamilton of Drumcairn 346 (1593–1603), but very much on a par with other principal members of his government, such as Alexander Seton of Fyvie 405 (1585–1603) and the earl of Montrose 392 (in the same period); those who were not officials of course appeared less frequently. These figures make one wonder why James VI has had such a bad press because of his supposed laziness. They also stand in total contrast to Mary's record.

Mary's most assiduous attendance came at the beginning of her reign. In the sixteen months between her return from France and the end of 1562, she appeared on seventeen out of the fifty-four recorded sederunts. By 1564, the number had dropped to five out of fifty. In 1566, it rose again, to a maximum of twelve attendances out of a known sixty-two. But of these twelve, it is not entirely clear that the queen was present on three, and of the remaining nine, five occurred in the immediate aftermath of the Rizzio murder in March 1566; at that time, as we shall see in more detail later, any semblance of normality had gone, and what passed for the 'council' was in fact the political faction who had taken control after the murder. The other four took place between July and October, and were concerned with the planned justice-ayre to Jedburgh. That in itself was fair enough; for a Scottish monarch to go in person on ayre (the peripatetic exercise of royal justice) was evidence of strong government. But in this case, Mary's journey to the border ayre at Jedburgh was accompanied by a dramatic ride to the great border castle of Hermitage, where she could spend a day with the earl of Bothwell; and it therefore became an occasion for scandal rather than a display of Stewart rule. It all adds up to a combination of lack of interest in the 'normal' years up to 1565, and too much intrusion of personal interest thereafter.

The same lack of direction is seen in the business with which the council dealt. The Scottish privy council as a single body retained enormously wide judicial, legislative and administrative functions; indifference to constitutional rules, such as were applied in England to distinguish between the business of council, lawcourts and parliament, and smallness of scale, which meant that a single council in Scotland could cope adequately, whereas in France and Spain the work came to be divided among several, may explain its unusually comprehensive nature. The Scottish government had an attractively casual belief in the need to get things done, rather than worrying about how they should be done, and thus one finds, for example, the parliament of 1592 cheerfully dumping its unfinished business – which included the tariff on wine and other matters – on to the council. This only serves to highlight the exceptionally limited amount of council business between 1561 and 1565: about one-thirtieth of the quantity which came before James VI's council in 1586–90, the early years of his personal rule. Mary's council was being comparatively underused.

Moreover, it is disturbing to find that very little of what was discussed was clearly inspired by the queen; a rare exception was the complaint in August 1566 that because her subjects were not observing acts prohibiting the shooting of deer, she and Darnley had 'na pastyme' when they went to the country on hunting holidays. If their respective council attendances put the charge of laziness levelled at king James into a perspective very different from the familiar assumption, so this ordinance raises the question of whether it should be Mary's son, rather than Mary herself, who is pilloried for putting love of hunting before devotion to duty. Hunting was itself a highly important social function of kingship. Certainly it was a priority shared by most medieval and early modern kings; Versailles and Falkland both, after all, began as hunting lodges. But the balance of political direction and more relaxed social contact had to be maintained.

In Mary's case, it was not maintained. As early as August 1562, only one year after her return to Scotland, a rota was drawn up by the council, so that there would always be a group of councillors with the queen, 'by whose advice the causes of her Grace and realm may be ordered as shall be thought most commodious and profitable'. It was a device which had been used in, for example, the minority of James V. It was not normally found necessary in the case of adult sovereigns. It was to be suggested three times in the six years of Mary's personal rule. But if her councillors had to consider resorting to such measures because she was not attending council meetings, what then was she doing? The answer suggests a situation which must have been infinitely frustrating. The council habitually met in the palace of Holyrood. There, in the royal apartments on the second floor, was the queen. Thus while her Protestant-dominated, pro-English council got on as best it could without the accustomed presence of the monarch in one part of the palace, Mary was living her life with a different group of people in another: she chose to spend her time with those close to her in her household and at court, like lord Seton, and the Flemings, who were never members of the council, and Bothwell, who was, but who attended only very rarely. So there was physical proximity to her councillors, but no more, given how rarely she actually came down the stairs from her private apartments to attend the council; and there was intimacy with her household friends.

Mary's lifestyle is a devastating example of the dangers inherent in the opportunities offered by the architectural layout of sixteenth-century royal palaces which enabled monarchs to withdraw to the remoteness of their private apartments and render themselves inaccessible if they so wished. Wise rulers maintained a balance between such remoteness and the availability which kept them in touch with the full range of political opinions within their court and government. Unwise ones remained aloof, and were therefore drawn down into the world of factional politics instead of presiding over and controlling it, because they allowed themselves to become too closely associated with one group within it. Mary clearly came within the second category.

But Mary did more than create a dangerous dividing line between her official council and her unofficial counsellors. That would have been political folly enough. But Mary compounded it, by continuing her mother's unpopular policy of surrounding herself with Frenchmen. She retained Mary of Guise's comptroller Bartholomew de Villemore, and her master of household Jean de Bussot, and had an apothecary, several valets of her chamber and a secretary who were also French. She could not be prevented from doing so because these people were financed from her French revenues as queen dowager. And strictly speaking, her retention of them did not break the letter of the law, in that the 'Concessions' of 1560 had bound the queen not to appoint Frenchmen to government office, but said nothing about her household. But it certainly broke the spirit of it.

Moreover, damaging as Mary of Guise's imposition of Frenchmen had been, at least it had an obvious *raison d'être*; there had been no doubt about the regent's pro-French and Catholic policy. There was every doubt about her daughter's. For this was a monarch whose public policy, if her council was any guide, was Protestant and pro-English, but who maintained a household in which there were Catholics and Frenchmen with whom she spent far more time; who would not ratify the acts of the Reformation parliament, but would do nothing else beyond insisting on her right to her private Mass for the Catholic faith. The kingdom of Reformation Europe necessarily contained religious dissidents as well as religious orthodox. But normally the religious disposition of the ruler made it clear which was which. In Scotland, the Calvinists seemed to be the orthodox, and the Catholics the dissidents. But the haze of uncertainty emanating from the throne made certainty among Mary's subjects impossible. And because such uncertainty was unique, so Calvinists and Catholics alike were in a uniquely disadvantaged position.

The state of the council was not, however, the only problem of Mary's personal rule. The other, and equally serious, was parliament. In general, the corollary to the rise of secretary and council was the decline of the representative assembly; the Estates in France, in the Spanish kingdom and in Denmark were far less frequently summoned than they had been in the fifteenth century. The exceptions to this trend were the parliaments of England and Scotland. Because of Henry VIII's use of it as the junior partner in pushing through the Henrician reformation, the English parliament got a new lease of life after its temporary decline in the reign of Henry VII.

In Scotland, there had also been signs of decline in the early sixteenth century; James IV in his later years visibly departed from the practice of holding regular parliaments. But the minorities of James V and Mary inevitably reversed the trend, and James V himself, during his personal rule, used parliament in something of the same way as Henry VIII had done, except that his junior partner was summoned to uphold, not to reject, the Roman church. Then came the unrivalled example of parliamentary power, when the Reformation parliament acted in defiance of the crown. What happened on that occasion was rightly a matter of considerable alarm for the sovereign; and it is only because there is no evidence that those who took part in the Reformation parliament regarded themselves as establishing a precedent for the future that it cannot be regarded as revolutionary. Once Mary was back in Scotland, it was expected that the normal relationship between crown and parliament would be restored. Once again, the queen failed to give a lead.

At first sight, the record looks reasonably good. During Mary's minority and absence in France, parliaments and conventions had met frequently; seventeen times in nineteen years. That pattern was apparently continued, with five meetings in the six years of personal rule. But of these five, only one – the parliament of 1563 – was in any way normal, for only in that parliament was there a range of legislation. Otherwise, the range of business dealt with by Mary's parliaments, though by no means unimportant, was quite exceptionally limited. A convention met in December 1561, and considered only two problems arising directly from the change in the religious situation, one relating to church lands and the other to the need to finance the Protestant ministers by taking part of the benefices of the old church. The parliament of December 1564 again addressed itself only to two matters; it reverted to the question of the church lands, and it declared that the queen had reached her perfect age (that is, age of majority) when she was twenty-one – a point which would be a political issue in 1567. Then a convention met in October 1566 solely to levy taxation for the baptism of Mary's son James. And the final parliament, of April 1567, had nothing to do with the government of the country, and related only to the crisis which followed the murder of Darnley.

So we are left with only one parliament that actually fulfilled its expected function. It passed twenty-seven acts. The first was an act of oblivion (indemnity), covering all civil and criminal actions between 6 March 1559 and 1 September 1561; thus did the queen who in March 1561 had sent a message to her subjects telling them to regret their past offences and begin to behave themselves properly let them off the hook. Indeed, although the act naturally did not specify what Mary had regarded as Protestant criminal activity, it perhaps gives us a clue to the reason why contemporaries believed that the Reformation had begun on 6 March 1559. Then there was a range of other matters, concerning fishing, the export of gold and silver, false coining, dearth, the admission of notaries, landholding – both ecclesiastical and secular – the setting up of a commission to visit the universities with a view to improving the teaching of languages and the humanities, and so on. Some of this business already indicates the nature of this parliament; it was underwriting the Protestant reformation, with its denial of papal notaries and its interest in education.

Other acts make this even clearer; there was legislation about the adequate provision of manses and glebes (the houses and strips of land for the ministry) and about the repairing of parish churches and maintenance of churchyards for burial – for the reformed kirk refused burial within churches. The first witchcraft act was passed, making not only the practice of sorcery but also consorting with witches a capital crime; and the penalty for 'notorious adultery', which had been outlawry in the 1551 parliament, was now death (though, perhaps unexpectedly, the divorce law in Reformation Scotland was less harsh than its English counterpart). In 1540, and again in 1551, parliament had been used to bolster up the needs of the old church, legislating on religious observance and moral behaviour. Now it gave its support to the desire of the new to make of Scotland a much tougher moral society: a godly community.

This brings out irresistibly the extraordinary lack of policy and ability to direct affairs which characterized the first four years of Mary's personal rule, and takes us back to the queen's attitude to religion. Whereas parliament had co-operated with a Catholic king in 1540, in 1563 it looks as though parliament and reformed kirk were acting in harmony, while a Catholic queen simply acquiesced. Despite the rhetoric about the 'great affection and love that her Grace bears towards her subjects', it is difficult to believe that Mary ratified at least some of the legislation of this parliament with any feelings of enthusiasm or affection. But she was certainly allowing the Protestants to consolidate a position which had still been very open when she returned to Scotland. Indeed, already in the previous year she had taken two positive steps which had been very welcome to them, and equally disheartening to the Catholics. The first related to the highly sensitive question of the financing of the kirk. In the 1561 convention, John Hamilton, archbishop of St Andrews, and the bishops of Dunkeld, Moray and Ross, offered the queen one-fourth of their revenues for one year, provided they were restored to their benefices and privileges. Actually, they had never lost them. But this curious offer, made by the Catholic primate not only for the kirk but also for the support of the queen, was the initial gesture which paved the way for the quite extra-ordinary deal worked out in February 1562. This was an agreement that two-thirds of the revenues of the old church would remain with the benefice-holders, while the remaining third would be given to the queen so that she could finance the new kirk.

It is actually easier to understand Elizabeth, who, despite her Protestant faith, was a grasping and parsimonious governor of her Protestant church, than it is to comprehend the spectacle of a Catholic queen paying for a Protestant kirk. Yet that is what happened. Admittedly, it was to Mary's advantage that it should happen; it did something, even if not very much, to offset the loss of revenue which the crown had suffered with the loss of ecclesiastical taxation. But more to the point is the fact that Mary did provide for the kirk, despite the sour complaints of the Protestant ministers that the queen frittered away too much of the 'Thirds' on her own concerns and entertainment. The piecemeal and complex solution of 1562 was of course no solution at all. But it was as much as the kirk could then get; and it got it from its Catholic monarch, who did not – understandably – take any initiative in finding ways to endow the kirk, and yet did not resist when one was imposed upon her.

The other action of 1562 was the assertive demonstration of the queen's political alliance with lord James Stewart. George earl of Huntly had been given the title and lands of the northern earldom of Moray in 1549. This most powerful northern magnate was now dispossessed of a substantial area of influence and control when the creation was set aside in the interests of lord James, whose grant of the earldom in January 1562 was made public in September. The Catholic Mary had already rejected the Catholic earl of Huntly in 1561. Now, not only would she not join with him in restoring the old faith, but she took positive steps to undermine his power by making her brother a northern earl. But she did not stop there. In August 1562, she went on progress to Aberdeen, where she was met by Huntly with a far larger retinue than had been stipulated. When she moved to Inverness in early September, she found the castle barred to her by its captain, who refused to allow her to enter without permission from Huntly or his heir lord Gordon. It was both a dangerous and a futile gesture; for a day later the castle was surrendered, and the captain was hanged. Mary remained in the north, returning to Aberdeen where she summoned levies.

Huntly's refusal to surrender the cannon from Huntly castle – and his wife's useless display of the Catholic vestments in her private Catholic chapel – did nothing to soften the queen. Huntly was outlawed. Provoked now to extreme measures, he gave battle to Moray and the queen's forces at Corrichie, near Aberdeen, on 28 October. He died – appropriately, perhaps, of apoplexy – on the battlefield. Two of his sons were captured. One, Sir John, was executed; the other, lord Gordon, remained alive, to be eventually restored to favour in 1565, when the queen's marriage to Darnley destroyed her close relations with her half-brother, and she thus found herself reversing the position of 1562 and seeking Gordon support against Moray. Huntly himself was posthumously forfeited, and therefore his possessions came to the crown; as a result Mary acquired a splendid collection of furnishings taken from Huntly castle. The justice of all this can be judged from the description of the English diplomat Randolph, when he wrote on 18 September 1562 – exactly the time of the conflict between queen and earl – that 'his house is fair, best furnished of any house that I have seen in this country; his cheer is marvellous great, his mind then such as it appeared to us, as ought to be in any subject to his sovereign'.

It is not the least of the puzzles that surround Mary Queen of

Scots that in this instance we find a Catholic queen treating a leading Catholic subject with outright hostility, one moreover who had a testimonial from a Protestant English diplomat. Randolph did somewhat overstate the case. Huntly's own loyalty had not been wholly reliable; he had, after all, temporarily joined the Protestants in the spring of 1560, and his own actions in the autumn of 1562 suggest a desire to retrieve his threatened position by a show of strength. And his son John had apparently contemplated seizing the queen, presumably on the grounds that if she would not willingly throw in her lot with the Catholic Gordons, she might be thus prevailed upon to do so. Nevertheless, Mary had clearly set out to reduce Gordon power in order to benefit her half-brother. This messy and curious episode is further evidence of the fact that she placed greater importance on the English succession, which the Protestant lord James might help her to achieve, than on the Counter-Reformation, for which she would need the support of the Catholic Huntly. It also shows her profound ignorance of the way in which successful Scottish kingship operated. For she intruded into the north a man with no landed or personal connection with that part of the country, and set him up against a line of earls whose record of loyalty to the crown was impressive and recognized by earlier Stewart kings with the formal title of lieutenant in the north. In so doing, she cut away the traditional reliance of the crown on the great family of Gordon as its representatives in the north. In its place, she created a Stewart-Gordon rivalry which would flare up again and violently disrupt the north in the reign of her son, in the late 1580s and 1590s. Stewart kings had moved against powerful magnates in the past. None had left a legacy such as this.

The events of 1562 and the acceptance of a parliament with strong Protestant leanings in 1563 show how far Mary was reinforcing and confirming her original choice, to allow her government and therefore her kingdom to be controlled by the Protestants. She had thrown away the opportunities which existed in 1561; instead, she merely ensured that her lack of public involvement and direction, and her close private association with foreigners and Catholics within her household left room for worry and doubt. But so long as she did no more than this, the policy of the Protestant politicians of letting this sleeping queen lie made very good sense. Knox's insistence in these early years of trying to bully her into ideological as well as political conformity with the Protestants was therefore an unnecessary embarrassment. Unnecessary – but also predictable; for Knox, who even managed to find grounds for complaint about the 1563 parliament, would never be satisfied by anything which involved compromise.

Admittedly it is only from Knox himself that we have an account of the series of famous interviews in which he trounced the queen; one suspects a degree of exaggeration here. His insistence on asserting his radical political views is not in doubt, however. 'So are not subjects bound to frame their religion according to the appetites of their princes', he felt it his duty to tell Mary in September 1561; 'if princes exceed their bounds, Madam, and do against that wherefore they should be obeyed, it is no doubt but they may be resisted, even by power'. 'Well then', replied the queen, after standing in amazed silence for a quarter of an hour, 'I perceive that my subjects shall obey you, and not me . . . and so must I be subject to them, and not they to me.' It was risky in the extreme to confront Mary with an outright attack on her own high sense of royalty, which she herself had expressed very clearly only three months earlier when she told Throckmorton that 'there is no reason that subjects should give a law to their Sovereign, and specially in matters of religion . . . for I have been brought up in this religion, and who might credit me in any thing if I should show myself light in this case'.

Understandably, the anxious lord James intervened at this point. For both this interview and the succeeding exchanges between Knox and Mary, and indeed Knox's relentlessly intransigent zeal for his cause, bring into focus the remarkable fact that potentially the greatest threat to the precarious new reformed kirk was not the Catholic queen, under whom it was trying to establish itself, but the leading Protestant reformer; for Knox was not only hated by the Protestant Elizabeth whose support the Scottish Protestant politicians sought, but was also a source of deep concern to those politicians who saw in Knox's uncontrolled outbursts against Mary's view of sovereignty and her personal religion the danger that he might drive her from the conciliatory policy, with its main focus on the English succession, which worked so well to their advantage. Thus in 1561 Secretary Lethington, writing to Cecil, lamented Knox's vehemence and unbridled spirit, fearing its effect on the queen he regarded as 'a young princess unpersuaded', with whom Elizabeth might do much in matters of religion. Elizabeth herself, like Lethington 'accounted politique', had her own problems with her hardline reformers. What made the Scottish situation unique, not to say bizarre, was that Mary, also 'politique' rather than zealous, as by necessity were most sixteenth-century rulers other than a Mary Tudor or a Henry II of France or a Philip II of Spain, was alone in interpreting her politic interests as being best served by support for a faith profoundly antipathetic to her own.

Thus, to the relief and good fortune of those who were desperately trying not to provoke Mary into antagonism to the new church, preferring to get their way by gentler persuasion, neither her own brave words to Throckmorton nor her shocked anger at Knox were to be translated into action. But Knox was not the only threat. Mary's treatment of the Catholic Huntly might do something to reassure the Protestants, but it did not remove the considerable Catholic presence in Scotland, not least within the capital itself. It was equally to the relief of the Protestants that in the first years of her personal rule, despite her insistence on her own private mass, the queen was making it clear enough that after all it was not they who would suffer from her return to Scotland. It was those who shared the religion in which she had been brought up whose hopes had been dashed.

In view of this, it is not surprising to find that the Jesuits who came to Scotland in 1562–3 spoke only of Catholic demoralization and despair in their reports to their General James Laynez. Thus on 30 September, Fr Nicholas de Gouda wrote describing his visit to Scotland between 19 June and 3 September 1562. It had taken him a month to see the queen at all, and when he did, it was an extremely private meeting 'at an hour when the courtiers were attending the great preacher's sermon, and could not therefore know of our interview'. A further difficulty was that Mary claimed that she could not speak Latin – rather curiously, in view of the fact that she had certainly learned it in France – and so a Frenchman and a Scot, Fr Edmund Hay, were brought in to translate. Then she insisted that it was impossible for her to do what the pope wanted, and follow Mary Tudor's example, because her position, her kingdom and her nobility were very different. Nor could she send representatives to the Council of Trent, nor give the pope's letters to the Scottish bishops, though subsequently she changed her mind on this point at least and agreed to deliver them. De Gouda's contacts with the bishops were equally depressing. The archbishop of St Andrews did reply to his letter. But the bishops of Ross and Dunblane refused to see him at all; Dunkeld was prepared to meet him, but only if he came disguised as a banker's clerk collecting payment of a debt – and then talked of nothing but money matters. On 2 January 1563, Hay wrote to Laynez, reinforcing de Gouda's account, and stressing even more forcibly that Moray was utterly dominant, and the Catholics, subjected to tyranny, were divided and hopeless.

As with Knox's description of his interviews with Mary, we have to allow for exaggeration in the case of the Jesuits' letters. 'Tyranny' is too strong a word. Nevertheless, the appalled reaction of these priests to what was going on in Scotland is readily understandable. They could not see how a monarch who herself insisted on her right to practise her faith could possibly distinguish her personal religion from that of the subjects within her kingdom. They knew very well that this was behaviour without parallel. Sneaking the Jesuits into a private room in Holyrood does indeed sit very oddly with Mary's insistence on her right to her Mass. Likewise, her denial that she could follow Mary Tudor's example reads very oddly when in fact she was on the point of doing something which Mary Tudor would never have done, and enhancing the power of a Protestant lord at the expense of a Catholic one. What she said to de Gouda was simply dishonest, a pathetic defence of an untenable position. Of course her kingdom was different from Mary Tudor's – just as Mary Tudor's was different from the kingdoms of France or Spain or Denmark. But there was one piece of common ground between the rulers of all these kingdoms: the recognition of their responsibility to maintain – by force, if necessary – their subjects within the church in which they believed. So the argument of difference carried no weight, and could not disguise the reality of Mary's position. It was not room for manoeuvre which was lacking. It was the will to act.

The despairing reaction of the Jesuits was entirely justified. Rulers in sixteenth-century Europe had – were indeed obliged to have – a deep awareness that defence of their faith, Catholic or Protestant, within their kingdoms had now become a fundamental part of their kingship. As religious unity was shattered and the papacy lost its role as head of the universal church, who else but the monarch could offer protection to the church within his kingdom? Even at the level of preserving social order, no monarch could afford to allow religious division to run riot; and for many, of course, it was far more than a matter of social control. The passionate desire of Charles V to re-unite Christendom, and when that failed, to crush the German Lutheran princes; the coldly determined dedication of Philip II; the sad and sometimes brutal emotionalism of Mary Tudor; even the 'politique' approach of Elizabeth and Henri IV: all testify to the new role of the ruler. So also does the stormy Huguenot propaganda warfare of the 1570s, which sought to confine the ruler within a contract with God and his people, precisely because of the fear created by the stupendous new power which the Reformation had brought to those who ruled. 'The powers that be are ordained of God' had given kingship a potentially sacerdotal as well as a temporal authority for more than a millennium. Now, the 'power ordained by God' had to guide the religious as well as the secular lives of a monarch's subjects, and for that he was answerable to God – only to God. As Mary's son James VI was later to write, this did not give kings untrammelled licence to do what they liked. It was a huge and awesome responsibility.

Set against that, the suggestion that Mary Queen of Scots

showed the attractive virtue of tolerance in an intolerant age emerges as wholly anachronistic. Her indifference not only to her kingdom but to the religion of her kingdom was not attractive; it was extraordinary, and it was profoundly irresponsible. In denying the doctrines of the traditional and universal church, men were gambling with their immortal souls. The Protestant attack, and likewise the Catholic defence, therefore had to be pursued with total commitment; there was no room for the attitude which Mary adopted, which showed such indifference to the souls of those over whom she reigned. The needs of her Catholic subjects, and the spiritual dangers which from her point of view faced her Protestant ones, were treated with equal lack of concern.

To this extent, Knox undoubtedly had a case when he invited Mary to show the same determined commitment as he had; in the end, that is why this most determined of men has always and justifiably had a reputation which towers above that of lesser men who chose the way of compromise. Of course rulers living in the political world could never rise to such heights. Their responsibility to protect the church did not and could not mean that they could eradicate all heresy; they had to accept the existence within their kingdoms of religious dissidents, and contain them as best they might. Their reactions ranged from the fanatic to the moderate. James VI and I, for example, was just as opposed to persecution as his mother, and therefore would tolerate Catholics within his kingdom – provided that they were prepared to show outward conformity; the Protestant Henri of Navarre changed his religion when he became Henri IV of France, and then allowed the Huguenots a carefully delineated and geographically restricted toleration. Such toleration is not the tolerance for which Mary has been so misleadingly praised. The fact is that Mary was unique in Reformation Europe; for it was she who ensured that the official religion of her country was not the religion of its ruler.

The difference between Mary and her mother is very clear. Mary of Guise had tolerated the Protestants because she wanted their support in achieving the marriage between Mary and the dauphin. But far more to the point, she had tolerated them because the international situation before the death of Mary Tudor left them too isolated to be a serious threat. Once that ceased to be true, she was prepared to fight to keep her daughter's kingdom not only pro-French but Catholic. At no time, therefore, was her religious policy actually in conflict with her secular interests, let alone subordinated to them. In stark contrast, Mary Queen of Scots' attitude to the religion which she was expected to restore to her kingdom can only be explained in the light of her main priority: her hope, however unlikely to be realized, of the English succession. She created a conflict of religious and secular interests for herself; and it was the latter which mattered more.

The lasting strength of Calvinism in Scotland, where it continued to flourish well into the twentieth century, long after it was in decline elsewhere, has too easily persuaded older generations of historians, as well as ministers of the kirk, that its success was assured from the moment of the Reformation parliament in 1560, *the* date of the Scottish Reformation. This was very far from the case. Leading Protestants might be able to take advantage of the particular political situation in 1560, but they knew all too well that this was by no means a guarantee of survival thereafter. Their Catholic queen held a strong hand of Catholic cards, dealt her by Catholics both at home and abroad. It was her refusal to play it which meant that in the years before the drama of 1565–7 it was the Protestants who were the sole beneficiaries of her sad combination of sins of omission and errors of commission. It was of course entirely to their advantage to allow her to fail as a monarch, and as a Catholic monarch, even if they can hardly have respected her for it. But Mary never stopped at one mistake where two were possible. As we shall see, she did not even stick wholeheartedly to the pro-English policy of her leading ministers, but began to add confusion to lack of direction by remembering that she was a marriageable female of European attraction, and even – belatedly – that she was not just a Catholic individual but a Catholic queen. The first four years of her personal rule were not just the relatively peaceful years, therefore. They were also the years when the seeds of disaster were being irrevocably sown.

CHAPTER SIX

Of Marriages and Murders
1563–7

The central fact of sovereignty, the ability to rule, was the critical area in which Mary failed. But in two other respects she did respond to the demands of monarchy. One was the question of her marriage. The other was the nature of her court. In the latter case at least, she certainly upheld the tradition of her Stewart predecessors. For obvious financial reasons, the Scottish court was more small-scale than its European, or even English, counterparts; but the combination of royal patronage and the sheer accident of genius, in the persons of William Dunbar, David Lindsay and others, had made it none the less a court of distinction. Indeed, the Stewart kings themselves included a poet of considerable ability, James I; and there is the enchanting comment written by Thomas Wode, one of the musicians at the court of Mary's father, that 'King James was a good musician himself . . . but his voice was harsh' – something which presumably the skilled singers had no choice but to endure. James V's widow, Mary of Guise, had continued to maintain court life, at least at the beginning of her daughter's minority, when the earls of Bothwell and Lennox, vying for her favours, took the lead 'sometimes in dancing, sometimes in shooting, sometimes in singing and jousting and running of great horse at the lists with all other knightly games'.

One very attractive aspect of Mary's personal rule, therefore, was the revival of court life. Her leading court poet and musician was Alexander Scott, already making his mark as a 'makar' – the Scottish word for a poet – in the early years of her minority. It was 'thy simple servant Sanderris Scott' who celebrated her return in his delightful 'A new year gift to the queen Mary when she come first home, 1562'. That poem is itself a reminder that the Scots were thinking of more than their political or even religious problems in their desire to get her back. For although the poet included a warning to the queen about the dangers of renewed idolatry – Catholicism – in his 'gift', he also had advice for her subjects:

'Let all thy realm be now in readiness
With costly clothing to decoir thy court.'

The visual display of the grace and grandeur of monarchy was once again possible. And even if Mary may not have wanted to be in Scotland at all, once she was there, it came as naturally to her as breathing to bring from France her ideas of what a court should be, and in so doing, therefore, to hold the kind of court which the Scots – apart, of course, from the sour and censorious Knox – expected of their monarch. There is no doubt that, whatever her political shortcomings, she fulfilled admirably the requirement that a sixteenth-century ruler should preside over a court which would impress both subjects and foreign visitors.

Unlike her Stewart predecessors, Mary has left us no visible signs of her court life; for she built nothing. Her court was held in the glorious settings of Stirling, Holyrood, Linlithgow and Falkland, which she inherited from former monarchs. But we can still know something of her court, and indeed of the personal devotion she could inspire from at least some of those who made it what it was. Even her later vilifier, George Buchanan, wrote Latin 'Pompae' and masques for her, and had a place in court frivolity not normally associated with this grave humanist when he produced the verses for Mary Fleming and Mary Beaton when they were chosen as the queens of Twelfth Night. The unfortunate David Rizzio began his career as one of the foreign musicians, Italian, French and English, at her court. She had a 'stand' – set of voices – for part-singing. And her pro-English policy was reflected in her addition of English musicians to the continental ones, who would live on to make the court life of her son James so brilliant.

At her wedding to Darnley, we first hear of the English family of Hudsons – a father and four sons – described as 'songsters, Englishmen, violers'. There was also a Scotsman, James Lauder,

OF MARRIAGES AND MURDERS

whom, like the Hudsons, James VI was to inherit as a court musician. But before that, Lauder accompanied the queen to England, and remained with her during at least the early part of her imprisonment, just as his bastard son John, player of the bass-viol, was with her in the later years. Indeed, even the greatest of all James's court poets and musicians, Alexander Montgomery, seems to have worked on Mary's behalf; in 1580, he went on a mysterious mission which, it has been suggested, was involved with a Jesuit plan for the restoration of the queen.

Like her father, Mary was a musician. Unlike him, she had a good singing voice; and she played the lute and the virginals. This musicianship was responsible for part of the barrage of questions about herself and Mary to which Elizabeth subjected Mary's ambassador Sir James Melville in September 1564. Whose hair was the better colour? Who was the fairer? Who was taller? ('Over high', said Elizabeth, on hearing that it was Mary, for she herself was neither too high nor too low.) Did Mary play well? 'I said', replied Melville, 'reasonably for a Queen.' And so the questioning and parrying went on, leading up to the scene when Melville was stage-managed into a room in which Elizabeth sat with her back to the door playing the virginals, where, after soothing her pretended anger, he admitted that, as between her and Mary, he 'gave her the praise'.

Yet even that was not enough. He was kept at court for two more days, so that he might see her dance; and again he acknowledged her greater gifts, for he told her that Mary 'danced not so high and disposedly as she did'. He had managed very circumspectly; but by now tact and diplomacy had been strained to their limits, and he went on to offer 'to convoy her secretly in Scotland by post, clothed like a page disguised, that she might see the Queen'. Yet this piece of cheek she 'seemed to like well'. And indeed, it appears that Melville was on remarkably good terms with the English queen. For comparisons with her sister of Scotland were not the only subject for discussion. It was on this occasion that he told her that he believed her claim that she was 'never minded to marry'. 'Madam', he said, 'ye need not to tell me that; I know your stately stomach: ye think if ye were married, ye would be but Queen of England, and now ye are King and Queen both; ye may not suffer a commander'. That also seemed to please her.

Various points of considerable interest emerge from this well-known and revealing interview. First, Elizabeth's persistent curiosity about Mary not only makes her own vanity obvious enough but has been assumed to be archetypally feminine. That is to miss the essential point of the rivalry between monarchs – male or female – which this episode encapsulates; when Henry VIII created that monumental extravaganza, the Field of Cloth of Gold, as the setting for his meeting with Francis I in 1520, he was doing on a vast scale exactly what Elizabeth did when she displayed her courtly skills to Melville for transmission to Mary. They were both concerned with the impact they made on their world. Second, her amused reaction to the suggestion that she should travel to Scotland in disguise masked a profound difference in attitude between her and Mary. From the last few months before her return to Scotland in 1561 right up to the time of her death in 1587, Mary was determined that she and Elizabeth should meet. On only one occasion, in 1562, did Elizabeth herself entertain the idea. The ostensible reason for the failure of that particular plan was the explosion of Catholic-Huguenot hostility in France; Elizabeth announced that the crisis meant that she could not possibly travel from London as far north as the designated place, Nottingham, and suggested postponing the meeting for a year.

To the abiding frustration of those ever since who have seen the lives of Elizabeth and Mary as an intertwined drama deprived of its greatest scene, neither that meeting nor any other ever took place. In 1562, Cecil had been strongly in favour, hoping for personal negotiations which would lead to the ratification of the Treaty of Edinburgh. It looks as though Elizabeth, with what was surely sounder instinct, allowed her initial willingness to give way to the suspicion that she would simply find herself tiresomely nagged about the point she would not openly concede, the English succession. Dealing with Mary's desire for her throne was better done from a distance, and through intermediaries. And third, Melville was in fact on dangerous ground when he talked of Elizabeth's refusal to marry. He dealt with it well, with a hard-headed compliment to a hard-headed woman whose *raison d'être* was the rule of her kingdom. But Mary did not have Elizabeth's 'stately stomach'; and the marriage of the Scottish queen was a matter which the English government was naturally anxious to control.

Mary's intention to marry was both expected and well understood. No one was under any illusion about the particular problems surrounding the marriage of a queen regnant; the English themselves had suffered from it in the reign of Elizabeth's predecessor, when Mary Tudor had tied England to Spain. But neither did anyone doubt that it was the duty of a ruler to provide an heir; and that took precedence over the potential difficulties, to the extent that, despite their recent experience, Elizabeth was constantly badgered by her subjects to marry. It was she who was out of line, not Mary.

It is therefore ironic that it was the reluctant Elizabeth who was besieged by suitors when she inherited her throne, the willing Mary who found it so difficult to acquire a second husband after the death of Francis II, even though the bachelors of Europe, from Sweden to Spain, who had failed to persuade Elizabeth of their attractions, were still on the hunt for a bride. The distressing fact was that no one was rushing to beg for her hand, as she herself rather pathetically said to the English diplomat Randolph in the spring of 1564. Certainly in the early part of Mary's reign in Scotland, nothing happened to advance her prospects. Not until the beginning of 1563 were positive efforts made, and it was not foreign suitors but the Scottish queen who took the initiative. For two years, Mary had agreed with a policy dictated by the English succession and therefore of great benefit to the Protestants. But she had never forgotten the prospect which she had so much wished for in the early months of 1561: marriage to Don Carlos of Spain, or Charles IX of France. Indeed, in January 1562, she had spoken of her intention to marry very highly, and made it clear that, despite her protestations to Elizabeth that she would not marry against her wishes, she still had Don Carlos in mind. Remarkably,

Lethington, one of the principal architects of the pro-English policy, was now prepared to back her.

For Mary herself, there was no necessary inconsistency in this. Her first policy was not working. Elizabeth was well aware that the supplicant is in the weaker position than the giver; she kept her head and refused to be manoeuvred into offering Mary the assurance of the succession which she wanted. Moreover, Elizabeth's hand was strengthened, that of the Scots weakened, by the solid antagonism shown by the English council to the prospect of Mary's succession when the English queen seemed on the point of death from smallpox in October 1562. This created a major headache for the Protestant leaders in Scotland. For them, as for Cecil, Anglo-Scottish amity was the cornerstone of their policy; and Mary's English ambitions had made both it and the Protestant successes within Scotland possible in the first two years of her reign. Now it was all too apparent that the English council, however enthusiastic about friendship with Scotland, was wholly unwilling to countenance the one thing which would ensure the Scottish queen's continuing friendship with England.

For Mary, there was an alternative. If the English would not accept her willingly, then they might be forced to do so; and that could be achieved by a marriage which would threaten them. There is, it must be said, a difficulty here. It is clear enough that a marriage alliance between Mary of Scotland and one of the two great Catholic powers would menace England. It is considerably harder to make the imaginative leap from that to Mary's position on the English throne. But such a leap did exist in Mary's mind. The only problem was to find the necessary husband, and – since by definition that husband must be Catholic – to demonstrate that she who maintained Protestantism in Scotland would benefit the Catholics of England.

The opening gambit came in February 1563 when Lethington turned up in England to propose a match between Mary and Don Carlos to the Spanish ambassador de Quadra. The attractions he dangled were not only Mary's personal charms, but her wealth from France and Scotland, and the addition to Philip's domains of Scotland, England and Ireland. He added an argument which in fact had no foundation: if the Spanish would not respond, he would seek, with the help of Mary's uncles of Guise, a marriage with Charles IX of France, thus threatening Spain with a restoration of the Valois alliance. In suggesting this, he was denying the real Guise policy, that if Mary were going to marry a Hapsburg, it should be Archduke Charles, younger son of the Emperor Ferdinand I; this was a scheme pushed by Charles of Guise, cardinal of Lorraine, without reference to Mary, and one to which she reacted with fury, not least because he was not rich enough to maintain her state.

Between then and August 1564, when Philip finally turned down the Don Carlos marriage on the ostensible grounds of his son's insanity – which had been obvious enough for some time – there were eighteen months of rumour, confusion, proposals and counter-proposals. De Quadra produced assurances of offers of help from English Catholics, but these in fact amounted to very little. And Philip's own total lack of conviction that Mary was going to provide him with a Catholic Scotland, let alone a Catholic England, can be seen in his consistent determination to keep the negotiations utterly secret. Since it was in exactly this period that, although other Scottish Catholics were still maintaining links with Rome, Mary's own contact with the papacy had become virtually non-existent, his doubts are readily understandable. But of course the secret was not kept.

The French were duly alarmed, reacting as they had done in the early months of 1561 against the Spanish match. Yet although, according to the Spanish ambassador in France, Catherine de Medici's initial response was that 'this was the greatest scare she ever had in her life', she had certainly got over it by the time Don Carlos's illness in the autumn of 1563 confirmed their doubts about whether it would ever take place. So they were not unduly alarmed. They had been preoccupied by far more pressing internal religious troubles. The first war of religion had broken out in April 1562. It ended with the Pacification of Amboise in March 1563, and a limited and, in the mind of Catherine de Medici, temporary toleration for the Huguenots. But in the course of the war, in February 1563, the duke of Guise had been assassinated by a Protestant, and that inevitably affected the power struggle between Catherine and the Guises. In the succeeding months, his brother the cardinal was, it was believed, prepared to oppose Catherine and countenance the Spanish marriage for his niece, thus linking Guise power to Spain; indeed, rumour had it that he and the pope intended to give her England for her dowry – to attain which, presumably, her would-be husband and father-in-law Philip II would duly fight. Fact wholly belied rumour. What the Guise family now wanted was a marriage between Mary and the new duke of Guise, but this never looked likely. What no one would consider was a marriage with Charles IX. And by far the most revealing reaction came from Catherine de Medici. Her candidate was Châtelherault's son Arran, by now lunatic. Her opinion of her former daughter-in-law could hardly have been made more clear.

It would obviously be wrong to suggest that Mary's marriage plans in 1563–4 were not a matter of concern – sometimes even of moments of panic – for France and Spain, and indeed England. If Mary had married a Hapsburg or a Valois, then the balance of power in Europe, and the prospects for the Protestants of the three kingdoms of France, England and Scotland, would have been potentially very seriously disturbed. So the question why she seemed such an unattractive proposition to France and Spain, despite all the obvious advantages, is extremely important. Part of the answer lay in the fact that neither French nor Spanish would willingly see her marry into the other of these two great houses. But neither could actually prevent such a marriage if there was sufficient determination by one or other for it. And Mary herself should have had a say in the matter. It therefore appears that the real problem lay with her.

It was not until July 1567 that the pope finally refused further dealings with her until he saw 'some better sign of her life and religion than he has witnessed in the past'. But by the beginning of 1563, there were certainly strong doubts about her religious commitment. Her initial pro-English policy and support for the

Scottish Protestants was itself a rejection of her French upbringing; she had not been trained by the Guises for that. Her behaviour in 1563, the very year when she was so enthusiastic about the Spanish marriage, was inexplicable if she wished to display herself to Philip II as a suitably ardent Catholic with whom it would be worth his while to ally. She did nothing to offset her total failure to advance the restoration of Catholicism in her kingdom, so clearly visible in 1561–2. Not only was there the parliament of 1563 whose legislation benefited only the Protestants, even if it stopped short of ratifying the acts of the Reformation parliament; but she actually imprisoned Archbishop Hamilton and other Catholics because their belief that her desire to marry Don Carlos presaged a change of religious policy at home had led them to celebrate Mass publicly at Easter. But there was more to it even than that. Questions were already being asked about her life as well as her religion.

Within the first two years of Mary's reign, long before the major scandals of 1566–7, there were two remarkable incidents. One is well known. In the winter of 1562–3 a French poet, Pierre de Châtelard, who had accompanied Mary to Scotland, and was clearly besotted by her, was twice discovered at night in her bedchamber. On the first occasion, when he was discovered hiding under her bed, he was let off with a warning. The second cost him his life. He was executed at St Andrews in February 1563, dying on a note of farewell to 'the most cruel princess of the world'. The 'cruel princess' had in fact reacted with understandable but ill-timed hysteria when he burst into her bedchamber to renew his advances; she shrieked for help, and when her half-brother rushed to her aid, screeched at him to kill Châtelard. The scandal was bad enough; Moray fortunately managed to prevent her from making it worse by insisting on the poet's imprisonment and trial.

That in itself, while being Mary's misfortune rather than fault, can hardly have encouraged the puritanical Philip II who, in this very month, was receiving the first overtures from the Scottish queen. But there was another incident, not now well known. On 10 August 1562, Mary, while in the company of the Englishman

Sir Henry Sidney, was handed a 'bill' by one Captain Hepburn, which contained 'as ribbald verses as any devilish wit could invent, and under them drawn with a pen the secret members both of men and women in as monstrous a sort as nothing could be more shamefully devised'. The account comes from Randolph, who was so shocked that he found it exceedingly difficult to report to Cecil: 'the tale is so irreverent that I know not in what honest terms I may write it to your honour'. Now it is certainly the case that any monarch might well be the target for scandal, if it could be found or invented. And inevitably a female ruler was particularly vulnerable. Elizabeth, for example, suffered from it because of her supposed affair with her favourite, Robert Dudley; indeed, scandal became uproar when Dudley's wife, Amy Robsart, died in mysterious circumstances – to which Elizabeth had the sense to react with the same dispassionate coolness as Moray.

But there is a considerable difference between scandal and the Hepburn incident. For that shows that within a year of her return to Scotland, Mary's reputation and prestige were already so low that she was not just the object of scandal spread about her, but the personal recipient of a direct gesture which was profoundly humiliating and insulting. One only has to consider whether anyone would have dared to do something similar to Elizabeth of England to get some sense of just what happened on that August day, and what it tells us about the lack of respect for her as queen which had already reached a very dangerous level.

Less dramatic, but equally extraordinary in terms of the treatment of a reigning monarch, was Knox's diatribe to her on the subject of her marriage. The negotiations of 1563, when, to Lethington's embarrassment, the secrecy Philip II had demanded was broken in Scotland, created further splits within the Protestant camp. Lethington, while using them as a means of putting pressure on Elizabeth, nevertheless does seem to have been willing to accept the Spanish marriage, if it could be brought about. Moray was very much less in favour, but in view of the English attitude to Mary as Elizabeth's successor, was left with little chance to oppose it. Knox, of course, was totally hostile. The result was a weakening of the partnership of Lethington and Moray, and a temporary breakdown of relations between Moray and Knox. But if Knox refused to communicate with Moray, he had no such reservations about expressing his views directly to the queen.

During the parliament of 1563, he preached a thunderous sermon to a large number of the aristocracy against a Catholic marriage, and against any Protestant nobleman who so far denied the cause of Christ as to support it, and followed this up, when Mary made the mistake of sending for him to tell him off, by reducing her to tears and 'howling', so violently did he criticize her. It was an amazing exchange. 'I have', said the queen, 'borne with you in all your rigorous manner of speaking . . . yea I have sought your favours by all possible means. . . . But what have ye to do with my marriage? Or what are ye within this Commonwealth?' 'A subject born within the same, Madam', came the devastating reply; 'and albeit I neither be Earl, Lord nor Baron within it, yet has God made me (how abject that ever I be in your eyes) a profitable member within the same.' And so Mary wept and stormed, while a page rushed for napkins to mop up her tears, and Knox left, throwing to her gorgeously apparelled ladies of the court as he went a reminder of 'that knave death, that will come whether we will or not'.

Again, comparison with Elizabeth is instructive. Elizabeth would never have made the pathetic appeal that Mary did to Knox, nor allowed any subject born within the realm to seize such an initiative in an interview with her. The English members of parliament who nagged her about her marriage and the succession in 1563 and 1566 were not treated to tears; instead, in 1566 when her patience snapped, they were subjected to a 'blistering speech' which reminded them all too clearly that subjects did not bully their queen. But for Mary, worse was to follow. In October, Knox reacted to the arrest of two Protestants who had disturbed the Mass in the queen's chapel at Holyrood by writing an open letter to the Protestants of Scotland, enjoining them to come to the support of their co-religionists when they were brought to trial. This was treason; Knox, without authority from the queen, was summoning the queen's subjects. Brought before the queen and council in December, he was acquitted.

The period of her attempts to negotiate a marriage alliance with France and Spain was therefore a particularly bad time for Mary. Her personal prestige was suspect, her political control even more so. In the early months of 1561, her failure to make a Hapsburg or a second Valois marriage may at least in part be explained by the desire of the Catholic powers to see her back in Scotland, where the prompt and firm exercise of Catholic monarchy might be strong enough to overturn the incipient success of Scottish Protestantism; the French who knew her personally may have had doubts, but still the effort was worth making. By the beginning of 1563, it had become all too obvious that such hopes were vain. She had helped only the Protestants; and, for all the charm which did make her personally attractive, as a politician she was already visibly regarded with a lack of respect which sometimes toppled over into open contempt. And since her actions in 1563 only confirmed Catholic doubts about her, it is not surprising that the lack of enthusiasm France and Spain had shown in 1561 was even more in evidence in 1563–4. Why should either entertain the idea of alliance with a woman who was still so visibly failing to control the Protestants – and even 'seeking the favours by all possible means' of the most famous Protestant of them all, John Knox?

This no doubt explains why the English were not so fearful as might have been expected. As long as the great Catholic powers regarded her as undesirable and unimpressive, so that they would not risk the war which marriage with her in order to restore Catholicism to Scotland and England would bring, the Protestant Elizabeth could draw breath; it was a risky business, but Mary, to what must have been Elizabeth's intense relief, remained the woman who could be kept more or less under control because her obsession with the English throne rather than the Catholic faith deprived her of independent bargaining power. Indeed, Lethington's negotiations with de Quadra, and his alternative threat, to persuade the Guises to arrange a marriage with Charles IX, had been at least in part intended to jolt Elizabeth into offering Mary what she wanted.

In August 1563 Elizabeth responded by making it clear that if Mary did marry any member of the house of Hapsburg, Spanish or Imperial, or the French king, then she would become her enemy. But if Mary took her advice, to marry an English nobleman or a Protestant prince, then she would stand her friend; and she threw in the sop that she would eventually enquire into her right to be regarded as her heir. A possible prince was Eric of Sweden, former passionate suitor of Elizabeth; but as with the Archduke Charles, he was not 'high' enough for Mary – and interestingly enough, despite the long-standing contacts between Scotland and Sweden, and the possible benefits for the Protestants of both kingdoms, Eric himself did not want to marry her, being prepared at most to offer his brother.

So the options narrowed. And after much general talk, Elizabeth eventually pronounced her choice of English noble. Early in 1563, she had joked about Robert Dudley as a suitable husband for Mary. In March 1564 she made a serious offer of this man, suspected murderer of his wife, supposed lover of the English queen, and certainly her favourite. In September, during Melville's visit to the English court, she created Dudley earl of Leicester, to make him more suitable as a husband for a queen – and interrupted the formal ceremonies by tickling his neck to demonstrate in the most public way her own affection for him. But it demonstrated more than affection for Dudley. It was also a distinct insult to Mary, showing Elizabeth's amused contempt for the sovereign to whom she was throwing him in marriage. For Mary, it was a horrid reminder of reality. This monarch with such a high sense of her royalty had been unable to establish her authority in her own kingdom; and her efforts in the European marriage market had, by the end of 1564, produced only one definite offer: marriage to the Master of Horse of the English queen. Indeed, even that was not certain. Mary was understandably unenthusiastic about such a match, but desire to please Elizabeth prevented her from rejecting it outright. The Master of Horse, on the other hand, was totally reluctant to marry her.

There lingered in the background, however, just one other

possibility. At the very moment of ennobling – and fondling – Dudley, Elizabeth suddenly turned to Melville and, pointing to Henry lord Darnley, told him that 'ye like better of yonder long lad'. Melville tactfully denied it. He was of course quite right. Leicester was not just Elizabeth's favourite because of his physical attractions; he was already emerging as a major political figure, and he was the friend and correspondent of Moray. But the ambassador kept the exchange as light-hearted as possible by replying in purely personal terms. How could any woman of spirit – that is, his queen – prefer to the new earl of Leicester someone 'that was liker a woman than a man; for he was very lusty, beardless and lady-faced'.

Darnley, the subject of the dialogue, was the son of Matthew Stewart, earl of Lennox. The earl had been an exile in England since 1544, victim of regent Arran's change of heart towards and defeat of the pro-English party. In the hope of using him to gain control of Scotland, Henry VIII had agreed to his marriage with Margaret Douglas, daughter of James IV's widow Margaret Tudor and her second husband, Angus. Lennox failed to do anything for Henry. But the marriage did something for Lennox. Not only did he have a claim to the Scottish throne, second to that of the Hamiltons' which was open to question, but now, through his wife, he had a claim to the English throne as well. Too much has been made of Darnley's place in the English succession. His claim, like Mary's, came through Margaret Tudor, and it was her line which had been excluded by Henry VIII; and as it was secondary to Mary's own, it can hardly be said to have strengthened it. But there was one thing to be said for it: Darnley, born in England, did not have the taint of being an alien, and his claim could not therefore be challenged by the English on these grounds. Moreover, this was not his only attraction. His father's religious commitment was far from certain. But his mother was a noted English Catholic. Thus when Mary's choice of husband had been narrowed down to Dudley or Darnley, the latter might well have greater appeal than the former; certainly his mother thought so, and indeed had had hopes of the marriage as far back as the death of Francis II, though Mary herself had shown no interest in him at that stage, when the hopeful countess had sent him over to France to meet and condole with her. The only problem was to get him out of England. This was achieved, for reasons which have never yet been adequately understood, in February 1565.

Already in June 1563, when Elizabeth was repairing the strained relations which had existed between her and the earl and countess of Lennox, she had asked Mary for permission for Lennox to return to Scotland. It was a request which she was to regret, and try unsuccessfully to withdraw; in September 1564, Lennox returned to Scotland. By December it was becoming increasingly apparent that the Leicester marriage was unlikely to happen; anxious for it in theory though Elizabeth was, the combination of Leicester's unwillingness and her refusal to link it to a formal acknowledgement of Mary as her heir gave it little chance of success. On 17 February 1565, Darnley met Mary at Wemyss Castle in Fife. In March, Elizabeth finally destroyed all hopes of the Leicester marriage, when she declared unequivocally – a rare event – that she would not pronounce on the succession until she had decided whether she herself would marry. It was a logical enough point, but a complete diplomatic mystery.

The most machiavellian interpretation, raised at the time, was that Elizabeth, well knowing Darnley's character, sent him north in February, and pushed him into Mary's arms in March, for Mary's destruction. This is very unlikely, however much subsequent events seemed to justify it. The Leicester marriage was certainly desired by the English government. It foundered on Leicester's own reluctance, and, in the end, that of the queen. Thus Elizabeth, for whom marriage was a deeply touchy subject, appears to have turned five years of careful and successful diplomacy into personal blunder, and taken a step which left her no room for manoeuvre. Her refusal to back the Leicester negotiations with acknowledge-ment of the succession – which everyone well knew would be overturned if she did have an heir of her body, without her having to say so in March – made their failure inevitable. There was no other likely suitor for Mary's hand. That, to the fury of the English, including the queen herself, left only Darnley.

Largely thanks to the marital antics of Henry VIII, and in particular because of his infatuation with Anne Boleyn, the idea that sixteenth-century royal marriages should be love matches looms larger than it should. Royal marriages were affairs of state. Although Darnley was not in the same league as the hoped-for Hapsburg or Valois husband, there were good political reasons for the marriage; and a case has indeed been made that this was why Mary decided to marry Darnley. Certainly it was approved of by the Catholic kings of France and Spain, and by the papacy, with whom contact was now restored – mainly because of the need for a papal dispensation for these two cousins to marry. But oddly enough, neither Darnley's place in the English succession nor his apparently Catholic leanings initially attracted Mary. Amazingly, at the beginning of 1565, she still had hopes of the lunatic Don Carlos, and her first reaction was to deny any desire to marry Darnley. Then came a dramatic change in her feelings. At the beginning of April, within two weeks of Elizabeth's rebuff about the succession, Darnley was smitten by measles. Mary plunged into an orgy of nursing and love. The years of stalemate were over. The period of romance, drama and crisis had begun.

It opened during Darnley's illness when Mary threw reputation to the winds by staying so late into the night with him that rumours of a secret marriage immediately circulated. These were false. But she did make her intentions very clear. On 15 May, she created him earl of Ross, a title associated with the royal house of Stewart since 1481; and the new earl was then allowed to create fourteen knights, including adherents of Lennox, but also including some who, like Stewart of Doune and Murray of Tullibardine, had been among those who fought the Protestant cause in 1559–60. It does look like an effort not just to please Darnley, by putting him in a position to hand out favours, but to create a party who would support the marriage from potential Protestant opponents; and indeed for Murray of Tullibardine there was an extra inducement, for he was made comptroller in August 1565. Then on 20 July she gave Darnley the further royal title of duke of Albany. And on 29 July, without waiting for the papal dispensation, she married him, in the chapel royal at Holyrood between five and six in the morning.

There were two notable aspects of the marriage, one curious, the other sinister. First, Mary emphasized her widowhood by turning up in a black mourning gown and hood; and so after the wedding there was an extraordinary ceremony in which those present began to divest her of her widow's garb, each man taking out one pin, before she departed with her ladies (presumably before her black clothes had actually fallen off her) to change into garments of joy rather than grief. Second, and much more alarming, although the marriage itself took place by Catholic rites, the new husband, so much approved of by the Catholic powers, refused to attend the nuptial mass. There is no evidence that Mary was concerned by this public demonstration of lukewarm Catholicism. On the day before the wedding, without waiting to seek the approval of parliament, and entirely on her own authority, she had pronounced him king of Scotland. She followed this up on 30 July with a public proclamation that in future royal documents would be subscribed by 'Marie and Henry'. Of all those who heard, only the proud father, Lennox, broke the resulting silence to cry 'God save his Grace'.

Nevertheless, although personal considerations were uppermost in Mary's mind between April and July 1565, the marriage to Darnley had a radical effect on the political situation in Scotland. Darnley himself hardly cut a convincing figure as a committed Catholic. Not only did he refuse to attend the nuptial mass, but he was prepared to go to St Giles on Sunday mornings, along with other members of the court, where their sins could be trumpeted at them by John Knox; on at least one occasion, the experience deprived him of his appetite for dinner. But neither was he a committed Protestant. And whatever else the marriage involved, it certainly meant the end of Moray's policy. He had been the great advocate in Scotland of the marriage with Leicester, and had pursued it to the end, with what feelings of bitterness as Elizabeth sabotaged it can only be guessed. Mary's infatuation with Darnley in April 1565 was accompanied by a breakdown of relations with her half-brother; his last attendance at the council was on 19–20 May 1565. On the 19th, in anticipation of a parliament planned for July, the council had to agree to chase up to Perth so that they could discuss with the queen 'all things needfull to be treated upon in the said parliament . . . and that her Highness may understand what they will require of her Majesty to be done, and by the contrary what her Highness will command them with'. It was the old problem of lack of communication. But it was now compounded by the new crisis created by the queen's choice of husband. Mary side-stepped a potential forum for opposition to the marriage, and did not hold the July parliament. But already, by the third week in May, Elizabeth's loss of influence with Mary and Moray's conflict with her had brought the Protestant control of the last five years to an end.

The result was a realignment of faction. Since 1560, the Protestants had not been solidly united; in particular there had been a split between the 'reformers' like Knox and the 'politicians' like Moray. But there was now a total split within the political camp. Despite the threat to Scottish Protestantism, which had seemed in the previous five years to depend so heavily on friendship with England, Moray did not have general support from the Protestants. He and Knox drew closer together. The strongly Protestant earls of Argyll, Glencairn and Rothes remained loyal to him. Châtelherault, in direct response to the ascendancy of Lennox, also joined with him. Otherwise he had the backing of some of the lairds from the Protestant areas of Fife and Ayrshire, but surprisingly few. Despite their hostility to Darnley's elevation as king, and despite the fact that already his petulant arrogance had made him deeply unpopular to all but Mary, other Protestants as well as the Catholics remained with the queen: not only the newly-created knights, but men like Morton and Cassillis, even lord Ruthven and, above all, Moray's closest political associate, Lethington. And Mary strengthened her party not only by her favour to the Lennox Stewarts, but by releasing from prison George lord Gordon, son of the forfeited Huntly, and subsequently restoring him to his earldom, and by granting to lord Erskine the earldom of Mar to which his family had been unsuccessfully pressing their claim against the crown since 1435.

Finally on 7 September 1565 there arrived from France James Hepburn, who had succeeded to his father Patrick's earldom of Bothwell, in 1556, to become the border earl and political trouble-maker whose ability to antagonize every section of the Protestant community, despite his own Protestant commitment, had kept him in exile in France since 1562, apart from a brief reappearance in Scotland in May 1565. Oddly enough, one of his few friends in these early years was Knox, who had tried to support him during one of his political rows, that with the earl of Arran in 1562; for Knox's ancestors had been adherents of the Hepburns and it appeared that claims of kinship and service, on this occasion at least, weighed with the man who normally rejected them in the service of God. Otherwise Bothwell was widely disliked. Now he was back, and visibly in the queen's favour, to play his notorious role in the last two years of the personal rule.

Thus for the first time in her reign, the queen appeared to be in an infinitely stronger position than her half-brother. Initially, the problem was that Moray's opposition to the marriage looked too much like a petulant and therefore unpopular reaction to his loss of political dominance. In the spring of 1565, that no doubt was the major consideration; for there was as yet no evidence that Mary, despite making a marriage which destroyed all he had worked for politically since 1561, was going to change into a ruler sufficiently decisive to mount a real threat to the Protestant cause. On 21 May, Randolph wrote of her in terms which suggested that if anything she was even less effective than she had been: 'I know not how to utter what I conceive of the pitiful and lamentable estate of this poor queen, whom ever before I esteemed so worthy, so wise, so honourable in all her doings; and at this present do find so altered with affection towards the lord Darnley, that she hath brought her honour in question, her estate in hazard, her country to be torn in pieces. . . . All men here stand in suspense.'

Admittedly Randolph praised her previous behaviour simply because she had, on the whole, done what the English wanted –

or rather, in 1563–4, found herself unable to do what they did not want. But the picture he gives suggests personal obsession rather than political intelligence at work. And on the same day, Throckmorton reported to Elizabeth not only that parliament would be held on 20 July, but that Mary intended to summon the ministers on 10 or 12 June 'to put in readiness for parliament some matters concerning religion and ecclesiastical policy'; the assumption was that in return for the old concession of her private Mass, and the new agreement for the Darnley marriage, Mary was as willing as she had ever been to allow the Protestant faith to remain unchallenged and perhaps even to give it the parliamentary recognition she had denied it since 1560. Throckmorton himself feared that there would be 'much ado'. But these two accounts of Mary in May 1565 show why there were many Protestants who still felt secure enough not to have to take the unpalatable decision to join with Moray in resisting their sovereign openly.

Events were to prove them wrong. For even if its political and religious advantages had not been the original motivating force, the Darnley marriage did have an unforeseen effect on Mary. Whether it was because she liked the warmer response she was now getting from France, Spain and the pope, or because she found the absence of the dominating Moray a release, or because the humiliations of the previous years had been too much, and pushed her into taking her own line at last, she did for the first time since she had come to Scotland show signs of departing from Catholic acquiescence in the advance of Protestantism.

It could not be said that her new policy was advanced with any great determination or result. But the juxtaposition of events in 1565 made this a deeply worrying time for the Protestants of Europe and Scotland, and therefore any hint of a more pro-Catholic attitude on the part of the Scottish queen would be a matter for great concern. On 29 July 1565, Mary married the Catholic – if vaguely Catholic – Darnley, with the approval of the pope, France and Spain. In this very month, France and Spain, in the persons of Catherine de Medici and the duke of Alva, were meeting at Bayonne. Their agreement, that there should be no compromise with heretics, immediately created panic; rumours of a Catholic league against the Protestants of Europe, a league in which the Catholic queen of Scotland had a part, flared up. There is in fact not a shred of evidence that Mary was involved in such a league; there was, indeed, no such league in 1565. But when religious positions were not yet fully established and still under threat, rumour was as potent as fact, in Scotland as elsewhere; five years later, for example, the Scottish Protestants were convinced that Alva himself was going to invade them. And in 1565, if rumours of a league were false, the continuing existence of Catholicism in Scotland was all too real; in March, Randolph had reported that there were still more Catholics than Protestants in Edinburgh itself.

Mary's new approach, therefore, could only create fears, both about what she might do in Scotland and about her possible foreign involvement. In June, she answered a petition from the General Assembly that the Mass should be abolished, according to the act of parliament of 1560, not only by refusing outright on her own account, but by defending her position with the ominous statement that she would not risk losing 'the friendship of the king of France, the ancient ally of this realm, and of other great princes, her friends and confederates, who would take it in evil part, of whom she may look for support in all her necessities'. That can hardly have inspired Protestant confidence in the renewal of her proclamation promising no alteration in the state of religion on 15 July 1565. The July parliament itself, from which the Protestants had hoped for much, never met.

It was therefore a further and very sharp twist of the knife when, on 29 July, Mary told the General Assembly of the Kirk that religion could only be established by the three estates in parliament – and when they did, she would confirm it; not only had parliament indeed established religion, in 1560, and she had never confirmed it, but her statement was made on the very day of the Darnley marriage. Moreover, she had already written to the pope on 24 July, protesting her loyalty to Rome and her intention to restore the Catholic faith. Undoubtedly she hoped for a papal subsidy, but this was not the whole point of her new attitude. During the summer, it was noted by English observers that even if she had not yet come out openly for Rome, she was nevertheless trying to convert individuals at court – a very dangerous policy, as her grandson Charles I was to find in the 1630s, when his wife Henrietta Maria was doing the same thing. On 1 August, Moray was summoned to appear, on pain of treason, by a council which for once contained a large number of Catholics; at the end of the month, she had the Protestant provost of Edinburgh, Kilspindie, replaced by the Catholic laird of Craigmillar. And in September, it was reported at the English court that her support for the papists and her avowal to please the king of France and her other friends were becoming increasingly ill-concealed.

By mid-August, Moray was in open revolt – the revolt known as the Chaseabout Raid. It was rightly named. In the next few weeks, both sides raced round southern Scotland without ever actually meeting. Mary thoroughly enjoyed herself. Darnley looked splendid in particularly elaborate armour. Moray was frantic. Earlier in the summer, Elizabeth had promised Moray support. But on this occasion, unlike 1560 and 1567–8, and despite her own fulminations against Mary which had included mutterings about war, she would not openly back rebellion; and Moray gave up and fled to England on 6 October. On the 23rd, he was received by Elizabeth, who put on a splendid public display of indignant horror about his treason to his queen. But both sides knew exactly how far their interests coincided. Moray was given asylum in England, and remained in Newcastle throughout the winter of 1565–6, to wait upon events.

In view of Mary's activities in the summer of 1565, there can be no reason to doubt Moray's own claim – a claim not denied by the Catholics, as the Spanish ambassador in England's report to Philip II makes clear – that when he rebelled, he was fighting for the Protestant cause. It was not, of course, a clear-cut matter. Even Moray's motives were not purely ideological. But lack of support for him does not mean that one may take a cynically political view of what he, a leading Scottish Calvinist noble, stood for; undoubtedly he was far more convinced of the dangers to Protestantism than those who still refused to join him. It is also understandable, however, that they did not, even although it was now clear that religion was a major consideration, as it had not been when Moray first opposed Mary in the spring.

Old rivalries, between Lennox and the Hamiltons, between Lennox and Atholl on the one hand and Argyll on the other, played their part in the disaster for Moray. But there was also a rather different ideological reason. At no time in late medieval and early modern Scotland did men lightly threaten that symbol of unity and stability, the crown, and never less so than in the 1560s when, however unsatisfactory the wearer of it, rebellion against the crown raised the spectre of the destruction of what could still offer certainty in a world which had become so uncertain. Memories of 1559–60 in Scotland, and the hideous spectacle of the religious wars in France, gave good grounds for caution, even in the face of what Mary was doing in the summer of 1565. And such caution was not necessarily unjustified. From the point of view of the Protestants who remained loyal to the queen, after all, Moray might well have been wrong to fear that Protestantism would go down with his carefully-nurtured pro-English policy. For although Mary had appeared to challenge the Protestant establishment, she could hardly be said as yet to have seriously threatened it; rumour and individual contacts do not make a Counter-Reformation.

It is, indeed, part of Mary's tragedy that when at last she did take a positive line, she did it so ineffectively. It has been suggested in her defence that she had good grounds for delay until she had fully established her rule in Scotland before making a move to defend, or even restore, Catholicism to her kingdom. Even if this line of argument was valid, it hardly rescues her from the charge of ineptitude; what Dr Julian Goodare has felicitously termed her 'Catholic interlude' was of very short duration, and marked by confusion rather than determination. But the argument itself is unconvincing. By waiting until 1565, she had in fact left it far too late; she had given the Protestants their head for five years. Moreover, she had less support than in the first years of her reign, when the Protestant success was still very fragile and the earl of Huntly who had died at Corrichie would certainly have been a strong ally, even if not a wholly satisfactory one; it was her misfortune that his son, restored to favour in 1565, was a Protestant, who refused to attend her Mass despite her blandishments. Her favour to the Protestants in 1561–2 ensured that the opportunity she sought through a Catholic marriage in 1563–4 was denied her; and the approval of the Catholic powers for her marriage to Darnley was no substitute for a solid alliance with one of them. She was left with Darnley; and by now even Mary was coming to realize what he was: immature, irresponsible and drunken. By the autumn of 1565, he had fulfilled one function as royal spouse by making her pregnant; but his behaviour was becoming an increasing liability, both to Mary personally, whom he insulted publicly, and to the prestige of the crown. Her insistence on proclaiming him king and giving him the right to sign royal documents was shown up for the hideous mistake it was when in November 1565, within four months of the marriage, a dry stamp had to be made of his signature because business was being endlessly held up by a king who was not there to attend to it.

In the winter of 1565–6, therefore, Mary's more openly pro-Catholic position of the summer was not followed up with any consistency. In the past, she had created confusion because of maintaining a Protestant-dominated council while consorting with a household which contained her Catholic and foreign friends. But at least it had been clear that her 'official' policy was that of her council; it was the Catholics, at home and abroad, whom she did not support. Now, the signals from the throne became even more conflicting. At last she extended her council. Moray had gone in May. Throughout the summer, Lennox turned up frequently. And there were also the Catholics John Leslie, later bishop of Ross, and Simon Preston of Craigmillar, provost of Edinburgh. But of the other new members, one, brought on to the council in October, was the Protestant earl of Bothwell; from the same month the Protestant Huntly began to attend regularly; then in November

Mary appointed that 'dangerous man', as she herself had called him, and undoubted Protestant, Alexander Gordon, bishop of Galloway: and there were also the Protestant lawyer James Balfour of Pittendreich and the Protestant laird John Maxwell of Terregles.

The council of 1565–6 was therefore slightly more broadly based than its predecessor, but it was not notably one which would take as strong a line on restoring Catholicism as the earlier one had in sustaining Protestantism. It is a measure of Mary's inability to understand the crucial importance of the queen's council that she did not capitalize on the strength of her position in the first months after the Darnley marriage by creating a council which could do more to back her in her pro-Catholic policy – and working with it.

Instead, the queen herself was now putting personal pressure on her nobles, though without much success, to attend Mass. And her renewed contacts with the papacy were maintained. Indeed, in January 1566, the new pope Pius V, distinctly over-optimistic about the situation in Scotland, paid her a warm tribute for 'the brilliant proof of your zeal by restoring the due worship of God throughout your whole realm'. She had not done so. All she was doing was to indicate that this was the direction in which she would now like to move, even if neither far nor fast. This in itself was a matter of concern for the Protestants who had stood by her against Moray in the autumn, although it was probably not enough on its own to turn them against her. But there was another problem, which left them no room for doubt and indecision. The methods which she was using to achieve her ends were the worst possible, in two ways. First, because she had not created a sufficiently broad basis of support, she was unlikely to succeed; all she could do was to antagonize and alarm the Protestants, while failing to satisfy the Catholics. Second, they were an outrage to all accepted political *mores*. For the old problem of separation between council and household and, even more dangerous, her reliance on the foreigners within it, was now revived in full and intolerable measure. The particular offender, the man to whom she gave her entire confidence once she had realized that Darnley was no possible aid to her, was David Rizzio.

Rizzio had been in Scotland since 1561. In 1564, he was advanced from being one of Mary's musicians to being her secretary for French affairs, operating within her household. When Darnley first came to Scotland, Rizzio liked him, and was indeed supposed to have influenced the queen in his favour. He was supposed to have done other things as well, including fathering the child which Mary was carrying in 1565–6. This was certainly not the case. But it was the case that once again Mary created the opportunity for scandal, for it was now Rizzio with whom she sat up late at night. Moreover, his haughtiness and closeness to the queen made him deeply unpopular, and by the winter of 1565–6 she alone protected him; for relations between him and Darnley, jealous of his position with the queen, had completely broken down.

This, in the year when she had broken with England and was favoured by the Catholic powers, was the 'politician' – and suspected papal agent – on whom Mary almost exclusively relied. The Scottish Protestants who had remained loyal to her in the summer and autumn of 1565 might not have existed. Nor indeed might the Catholics. Among the Scottish aristocracy, the queen's contacts had now narrowed down to the Protestants Bothwell and Huntly who would not attend her Mass, Lennox, and that negative Catholic who in 1561 had refused to support the move for Catholic restoration, Atholl. Already in September 1565, Randolph, who in the previous May had expressed sympathy for her, had written of the dangers: 'how she, with this kind of government, her suspicion of her people, and debate with the chief of her nobility, can stand and prosper, passes my wit. To be ruled by the advice of two or three strangers, neglecting that of her chief councillors, I do not know how it can stand'. He was to be answered in March 1566.

Mary does appear to have been living in a world of totally unreal self-confidence. Despite the isolation within which she was now operating, she felt strong enough to have a trial of strength with those Protestant lords who had controlled events in Scotland until 1565 and then been ousted from power after the Darnley marriage – Moray, Argyll, Glencairn, Rothes and others – summoning them to stand trial in parliament on 12 March 1566. That determined the date of the showdown with the queen, in which Rizzio was the sacrificial victim. The lords did not wait to be tried. They acted first. Their weapon was the wretched Darnley, whom they attracted to their side by promising to persuade parliament to grant him the crown matrimonial – a much more authoritative recognition of kingship than Mary's proclamation. On 1 March 1566, Darnley made a bond addressed generally to earls, lords, barons, freeholders, gentlemen, craftsmen and merchants, stating his intention to rid the country of those who abused the kindness of the queen, especially 'a stranger Italian called David' who might happen to be killed in the course of Darnley's enterprise against him, which might 'chance to be done in the presence of the Queen's Majesty or within her palace of Holyroodhouse.'

To this quite amazingly explicit advance account of murder, Moray and his associates responded with a bond made at Newcastle on 2 March, promising general support and the crown matrimonial. The deed itself took place on the 9th, when Patrick lord Ruthven, Morton, lord Lindsay and others broke in on a private supper-party held in the tiny ante-room to the queen's bedchamber in Holyrood, dragged Rizzio out, and stabbed him to death, carefully leaving Darnley's dagger in the body. The extent of the opposition which had built up against her was dramatic. Over 120 people were involved, including two of Darnley's knights, and – ominously – Mary's own officers of state. On the 10th, Moray and his associates arrived from England, and entered Holyrood.

Much has rightly been made of the threat to Mary herself, then six months pregnant, and of her very considerable personal courage. As is well known, she very quickly detached Darnley from the conspirators by pointing out, correctly enough, that he was merely a tool who could hope for nothing from them; on the night of the 11th she escaped with him from Holyrood and rode to Bothwell's castle of Dunbar, arriving early the next morning and – at least as legend has it – cooking breakfast for everyone. For once she acted with utter decision and determination. But the real point of the Rizzio murder is not in the savagery and drama of the event, substantial as these were. Rizzio, singled out for opprobrium and violent death, was not an isolated and unique figure. He was the man who suffered for the five years of dangerous political divide which Mary had created, culminating in the disastrous year 1565–6 when she made that divide absolute. It was indeed a physical as well as a political divide; for one might almost say that Patrick lord Ruthven, assiduous attender at the council since December 1563, got his best chance to make his views known to the queen when he broke through the barrier between the public apartments where the council met and the private apartments where the queen spent so much of her time, bursting up that famous stair which separated them at the head of the band who murdered Rizzio on 9 March 1566. The Rizzio murder was not just the immediate comment on a queen's folly in putting too much trust in one foreign servant. It was a general comment on a refusal to consult and communicate with the political nation which had gone beyond the point of toleration. It was also the effective end of any semblance of policy or government by the queen.

The immediate aftermath seemed to favour Mary. She was back in Edinburgh by 18 March. On the 20th, Darnley repudiated his bond of 1 March; he denied all knowledge of the Rizzio conspiracy, and claimed that his only offence was to consent to the return of the exiled Protestant lords without consulting the queen. It was a denial which would be remembered with bitter resentment by those whom he had deserted. Eight days later, showing that she had learned nothing, Mary appointed Rizzio's brother Joseph as her French secretary. In late March and early April, she held a series of council meetings, at which Bothwell, Huntly and Atholl were notable attenders, and at three of which she may herself have been present, to pronounce on the need for justice for the murder of Rizzio, and to fuss about disorder in the realm. But the appearance of control by the queen and her supporters was short-lived. Reality was very different; and those who had regularly attended her council in 1565–6 recognized this. On 15 April they suggested a measure which was certainly designed to ensure Mary's safety, but undoubtedly also reflected their awareness of the need to bring her back into contact with a wider range of her Scottish subjects; it advised that she should stay in Edinburgh castle until after the birth of her baby, but added that if she went elsewhere the council would remain in Edinburgh, but 'some noble men' should always be in the company of the queen. And although the murderers themselves remained unforgiven, she had to restore Moray, Argyll and Glencairn to favour and to political power. All were present at the council meeting of 29 April. From then until the final crisis of her reign in the spring of 1567, it was these men who, in uneasy coalition with Huntly, Atholl and Bothwell, and from September, Maitland of Lethington, were the queen's government.

It was a period when, with one notable exception, nothing happened. Mary's pro-Catholic approach ended. Relations with Elizabeth became more cordial. Darnley continued to drink and make himself a nuisance. But on 19 June came the one great success of Mary's queenship. She gave birth to a son, James. The event was signified by two famous statements. One was Elizabeth's despairing outburst, 'the queen of Scotland is lighter of a bonny son, and I am but barren stock'. The other was Mary's own; showing the baby to Darnley, her hatred burst forth in the bitter comment 'for he is so much your own son, that I fear it will be the worse for him hereafter'. Fortunately for two kingdoms, it was not Darnley's characteristics, nor indeed his mother's, which determined what her son would be.

The next eight months were dominated by the mounting problem of Darnley, from whom by now Mary was entirely estranged. By the autumn of 1566, he appears to have been writing to the pope and the kings of France and Spain, accusing his wife of failing to restore Catholicism to Scotland. That they knew already. But such letters from the 'king' of Scotland were intolerable for the Scottish government. Even more dangerous was his intention to go abroad himself. Thus on 20 November Mary and her principal councillors met at Craigmillar, to discuss ways of getting rid of him. For Mary, the stumbling-block was the fear that divorce or dissolution of the marriage might bastardize her son. Lethington assured her that her honour and conscience would be preserved, and that she would see 'nothing but good and approved by parliament'. It was on this occasion that he provided the well-known thumb-nail sketch of Mary's half-brother, when he said that Moray would 'look through his fingers thereto, and behold our doings, saying nothing to the same'. Mary herself, in deep distress, and recently recovered from the severe illness to which she had succumbed when going on justice-ayre to Jedburgh in October, talked of her wish for death – or retirement to France.

It was later claimed that a murder bond had been drawn up at Craigmillar, a copy of which was given by Bothwell to Mary after the battle of Carberry in June 1567. Moray, later accused of being party to it, naturally denied its existence. There may or may not have been such a bond. But the idea of killing Darnley was in existence, if not in November, certainly by late December. On 17 December, Darnley had committed his final outrage; although present in the castle of Stirling, he refused to attend the baptism of prince James, thus casting doubts on the legitimacy of Mary's son, which she herself had been so careful to assert publicly at the time of his birth. Mary was still creating a certain confusion about her attitude to religion; James was baptized as a Catholic, but already on 3 October she had conceded that all benefices worth less than 300 marks should now go to Protestant ministers, and on 20 December she made an outright gift to the kirk of £10,000 in money and victuals to a considerable value. Where once she had helped the Protestants in the hope of recognition of the English succession, now it looked as though she was helping them in the hope of getting rid of Darnley. Certainly there was no doubt about the significance of what she did on 24 December, when she pardoned Morton and the other murderers of Rizzio, those who had most reason to hate Darnley for his desertion of them after the murder; her intentions, given her own hatred of them, can hardly have been made more clear.

Darnley was then in Glasgow, heartland of Lennox influence. On 20 January, Mary set out to visit him. There, she persuaded him of her change of heart towards him. Undoubtedly there had not been a change of heart; but Darnley was convinced, writing to his father Lennox on 7 February about 'my love the Queen which I assure you hath all this while and yet doth use herself like a natural and loving wife'. During 'all this while', at the end of January, he had therefore agreed to return to Edinburgh with Mary. There he was lodged in the house known as Kirk o'Field. On 9 February, the night before Darnley was to return to Holyrood, Mary changed her mind about spending the night there, and went to attend a court masque, devised by her servant Bastian in celebration of his own marriage that morning. At about 2 a.m. on the 10th, the house was blown up. Darnley escaped into the garden where his body was found; he had been smothered by, it was suspected, the Douglas kinsmen of Morton.

Whoever else was involved, it is significant that no one doubted that the principal conspirator was Bothwell, although the damning evidence – by no means all of it as controversial as the Casket Letters – was only assembled later; and, because of her estrangement from her husband and her visible affection for Bothwell, it was equally assumed that Mary herself had a hand in it. It was a dangerous moment. But it was not the Darnley murder which brought Mary down. The fact was that an embarrassment had been removed, a problem resolved. There is no doubt whatsoever that Mary could have continued her reign, free of the albatross, because that was precisely what people wanted. What she had to do – as Elizabeth and Catherine de Medici, both of whom stood by her in February 1567, begged her to do – was to preserve an appearance of innocence, allow the scandal to burn itself out, enable stability to return. Rulers did recover from great scandals in the sixteenth century; the murder of Amy Robsart, the St Bartholomew's Day massacre, the execution of Mary Queen of Scots herself, were headline news in Europe, and in at least two of these cases, infinitely more dangerous to their perpetrators than the murder of Darnley. The problem, therefore, was not the murder. It was the infinitely unwise behaviour of his widow.

She should have been in the seclusion of strict mourning in Edinburgh. Instead, she attended a wedding on the day after the murder; and she then went off to Seton. She allowed Darnley's father Lennox to accuse Bothwell of the murder, and bring him to trial. It was a total farce; and Mary's refusal to receive Elizabeth's messenger when he arrived at Holyrood with a letter of advice on the morning of the trial only ensured conviction of her guilt. Worst of all was the parliament she held in April. It was well attended; and it certainly offered the chance to re-establish a semblance of normality, had Mary behaved like her ancestor James II in the first parliament held after his sensational murder of the mighty earl of Douglas, when every nerve was stretched to show that business was being done as usual. Instead, what was staged was an extraordinary political event. There were three acts. One proclaimed the benefits of Mary's rule since her return to Scotland, on the grounds that she had not tampered with the state of religion; it annulled all acts contrary to the kirk and at last – after seven years of uncertainty – took the kirk formally under the queen's protection. The second dealt with the law of indemnity. The third thundered against anti-Marian placards and bills, not surprisingly in view of what was then on display in the streets of Edinburgh; it is a measure of the dangerous state to which Mary's actions had brought her that the culprit named in the act was the brother of her own comptroller, William Murray of Tullibardine.

The remaining business of this parliament only made matters worse. It ratified earlier grants, nineteen in all. One theory which has been advanced to explain why Mary was brought down is that she was approaching her twenty-fifth birthday, the age at which she would be expected to issue her act of revocation; those who feared to lose by it therefore struck first. This hardly seems convincing, not only because it suggests a degree of strength and control which Mary certainly did not possess at any time in her reign, but also because of the April parliament. For if Mary did possess such a potential trump card, she promptly threw it away as she issued ratification of grants not only to Bothwell, the principal suspect, but to Morton, whose Douglas kinsmen were the principal suspects of the actual killing, and to Moray and Rothes; and to leave no doubt on the point, even though the queen was said by the parliament of 1564 to have reached her majority when she was twenty-one, the ratifications which involved earldoms were now pronounced to be as authoritative as if she were already twenty-five. It did look suspiciously like the pay-off for the deed. The same point can be made about the final business of parliament, the reduction of forfeitures; of the eleven agreed, nine went to Gordons. It could well be argued that this was a way of buying Gordon acquiescence in the forthcoming divorce between Bothwell and Lady Jean Gordon, Huntly's sister. And that, of course, was the essential prelude to Bothwell's marriage to Mary herself.

This parliament made it quite clear that no member of the political nation had anything to fear from the queen. It also indicated once again how little attempt she herself was making to keep a grip on events; others demanded, she agreed. Parliament was in session from 14 to 19 April. On the 19th or 20th, there appeared one of the most famous examples of the political bond, used during Mary's minority for major political and sometimes ideological reasons, but in the crises of 1566–7 for immediate and even murderous gain. On this occasion, the archbishop of St Andrews, six bishops, eight earls and a number of lords signed the bond known as the 'Ainslie's Tavern bond' accepting Bothwell's innocence of the murder of Darnley, and promising to persuade the queen to humble herself to marry him. One can hardly imagine a more dramatic night in a pub. On 24 April, Bothwell seized the queen, returning from Stirling where she had gone on the 21st to visit her son, and carried her off to Dunbar, where he apparently raped her. What certainly happened was that on 15 May she married him. Bothwell was Protestant. Mary had always insisted on her right to her personal Catholicism, whatever happened to anyone else in Scotland, and had created considerable problems by doing so. The marriage took place by Protestant rites. The end was now very near.

Lady Antonia has written very convincingly of Mary's state at this time, lethargic, bewildered, her political judgement gone. Her description is undoubtedly correct. But apart from particular moments of dramatic activity such as the attack on Huntly in 1562, the Chaseabout Raid and the immediate aftermath of the Rizzio murder, and the brief period of positive royal policy after the Darnley marriage, these are characteristics which had been in evidence throughout her reign, if never before in such extreme form as in the period after the Darnley murder. Lack of direction, lack of clear policy, the destruction of any hope of the political balance which effective rulers maintained, because she relied too much on one man: these had been problems since August 1561. Up until 1565, the man had been her half-brother. In 1565–6 it had been, much more offensively and dangerously, the Catholic foreigner Rizzio. Now, and wholly unacceptably, it was Bothwell, the Protestant earl, but one without real allies, whose political prominence depended, like Rizzio's, wholly on Mary's personal predilection for him. Those who had signed the Ainslie's Tavern bond had done so, almost certainly in desperation, turning to a strong personality who alone had the queen's trust, and probably more than that. The gamble failed.

The last council meetings of Mary's reign, in May and early June 1567, were purely meetings of the small Bothwell faction, presided over by the earl, now elevated to be duke of Orkney. Bothwell himself made one strenuous and final attempt to recreate the political consensus which he himself, with the queen's passive acquiescence, had destroyed. On 22 May, his council drew up a rota of councillors to be permanently resident with the queen; it included men like Morton and Rothes. It had no hope of working. And so the council fell back on the assertion of the blessings of Mary's rule, just as the act concerning religion in the April parliament had done. The second of its ordinances on this theme, on 4 June, went further, reaching a high note of shrill complaint that her subjects did not understand their queen. No doubt they did not. For still she could not be pinned down to a consistent policy; having taken the kirk under her protection in April, in a desperate effort to gain support, she had then promptly proceeded to dispense individual Catholics from it, while herself departing from her faith to marry as a Protestant. Her political judgement, always suspect for precisely this kind of action, was now indeed entirely in abeyance. Rulers who have to explain, defend themselves, protest that their actions are not understood, have reached a nadir. Mary Stewart had done so.

On 1 May, the Ainslie's Tavern bond had been answered by one made by Argyll and three other earls, including Morton, unlikely signatory of the bond for the Bothwell marriage, and Atholl, formerly strong supporter of Mary; it also included her comptroller, Murray of Tullibardine. It was made for the purpose of freeing the queen from captivity by Bothwell – and for maintaining her son. It was followed up by a second, undated, but made after the Bothwell marriage and designed to ensure that James Balfour of Pittendreich, advanced by Mary in 1565–6, and now holding the key position of keeper of Edinburgh castle, would support Bothwell's opponents, as indeed he did. Then on 6 June 'we of the nobility and council' issued a proclamation announcing their intention to resolve the troubles which beset the realm by rescuing the queen from captivity and punishing Darnley's murderers. This group, known as the confederate lords, contained twelve earls and fourteen lords. It was a very powerful party.

Rescuing the queen meant using force. And so on 15 June, two armies, Mary's and the confederate lords', faced one another at Carberry. Among the confederate lords were Mary's officers of state. Absent from the queen's army were men like Huntly and Erroll; like their ancestors when the crisis of James III's reign came at the battle of Sauchieburn in 1488, they would not fight against their sovereign, but would not at that moment support her. There was no battle. Mary's forces gradually deserted. Bothwell agreed to accept a safe-conduct and depart, in return for the lords' promise to treat the queen with honour. They brought her back to Edinburgh, through streets lined with people hurling abuse at her. From there, she was immediately taken to the island castle of Lochleven where, at some date in mid-July, she miscarried of twins. In grievous personal distress and illness, she was forced to abdicate on 24 July in a scene when she was treated with considerable brutality by one of Rizzio's murderers, lord Lindsay. Whatever her failures which had brought her to this point, her state in the summer of 1567 is intolerable to contemplate. Even so, those who knew her managed to do so with tolerable equanimity; in different, and admittedly less heart-rending ways, they too felt driven beyond endurance.

Meanwhile, there were more pressing problems. Mary herself was not an immediate threat, ill as she was, and – as they thought – securely imprisoned. Since 21 June, a government of sorts had been kept going by the anti-Marian faction constituting itself as the council. The abdication – or, as it was called, voluntary demission of sovereignty by Mary made in favour of her son and naming Moray as regent – improved matters, as did the coronation itself, and Moray's formal acceptance of the regency on 22 August; everything began to look rather more legal. The new government was also amazingly lucky in the reaction of foreign powers. Unwittingly, the confederate lords had chosen their moment well. The summer of 1567 saw the outbreak of the second war of religion in France. Spain was fully occupied in its attempt to control the revolt which had broken out in the Netherlands in the previous year; this was exactly the period of Alva's great march north from Italy to subdue the rebels. In any case, it is unlikely that either the French or the Spanish would have dissented from Pius V's view of Mary, expressed in his public repudiation of her in July.

There remained England. Throckmorton was rushed north to Scotland in mid-July. He was not allowed to see Mary, and he failed, from a distance, to persuade her to retrieve her position by divorcing Bothwell. But the presence of an English diplomat undoubtedly helped the ruling clique; for he found such widespread hostility to Mary, including among the 'people' – and particularly among the women, who were, he said, 'most furious and impudent against the queen' – that it was all too obvious to him that there was no hope of restoring her. Indeed, he believed that only his pleas on her behalf saved her life. Elizabeth, therefore, accepted the inevitable, that the rebels had won, and although she refused to recognize them as a legitimate government, neither did she do anything further for Mary. Instead, she revived memories of Mary's minority, as she dangled the idea that the young king should be brought up in England by his grandmother, the countess of Lennox – the woman she had sent to the Tower in 1565, in an excess of rage over the Darnley marriage. The French had the same notion, and suggested taking him over themselves.

Neither prospect appealed to the Scots; this time, their young ruler remained at home, to be given a brilliant and brutal education by George Buchanan.

Nevertheless, the appearance of normality and the lack of challenge from abroad by no means resolved the problems for Moray and his associates. The major part of the political nation had seemed to be ranged against Mary in June 1567. Actually, it had been ranged against Mary so long as she was dependent on Bothwell. And not all the confederate lords at Carberry shared the same determination thereafter that she should be deposed. There were two reasons why some men had doubts. The first was ideological. The attempt to control the actions of a wayward sovereign was one thing. Deposing her was quite another, and infinitely more unpalatable, for this was even more of an outrage to political *mores* than Mary's own actions in the winter of 1565–6, when she had relied so heavily on Rizzio. The Protestant lords had stopped short of doing so in 1559, and even though one of the considerations then weighing with them no longer applied, because Mary now had a child of her body to continue the Stewart line, nevertheless – as Moray had found to his cost in 1565 – rulers in Scotland had to drive men to extremes of provocation before they were faced with opposition sufficiently determined to bring them down. The two previous Stewarts who had done so, James I and James III, had been exceedingly aggressive rulers. Mary herself was quite the reverse. If, therefore, she could be persuaded to rid herself of Bothwell, then it could be argued that there was no obvious reason not to restore a monarch who was undoubtedly unsatisfactory but not, in her own right, threatening; this solution was distinctly preferable to one which involved an attack on the prestige and authority of the crown itself.

The second reason for hesitation was more self-interested, though linked to the first. Without Bothwell, she might once again be as malleable as she had been in the eleven months after the Rizzio murder and, even more to the point, she would be available for marriage; that certainly suggests why the Hamiltons, whose brief adherence to the confederate lords – on condition that they, not the Lennox Stewarts, were acknowledged as heirs presumptive – had looked unbelievable even while it was happening, changed sides. Both considerations help to explain a much more surprising defection, that of Moray's hitherto consistently loyal ally, Argyll. Even men like Lethington and William Kirkcaldy of Grange, who did remain with the confederate lords, were clearly deeply worried; hence Kirkcaldy set off to pursue Bothwell up to Shetland, in the hope that the political situation would immediately become more flexible if he could be brought under constraint. Such doubts and considerations were to keep the political situation in Scotland unstable until 1573. Meanwhile, it was all too clear how quickly the political barometer had changed, at least as far as the greatest nobles were concerned, even between 15 June and 29 July 1567. Twelve earls had signed the order for Mary's imprisonment in Lochleven. Five attended the coronation of James VI. The only comfort for the hard-line opposition to Mary was that one of the earls was her former adherent, the Catholic Atholl; and there was much less defection from the confederate lords to Mary among the lesser lords and greater lairds, and – significantly – from her former officers of state.

A combination of Moray's assumption of the regency, Bothwell's escape to Norway, and the lack of coherent opposition to the new regime, ensured that doubts were not at this stage translated into positive action. In September, Argyll came back into line, and Huntly came over to Moray; and gradually, during the last months of 1567, Moray's regime was increasingly widely accepted. But the wide-spread unease of the summer left two legacies. One was Moray's strenuous and highly intelligent use of his authority. In November, he made a punitive raid on the borders, which had the double advantage of demonstrating his determination to maintain order and strong rule at home, and attracting a grudging recognition from Elizabeth; for the borders were an Anglo-Scottish problem. The other was the effort to switch the burden of guilt for the Darnley murder away from Bothwell and on to Mary herself; the danger that her absence was literally making men's hearts grow fonder was to be counteracted by a reminder that as queen she was wholly unacceptable.

From June 1567, the confederate lords had done what Elizabeth and Catherine de Medici had begged Mary to do in February: they followed up their promise in their proclamation of 6 June to punish Darnley's murderers. As they themselves included Darnley's murderers, what they were demonstrating was their skill in using the political lie, which would be believed because believing it meant the hope of returning to normality; it was because Mary had never learned that political lesson that she had totally lost political initiative. It is a considerable irony that had Mary taken the advice given to her, the resolution of what everyone agreed before February 1567 to be a massive problem – the existence of Darnley – would have been quickly followed up by exemplary trials, and that would have been the end of the affair. Instead, Mary allowed a temporary embarrassment to become an intolerable reproach. Because the queen married Darnley's supposed murderer, Darnley himself came to be seen as an innocent victim rather than the threat to the crown that he actually was. The result was that the murder became a *cause célèbre*, and the pursuit of his murderers a major political necessity; indeed, so far did the queen's actions after the murder distort reality that Darnley's ghost walked the world of Scottish politics as late as 1581, when the earl of Morton was executed ostensibly on the grounds of his involvement in the murder.

The effective response to the political necessity was not of course the justice that is blind and impartial. But the 'justice' used to resolve a political crisis is not normally blind, in any century; the Scots' actions in 1567 were no unique outrage. Bothwell himself, the man whose trial and conviction would alone have done so much to calm the feelings which were running so high in the summer of 1567, was never caught by the Scots. His fate was different, and much more horrible; in Norway, he fell foul of the kinsmen of a former mistress, was imprisoned by Frederick, king of Denmark and Norway, and died in 1578 in the fortress of Dragsholm, chained to a pillar and quite mad. But his adherents were rounded up. They included William Powrie who had brought the gunpowder to Kirk o'Field, and, in 1568, Bothwell's page and a key witness, 'French Paris'. Their evidence not only confirmed what everyone believed anyway, but provides sufficient detail to suggest that later attempts to shroud the events of 9–10 February 1567 in mystery are distinctly misplaced. The only possible mystery, for those who insist on looking for it, is the queen's part in it all. In June 1567, the confederate lords presumably knew the answer already. But on the 20th, they picked up a real prize, something which could be used to convince others; Bothwell's tailor George Dalgleish, who had helped his master change out of his court dress into clothes more suitable for murder on 9 February, was captured. He handed over a silver casket, produced from under his bed, which contained letters to Bothwell apparently from Mary.

Interestingly, no attempt was made at this stage to use them against the queen; the confederate lords were doing an effective enough job already in bringing her reign to an end, and clearly had no desire to trumpet to the world the shattering personal scandal which publication of such letters from their ex-monarch would create. By December, however, there was more need to remind at least those in Scotland of the involvement with Bothwell which had made her rule finally impossible. So, on 4 December, the council referred to 'privy letters written and subscribed with her own hand and sent to James earl of Bothwell, chief executioner of the horrible murder'. They were still being very guarded; but for the first time, they openly hinted at Mary's direct part in the murder, and let it be known that there was evidence for it. It was an action clearly taken to sway the minds of any waverers among the seventy-three people who came to parliament on 19–20 December, to re-enact the acts of the Reformation parliament of 1560, restate the Confession of Faith, and formally pronounce the legality of Mary's abdication and Moray's regency. In addition – carefully reiterating the existence of the 'privy letters' – they justified the detention of the late queen. They even repeated the act of 1564 which had declared the queen to have reached her age of majority, because a negligent printer had botched its original publication; there was to be no doubt that it was a queen of full age who had abdicated.

None of this removed the unease shared by Protestants and Catholics alike about the fact that a reigning monarch had been deposed. It did, however, finally cover the constitutional nakedness of the new regime, and it did remind the Protestants that their position, never wholly certain under Mary, was now secure. Even so, two Protestant earls, Huntly and Argyll, along with the archbishop of St Andrews, two other bishops and five lords, demonstrated their continuing, if impotent, dislike of what had happened when, on 25 December, they made a bond to free the queen – while ensuring the safety of the 'prince'. It was an empty gesture. Moray was fully in control, and the early part of 1568 was an infinitely less disturbed period than the whole of 1567. Then, on 3 May, came the stunning news that Mary had escaped from Lochleven. Since the previous July, she had recovered her health. The pathetic invalid of the summer of 1567 was once again the woman of great personal charm; and that had been used to considerable effect on certain members of the Douglas family at Lochleven, supposedly reliable, but actually highly susceptible. The escape was engineered by George Douglas, brother of the laird of Lochleven, who undoubtedly hoped to marry her, and 'the little Douglas', Willy, an orphaned kinsman, whose devotion to her was such that he was to remain in her service until her death. On 2 May, disguised in the clothes of an ordinary country-woman, she walked out of the castle and was taken across to the mainland, where she was met by one of the men closest to her during her reign, lord Seton. She spent her first night of freedom at his castle of Niddry; and from there she went west, to Hamilton.

The extent to which men rallied to her, once she was at liberty, does not entitle us to assume that they regarded her as a successful ruler. It is simply a powerful comment on Scottish attitudes to the authority of the crown. At Hamilton, on 8 May, a bond was made praising God for setting her at liberty, and promising mutual support in restoring her to her throne. It was signed by nine bishops, nine earls, twelve abbots and commendators (secular holders of monastic property) and ninety lords and lairds. It included men who had opposed her to the point of rebellion during her personal rule, notably Argyll and Rothes; rebellion against a queen who had never commanded respect and then abused her position as Mary did in 1565, was possible, even justified, but deposition was not.

Not everyone, of course, agreed with this. There survives an opposition bond, made on the same day in Edinburgh. It is a very much smaller affair, but still a very revealing one. It involved Kirkcaldy of Grange, for all his earlier agonies about what the confederate lords had done, and, on behalf of the burgh, Mary's Catholic provost, Simon Preston of Craigmillar; for these men, who bound themselves to defend the king and the regent, practical considerations about Mary as a ruler took precedence over political and even religious ideology. Even Preston, so loyal to her throughout the Rizzio crisis, had now had enough.

With the backing she had, however, and with men pouring in to join her army, she should certainly have won. Had success followed from the ideological commitment to the monarchy shown by those who supported her, there would presumably have been a return to the position of 1561–5 – worried Protestants, dissatisfied Catholics, and a lack of direction from the throne – until there was another crisis, or until she died. She did not win. Moray was then in Glasgow. The queen made the fatal mistake of passing too close to the town when moving her forces from Hamilton to Dumbarton, the castle held by her adherent lord Fleming who, like Seton, was one of her old household friends. Moray, who had repulsed her attempts to negotiate, brought his rather smaller army out to meet her on 13 May, and won a resounding victory at Langside, largely because of the superior generalship of Kirkcaldy of Grange, but also because at this critical moment Argyll's determination failed him; he who commanded the main body of Mary's army did not fight. He had not wholeheartedly supported Moray after Mary's downfall in 1567; he had found it more acceptable in principle to maintain loyalty to the queen rather than to the regent. But when the choice became stark, it seems that doubts about Mary became too insistent to be ignored.

Mary panicked completely. She fled south, reaching Dundrennan abbey in Galloway, a mile from the Solway Firth, on 15 May. None of those with her could deflect her, hard though they tried.

On the 16th, she crossed the Solway in a small, inshore fishing boat, and arrived in England. Her comeback had lasted for exactly two weeks. She was later to agree with those who had tried to insist that her best chance lay in remaining in Scotland; and the point has been rightly emphasized by later historians, for her departure left her supporters leaderless. Her decision to make for England rather than France has also been questioned. But this is to put too much weight on the idea that because she had been brought up in France, France would always stand her friend. That had manifestly not been the case during her personal rule; and she herself knew very well that she was no favourite of Catherine de Medici. She did not actually know what Elizabeth's attitude would be, but for eight years she had indulged the romantic notion that, if the two queens met, there would be firm personal friendship between them, and that, along with the fact that England was the kingdom which to her had long represented her future, seems to have determined her decision now. Even so, it is possible that she had a last moment of doubt, and tried to persuade the captain of the boat on which she had embarked – a vessel wholly unsuitable for a long sea voyage – to take her to France. Whether that is true or not, the undoubted fact is that her political judgement had once again completely failed her.

She does not appear to have had any awareness of the enormity of the problem which her arrival in England would create. One reason why Mary as a political figure was never successful was that personal and political considerations were always too much inter-twined in her mind. Moray's seizure of her jewels in the summer of 1567, for example, was a grievance which rankled with her to the end of her life; she seemed to regard their loss as seriously as the loss of her kingdom. Now, when she reached England, and a horrified Cumberland gentry had to house her and await their queen's pleasure, she showed more annoyance at Elizabeth's undoubtedly stingy gift of a few old dresses than awareness of her desperate political predicament. Apparently she simply assumed that Elizabeth would restore her to her throne. But no one else, in Scotland and in England, was in any doubt about the political predicament into which her flight had plunged them.

Elizabeth's own position was certainly intolerable. The fully developed ideological battle between the extreme Calvinist resistance theorists and the exponents of divine right monarchy did not begin until after the massacre of St Bartholomew's Day in 1572, when Huguenot writers such as François Hotman and Philippe du Plessis-Mornay, backed up by Théodore Beza and George Buchanan, argued for a sophisticated form of contractual kingship in which the king could be constrained – or removed – by his leading subjects, lesser magistrates or nobles, and were answered by a host of theorists, beginning with Jean Bodin and including a king, James VI, who produced a full-blown justification of kingship by divine right. But Calvinist resistance theory had already had its first airing, in the 1550s, when the Protestant Marian exiles – including John Knox – had asserted it in a cruder, less controlled and therefore more dangerous form. There was no doubt where Elizabeth's ideological sympathies lay. Yet on four occasions in her reign, she was faced with the massive problem of reconciling that ideology with practical politics. Three involved Mary Queen of Scots, the fourth being her reluctant aid to the rebels of the Netherlands against Philip II in the mid-1580s. The first Marian problem had happened in 1560, when Cecil had pushed his worried and unwilling monarch into aiding the Scottish Protestants, technically rebels against their divinely ordained queen. Now, that queen had turned up in England, to seek aid from her sister monarch. It was the beginning of a major political headache, even a nightmare, which would end only with the execution of Mary in 1587.

In 1568, Elizabeth was caught between Moray, whom she obviously much preferred as the person controlling events in Scotland, and Mary, who could appeal to her most basic instinct, the sanctity of legitimate authority – an instinct perhaps all the stronger in her because of doubts about the legitimacy of her own authority which Catholics, who had never accepted the validity of her father's marriage to her mother, were all too happy to voice. Her initial attempt to find a way out of the *impasse* was to hold what was called a conference, but has not unfairly been described as the first trial of Mary Queen of Scots. It met at York in October 1568, and was then continued at Westminster between November and January 1569. At Elizabeth's insistence, the matter to be discussed was whether Mary was innocent or guilty of the murder of Darnley; for that alone provided straightforward grounds for deciding whether she should be restored to her throne or not. Moray was there in person. Darnley's father, Lennox, was refused leave by Elizabeth to appear. Mary also, to her understandable fury, was not present. She was represented by commissioners, principally lord Herries and John Leslie, now bishop of Ross; both were genuine defenders of her cause, but both had doubts about her innocence of murder. Since in February 1567 her guilt alone would certainly not have lost her the throne, this is a measure of how far the real reasons for Mary's failure and downfall had been conveniently hidden behind the chance that her mistakes had given first her Scottish opponents, and now the English queen, to make the murder of Darnley, which might have been politically acceptable, into a moral outrage.

It is not surprising that in 1567–9 this is what they did. Branding Mary as an adulteress and murderess shifted the debate about her rule away from a very real problem: that deposition on the grounds of her political and religious failures might be entirely justified in practice, but it left unresolved the murky ideological question of whether any actions could be justified in theory when taken against legitimate authority. The Scots themselves were clearly in some perplexity about this; they were unhappy about acknowledging to the world that their queen was a personal scandal. But Elizabeth was in no doubt. She would not allow the case to turn on the justification of rebellion. The 'rebels', Moray and his supporters, could only accept her position. The real sufferers were those who had remained loyal to Mary despite all her mistakes, while deeply suspicious of her involvement in the plot to dispose of Darnley, for they now found themselves in the awkward position of having to defend her on the wrong grounds, and to make what they could of a very dubious case. What is unfortunate is that so much writing about her since has mistaken the necessary political manoeuvring of this period for the real issue, and has assumed that the Darnley murder actually did matter more than the long run of evasions and misjudgements which had characterized her rule, and which merely reached a climax in 1567.

In 1567, those who knew of the existence of the famous casket and whatever it contained had been remarkably reluctant to do more than hint at it. Even now, Moray showed the same reluctance. But he had to make his case to Elizabeth; and under English pressure, he revealed the Casket Letters, unofficially in October and then officially in December, by which time he had already openly accused Mary of murder. Armed with this evidence, Elizabeth made her remarkable decision in January 1569, which was in fact no decision at all except to maintain the status quo. The letters had persuaded her of Moray's honour. But she chose to ignore the logical consequence of this, that Mary was therefore guilty, and instead declared that there was no reason to doubt her honour either. The upshot was that Moray went back to Scotland, with £5,000 from the English queen. Mary remained in England. In the short term, it was a decision which was legally ludicrous but politically very sensible. Elizabeth had given a display of helpfulness to the Scots. She had avoided any risk of offending the Catholic powers by refusing to condemn Mary. She had also averted the Anglo-Scottish war which would have undoubtedly resulted from any attempt on her part to restore Mary. And she had ensured an amenable government in Scotland. In the long term, however, she had created for herself a problem which was not to be resolved for eighteen years.

The Casket Letters themselves were exceedingly useful to the English government in 1568–9. They have also provided a wonderful subject for historical detectives since the eighteenth century. What the English saw in 1568, when Moray revealed the contents of the casket (which may or may not be the one now in the possession of the duke of Hamilton at Lennoxlove – and is in any event now empty) were eight letters from Mary to Bothwell, a long sonnet expressing her emotions, and two marriage contracts between her and Bothwell. Their authenticity cannot be judged from the originals, for these disappeared in 1584 and have never been seen since. What the intrepid sleuths have had to work from is a series of copies and translations, from Scots to French and from French to Scots, and all existing in English copies. The debate will of course go on; no individual contribution will ever end it. Only three things will be said here. First, if we look at them without an urgent sense of the need to prove Mary innocent or guilty, and simply observe what is known about the contents of the casket, from their discovery on 20 June 1567 to their disappearance in 1584, one fact stands out with remarkable clarity. The Scots were exceedingly reluctant to make them public. They had not used them when they were first discovered, referred to them only generally when, in December 1567, they would have been of obvious political value, and produced them in 1568 because Moray was left with little choice. Their subsequent disappearance is certainly connected with Mary's son James; having been in the possession of the earl of Morton, they came, after his death, into the hands of the earl of Gowrie, forfeited and executed in 1584, and so to the crown.

Scottish reluctance, from June 1567 to October 1568, does not suggest a rush to forge damning evidence. James VI's ability to 'lose' them implies his own belief in their authenticity; for they disappeared just at the time when Elizabeth was desperate to get her hands on them, precisely because this was exactly the period when first the English parliament of 1584 and then the Babington plotters of 1586 were forcing her towards acceptance of the hideous proposition that Mary must die, and she therefore needed every possible justification she could find. Elizabeth already had the copies. There was no reason for her to press for the originals, nor for James to deny them to her, unless both were aware that they had something more to offer.

For his part, James had every reason to trumpet them to the world as forgeries, if this was what a sight of them suggested, for to do so would have enabled him to protect his mother's reputation, without threatening his own hold on the Scottish throne. It was in 1584, the very year of their disappearance, that the king was showing his determination to restore the prestige of Scottish kingship; for parliament passed an act against calumnies which traduced the king and his estate, to the 'dishonour, hurt or prejudice of his highness, his parents and progenitors', and specifically censored two of the works of George Buchanan. The offensive political theory, *De Iure Regni apud Scotos*, which justified the deposition of James's mother, and the *History*, which included an account of her misdeeds, were no longer to be available to the king's loyal subjects. Nothing, therefore, would have suited James better at this point than a public demonstration that the damning letters were forgeries – if only they had been. What it all amounts to is this. Outright forgery of the originals – as opposed to the odd interpolation in the copies – can only have been done by the Scots; and to suggest that her Scottish enemies forged something that they were then very unwilling to use, and managed in the process to fool Mary's own son and cousin, both of whom knew her handwriting, into believing that they were undoubtedly genuine, simply does not make sense.

Second, if they were forgeries, where did the forgers get their ideas from? The woman portrayed in the letters and the sonnet is a woman utterly dominated by a man, one who would renounce everything for him, who masochistically dwells on her sacrifice – 'my peace, my subjects, my subjected soul' – and on the fact that he had raped her before she first loved him: the archetype, in other words, of the woman who adores the man who tramples on her. In the twentieth century this is not an unfamiliar concept; Barbara Cartland and a host of lesser lights have made their reputation from it. And because it is now so familiar, not enough emphasis has been given to the fact that it was *not* a common theme in the sixteenth century, and that if Mary's opponents were setting out to fabricate evidence against her which they wanted to appear convincing, it is curious that they should think up this kind of image, rather than, for example, that of the sort of malevolent schemer typified by Catherine de Medici in Protestant tradition.

In a bibliographical study of women in medieval and early modern western literature, *The Crooked Rib*, it has been shown that there were two images of woman, one deriving from the Virgin, the meek and good, and certainly not responsive to rape, the other from Eve, the taunter, the instrument of man's destruction, and thus scarcely a candidate for rape. Sixteenth-century Europe had no cultural tradition of love awakened in the woman taken by force. One only has to think of that familiar theme in Renaissance painting, the rape of Lucretia – who killed herself because of it. There is therefore an absence of any tradition, cultural or propagandist, on which the supposed forgers of the Casket Letters could draw. There is, however, an account by Kirkcaldy of Grange of a saying by Mary herself which does chime with the contents of the letters; she had announced, he said, that she would follow Bothwell to the end of the world in her petticoat. It is on the whole easier to believe that the same mind wrote such letters and said such a thing than that her enemies carefully constructed and foisted on to Mary the sort of besotted and irresponsible devotion for which their culture offered no model. Moreover, if the letters were forged, then the forger not only displayed a level of originality which amounts almost to genius, but also an infinite but quite superfluous capacity for taking pains: eight letters, including one which contains a vast (and if forged, quite unnecessary) amount of detail, a sonnet and two marriage contracts, where any of these (or at least two of the first and one of the last) would do.

A final point is this. If the letters were genuine, Mary clearly conspired to murder Darnley. If they were not, there still remain good grounds for suspecting her involvement. Either way, the purpose they served at the time was political. The continuing debate, for all its fascination, serves none.

Elizabeth's decision, and Moray's return to Scotland, left Mary in what seemed a hopeless position. On 4 January 1569, before the result of the conference was known, the burgh of Aberdeen made a bond to Huntly as the queen's lieutenant in the north, asserting their loyalty to her and promising to support Huntly in resisting those who opposed her; and in the same month Huntly wrote to Mary herself, a letter which was intended to be encouraging but ended on the depressing note that he had been able to do nothing recently because 'the weather has been so evil here these twenty days that it was not possible for one to travel'. But it was not the weather which destroyed Mary's chances. Moray was now too firmly in control. In April, Châtelherault's refusal to acknowledge

James VI landed him in prison; and during the spring, Huntly, Crawford, Cassillis and several Marian lords and lairds found it prudent to make a quite different bond, promising to serve the regent and accept the king's authority, and annulling any previous bonds made to any other authority. Thus Moray was able to resist Elizabeth's sudden attempt, sprung on him in May, to end the stalemate and get Mary back to Scotland, restored to her throne although with the Protestant religion guaranteed. Mary herself backed this up, promising to abide by the guarantees – she was, indeed, at this time going through what Gordon Donaldson has called 'a kind of Anglican phase' in response to Elizabeth's insistence on linking this to her possible restoration – and announcing her desire for a divorce from Bothwell. The proposals were put to a convention at Perth at the end of July. They were overwhelmingly rejected, by forty votes to nine; even though the nine included Huntly and Lethington, the result was a clear demonstration of the weakness of the Marian party and the strength of Moray. Elizabeth was left with Mary on her hands; Moray remained in power.

And then in January 1570 the situation once again changed dramatically. On the 23rd, Moray was assassinated at Linlithgow by James Hamilton of Bothwellhaugh, with the foreknowledge of John Hamilton, archbishop of St Andrews. Mary was delighted, and rewarded the murderer with a pension. Moray was a true Stewart: tough, able, masterful, self-interested. To these formidable and familiar qualities was added the ideological commitment to a new faith which transformed the perceptions of many great sixteenth-century aristocrats; Moray himself was described with some awe by Throckmorton in 1567 as one who 'seeks to imitate rather some who have led the people of Israel than any captains of the age'. Like others among history's royal bastards, he could have been pardoned for cursing the perverse fate that had made his sister a queen and himself merely a leading noble. Yet it must be said that there is no evidence that he aspired to the crown, though Englishmen, with their own dynastic tangles, thought he might. And there is no evidence either that hidden personal ambition rather than professed

Protestant convictions inspired his behaviour between 1558 and his death. He had been Mary's effective servant so long as the Protestant cause prevailed, and her enemy only when hints of a change of policy were accompanied by ever clearer evidence of the incompetence which in the end he was to denounce to her face.

Mary's reaction to his murder may be understandable, but it is not edifying. Nor was it the general reaction, in Scotland and elsewhere. Elizabeth regarded his death as a disaster for her; she had, she said, 'lost the best and most useful friend she had in all the world'. She had not always treated him so; his rejection of her plans to restore Mary had made her as furious in the summer of 1569 as she was grief-stricken now. But in the intervening period the Rising of the Northern – Catholic – Earls in England and Mary's involvement in this had clarified her mind. She would not press for Mary's restoration. It was the Moray government in Scotland which she had wanted to sustain.

Moray's death was followed by a civil war, as Mary's adherents – now with the addition of Lethington and Kirkcaldy of Grange – once again renewed their efforts on her behalf. But in the renewed conflict between the king's party and the queen's, it was the former who had Elizabeth's support. In the spring, she sent English troops to southern Scotland; and it was her intervention which ended six months of political vacuum in Scotland, when she insisted that Lennox become regent in July 1570. Lennox himself was killed in September 1571, and succeeded by the somewhat ineffectual earl of Mar. But by then the king's party was proving the stronger. In April they had taken Dumbarton castle, a serious blow for the Marians for its position in the south-west made it a possible point of entry for the French; and there they captured and hanged the ablest of the Hamiltons, the archbishop of St Andrews. Of the rival parliaments held in May and June, it was the king's which was better attended. The war was to grind on until 1573, but there was increasingly little doubt about who was going to win it.

The final, formal capitulation of Argyll, Cassillis and others was made to regent Mar and the earl of Morton in their bond of

12 August 1572. The last Marian stronghold, Edinburgh castle, held by Kirkcaldy and Lethington, was eventually taken, with English help, in May 1573; it was on this occasion that Elizabeth decided to cut costs by sending her soldiers on the dangerous business of crawling round the foot of the castle rock picking up cannonballs for re-use. When the castle fell, Kirkcaldy was hanged. Lethington died, possibly by his own hand. The Marian party no longer existed. Throughout the 1570s, Scotland was ruled by Morton, who had succeeded Mar as regent in October 1572. Exceedingly tough, highly favourable to and favoured by Elizabeth, he imposed the order and stability which Moray was only beginning to achieve at his death. For the Scots, Mary was a thing of the past. Whatever the Catholics thought of the matter, the Scots were to be a Protestant people with a Protestant king, and the curtain had been finally rung down on the drama starring their former queen. Even the reintroduction of the Darnley murder as a means of getting rid of Morton in 1581 was in no sense a revival of the personal and political passions of the late 1560s; it was an immediate political device, used once the regency was at an end by a powerful clique for whom Morton's actions as regent had been intolerably harsh, and all too effective.

But Mary was not a thing of the past in England; she was a very present menace. 'The poor fool', said Charles IX of her in 1572, 'will never cease [from plotting] until she lose her head. In faith they will put her to death. I see it is her own fault and folly.' It was one of this king's few wise remarks, although it was to be another fifteen years before Elizabeth was persuaded to let what he foresaw happen. From Mary's point of view, however, Elizabeth's refusal either to release or restore her gave her every reason to do what she could on her own behalf; and if that meant killing the queen on whom she had imposed herself, and replacing her on her throne, that too was justifiable. She had always wanted to be queen of England. In Scotland, she had ignored her obligations as a Catholic ruler for the sake of the English crown. But once she was in England, different considerations came into play. What she could not get by agreement and by living with heresy in Scotland, she could now get by force as the champion of orthodoxy in England. It was an altogether characteristic combination of heedless ambition and hopeless political judgement.

Elizabeth was in a much more invidious position. She owed her throne to dubious and inconsistent manoeuvres with the rules of succession – manoeuvres which had successively bastardized, and then legitimized, her sister and herself. As a Tudor and as the granddaughter of Henry VII, she was all too well aware of the problems that the English had created for themselves by successive depositions since 1399, and of the abstruse and barely plausible reasoning used to justify them. Her understandable, if not entirely logical reaction was to abhor all tampering with legitimately constituted monarchy, a feeling held all the more strongly because she knew better and better, as the sixteenth-century catalogue of European rebellions lengthened, that there were powerful views to the contrary. Her attitude to Mary can be criticized as vacillating and half-hearted; these were certainly criticisms levelled at her policies in other fields throughout her reign. Yet her agony commands respect as well as sympathy. Mary's can arouse only sympathy – if that.

The story of the nineteen years of Mary's captivity in England is on the one hand familiar, and on the other undergoing further much-needed research. But it belongs to Mary's biography and to English history, not to a study of Mary as queen of Scots. Queen of Scots she had ceased to be. All the wild plotting, by her and on her behalf, was aimed at the throne of England, and will thus be treated only very briefly here. In 1568, within the first few months of her stay in England, as has recently been shown by Mr Mitchell Leimon, Sir Francis Walsingham, then a private citizen, was sufficiently alarmed by her to intercept her correspondence and transmit information about her to Cecil. He was right to be concerned. She made her intentions perfectly clear from the moment of the break-up of the York-Westminster conference. The final stages of the conference were accompanied by a minor outbreak of hostilities between Spain and England. Mary instantly assumed an Anglo-Spanish war, in which English Catholics would fight, with Spain, to put her on the English throne. In January 1569, the queen who had not restored Catholicism to Scotland was therefore announcing to the Spanish ambassador that 'if his master will help me, I shall be queen of England in three months, and mass shall be said all over the country'. There was no war. Indeed, her very existence would always give Philip II pause, because he could never be certain that, if she did become queen of England even with his help, she would not then create an Anglo-French alliance. But Elizabeth could not be sure that Philip would continue to stay his hand for this reason. What she was in no doubt about was that in the autumn of 1569, and again in 1571, Mary was heavily involved in two very major plots against her, the Rising of the Northern Earls, and the Ridolfi Plot.

Both depended on the marriage of Mary to Thomas Howard, duke of Norfolk, not himself a Catholic, but a man perfectly willing to head a Catholic rising in order to ensure at least Mary's right of succession to Elizabeth, and indeed to remove Elizabeth to the immediate benefit of Mary and himself. The idea of Mary's marriage to Norfolk had first been raised during the York-Westminster conference; at that point, Moray had seen some advantage in having Mary married – and remaining – in England. But nothing had come of these initial discussions; and the secret that both Mary and Norfolk intended to go ahead with the marriage, which Norfolk had absolutely denied to the English queen, was kept from Elizabeth until the autumn, when she discovered it just as she was faced with a major Catholic revolt in the north, led by the earls of Northumberland and Westmoreland, and designed, it seems, to create a Catholic England which would therefore not be under threat from the Catholic powers of France and Spain. It was put down, savagely, by the government, with some help from Moray who apprehended Northumberland when he fled to Scotland, and handed him back to the English. But Elizabeth could not bring herself to execute Norfolk. She left him alive, to be the major figure in the Ridolfi Plot.

The rising of 1569 had involved discussions with the Spanish ambassador. The Ridolfi Plot was an even more serious affair.

Ridolfi himself was a Florentine banker resident in London – one of an ancient line, regularly bankrupted by their improvident English hosts. He was also a papal agent. In 1570, Pius V made the grievous error of excommunicating Elizabeth, to the considerable annoyance of France and Spain; they saw clearly enough that it was a pointless and provocative gesture. But Ridolfi thought otherwise, and so, of course, did Mary; the pope had now provided them with complete justification for their actions. What Ridolfi wanted was a Spanish force, led by Alva, to land in England, whereupon Norfolk would raise the English Catholics in support; it was an idea dreamed up during his deliberations with the Spanish ambassador in England and with John Leslie, bishop of Ross. In March 1571, he set out to persuade Philip II, Pius V and Alva to agree with it. The pope was enthusiastic. Alva told Philip that he was prepared to countenance the plot, but only if the English rebels could hold the field for forty days; then Spain might join in. In the event, nothing happened; Cecil, now lord Burghley, got his hands on Ridolfi's messenger, an agent of the bishop of Ross, and the existence of the plot was discovered.

Three people suffered direct consequences, though in very differing degrees. The Spanish ambassador, the pompous and stupid de Spes, was flung out of England. There remained Mary and Norfolk. In 1571, parliament had already shown their hostility to Mary. In 1572, they howled for her blood, and Norfolk's. Elizabeth finally agreed, in the second case; Norfolk was executed on 2 June 1572. She refused the first. Both Lords and Commons had wanted a bill attainting Mary of treason; they toned this down – if such a phrase can be used – in favour of one which they thought might be more acceptable to Elizabeth, denying Mary any claim to the English throne, and making her responsible for any future plotting on her behalf. That too Elizabeth rejected. Yet she had already made it clear that her efforts to maintain Mary's dignity and honour were over. In 1568 the Scots had broken with a tradition which differed fundamentally from that of the English. When kings were deposed in Scotland, there was no effort to produce constitutional justification for it, such as was done in the cases of Edward II and Richard II. They were forced to do so, however, when Mary was deposed, because they had to justify their action to Elizabeth. They used George Buchanan, who anticipated the Huguenot propaganda of the 1570s when he asserted the idea of an ancient Scottish constitution by which the people had the right to depose unsatisfactory kings, and gave examples of the forty-five early kings to which this had happened, every one of them monsters of vice. It was a dangerous argument to use to Elizabeth. But it was an argument which provided some grounds for what had been done to Mary, and it was backed up by Buchanan's *Detection of Mary Stewart*, written to leave no doubt that Mary was the present-day equivalent of those early examples of intolerable immorality. At the end of 1571, after the discovery of the Ridolfi Plot, Elizabeth at last allowed the *Detection*, and the Casket Letters, to be published.

The following decade saw something of a lull. Mary lived mainly in Sheffield castle, though occasionally spending periods elsewhere, at Tutbury and Chartley. She was under the guardianship of the earl of Shrewsbury and his redoubtable wife, Bess of Hardwick. The two women spent time together embroidering – an art in which Mary was highly talented – and gossiping. Mary was later to try to report to Elizabeth Bess's outrageous comments on her monstrous vanity; fortunately for Bess, Elizabeth never saw the letter so clearly intended to wound her. Mary was still treated as queen, dining under her cloth of state; she cost the English government £52 per week, and during her English imprisonment, unlike her French upbringing, the Scots were not asked to contribute to the bill. She hunted; occasionally she went to Buxton, to take the waters for her declining health. It was a placid and infinitely frustrating existence, during which she contemplated the excitement of plotting, the secret letters smuggled in and out in the heels of shoes and so on. And she never gave up either contacts with potential supporters, or hope.

In 1582, it all began again. In that year, which saw the first attempt to assassinate the leading Protestant ruler William of Orange, Walsingham – now no longer a private citizen, but a major councillor and Elizabeth's greatest bloodhound in smelling out conspiracies – came upon a plot known as the 'Enterprise', involving Mary, Francis Throckmorton, nephew of Elizabeth's diplomat, and the Spanish ambassador. English determination to have Mary executed, so long rebuffed by Elizabeth, was now revived with explosive force. Elizabeth held out, and made a last desperate effort to resolve the problem which Mary created for her by removing it elsewhere. By 1583, she was resurrecting the old scheme of getting Mary back to Scotland; she was to be co-ruler with her son James. Mary herself, using the duke of Guise as her intermediary, had first raised this idea with the Scottish government in 1581. It had fallen on very deaf Scottish ears, and continued to do so; all that happened, now that Elizabeth was in favour of it, was that the Scots took a little longer to say no. But in May 1585 they finally made it clear that this 'Association', as it was hopefully termed, was unacceptable.

James, now in his late teens and already a ruler of sufficiently obvious skill and ability to impress English observers and infuriate Elizabeth, had no intention of sharing the power he was exercising on his own behalf, now that his minority was over, with a mother who was a scandal, an embarrassment, a Catholic and, above all, a woman of proven political inability. He would not, therefore, take on to his own shoulders the burden of Mary; from his, and the Scots', point of view, she was undoubtedly much better left in England. Understandably, it was a very different matter for Elizabeth.

In 1584 in England, there was another 'Association': the Bond of Association, proposed by the council and enthusiastically accepted by parliament. This was sent throughout the country for signatures. It allowed the killing of any person on whose behalf a plot was made with the intention of putting him – her – on the English throne. It was lynch law. But only Elizabeth's direct intervention persuaded parliament to introduce into the act, which would give the bond legal force, a clause providing for a tribunal to try the person in question. English reactions to Mary were now at a level of hysteria. It was hardly surprising. William of Orange was assassinated in this year; and the question of English intervention in the Netherlands, thus offering aid to rebels against the might of Spain, was already very much a possibility, which was translated into reality in 1585 when Leicester led an English army into the Netherlands, and became lieutenant-general. In this highly tense atmosphere, Mary walked straight into the last trap. She was an enthusiastic party to the third and final major plot on her behalf, the Babington Plot, simpler than the two earlier ones but probably all the more threatening for that: Elizabeth was to be assassinated, and Mary was to become queen of England, the political nation sworn to kill rather than to accept her. Whatever perception of the real world she had ever possessed was now lost. She was in fact ensuring her admission to the next.

Walsingham knew about it from the beginning, having introduced a spy, Gilbert Gifford, into Mary's household. Between January and July 1586, while Mary once again enjoyed the heady excitement of plotting, with coded letters transmitted in a beer-keg, Walsingham was informed of every step. The end came with Mary's letter to Anthony Babington on 17 July, enthusiastically approving of the assassination of Elizabeth. The copy sent to Walsingham was endorsed by his agent and decipherer Thomas Phelippes; on the letter, he drew a gallows.

Mary, throughout this period housed at Chartley, was now moved to Fotheringhay and there, in October, put on trial and convicted. Elizabeth was in an agony about Mary's death which stands in stark and instructive contrast to Mary's cheerful willingness to countenance hers. Even now, she tried to hold out against the inevitable, the point to which she had been brought by the insistence on the one hand of her council, her parliament and her subjects and, on the other, Mary's actions. She was being asked to undertake what was for her, or any ruler, a monstrous act, and it was not her importunate subjects who would be left with the responsibility for it. In 1649, Cromwell and his associates were to insist that the execution of Mary's grandson Charles I must be done openly and in the full light of day, to show that they were utterly convinced of the justice of their action. The great hall at Fotheringhay was not quite as open as the scaffold erected outside the Banqueting House in Whitehall. But the trial and execution of Mary were just as formal. For the first time, a divinely ordained monarch was condemning and putting to death another equally divinely ordained monarch. But Elizabeth did not share Cromwell's conviction of the rightness of the cause; that consolation was denied to her.

Her last, frantic effort to avoid the terrible decision was her attempt to persuade Sir Amyas Paulet, keeper of Fotheringhay, to have Mary quietly killed. Paulet, that rigidly loyal subject, would not agree to murder. And so on 1 February 1587 Elizabeth signed the death warrant. Exactly a week later, Mary was dead. At her execution, she was the only person who showed no reaction to the fearful tension surrounding the event. The earls of Shrewsbury and Kent, sent to Fotheringhay to preside over the proceedings, were visibly nervous. The executioner botched his job; it took him two blows of the axe to kill her, and three to get her head off, and he then suffered the shattering experience of picking up the head to display it according to accepted ritual, only to find that what he was holding was a wig, while the head itself dropped from his hands. The queen herself, however, had gone to her death with serene confidence, clothed in red, the liturgical colour of martyrdom. It was, finally, as a Catholic martyr that she saw herself.

The news was greeted in Scotland with appropriate horror; at the parliament held in the summer of 1587, the members present knelt and swore to avenge her, although they quickly changed their tune when it became necessary to prevent Francis Stewart, nephew of James Hepburn and now earl of Bothwell, from actually trying to do so. In Paris, her black-draped portrait was widely displayed, and crowds surrounded the Louvre, howling for revenge. In Spain, Philip II, already provoked by English intervention in the Netherlands from 1585 into considering a departure from the policy of leaving England alone which he had pursued since 1558, and in whose favour Mary had revoked her son's claim to the English throne, at last moved decisively into his heroically disastrous 'Enterprise of England'. In England itself, the populace rejoiced; but the queen sat alone in stunned grief, from which she emerged to turn like a tigress on the unfortunate under-secretary William Davison, to whom she had given the death warrant. In Fotheringhay, Mary's body lay, embalmed, until the end of July, when it was buried, with all due ceremony, in Peterborough Cathedral. After her son James succeeded to the English throne, it was moved to Westminster Abbey, where splendid monuments were put up to both her and Elizabeth. It seemed fitting, to the first king of Britain, that the last two independent sovereigns of Scotland and England should lie together in glorious repose.

What then are we to make of Mary? There can be no doubt of her failure as a ruler. This sovereign, of the blood of two great families, the Stewart kings of Scotland, and the most influential and able of all aristocratic lineages of the sixteenth century, the house of Guise, showed nothing of the quality of either. Instead, we find an inability to make or keep contact with political reality which was rare in the Stewart line hitherto, though evident in two of the Stewart kings of the next century. In the event, she was always unable to foresee crisis, and nearly always unable to do other than than collapse when crisis erupted. Thus at one of the most critical moments in their history, the Scots were faced with a ruler who displayed an incompetence which they had not experienced since her great-great-great-great-grandfather, Robert III, who had died in 1406, pronouncing himself to be 'the worst of kings and most miserable of men'; it is an improbable though not impossible case of inherited weakness to set alongside the upbringing she shared with her feeble first husband and his brothers.

Moreover, although throughout her life she created distress and drama for those who had to deal with her, the sad fact was that in the end she amounted to so little. Elizabeth, who suffered from fear of her for eighteen years; Rizzio, on whom she put too much dependence; Darnley and Bothwell whom she married, to their misfortune even more than hers; Moray and the other Scottish Protestants determined to maintain their religion, yet never sure whether their ruler was friend or foe: to these people, in her lifetime, she mattered greatly. Yet she neither restored the religion in Scotland for which she later claimed to die, nor achieved the English succession for which she was prepared to sacrifice its cause. It is indeed ironic that, even in the early years of her personal rule, when she tried so hard to make herself acceptable to Elizabeth, she failed to get what she wanted; while her son James, equally enthusiastic about his future as king of England, but never for a moment forgetting his present as king of Scotland, constantly infuriated and maddened the English queen precisely by pursuing his own independent policy – and not only achieved his ends after her death, but, during her lifetime, extracted from the most parsimonious ruler in Europe the handsome sum of £58,000. Mary's apologists have made the case for understanding her difficulties, even sharing her passions. No apologist has ever convincingly established positive aspects of her government, such as have been argued for Æthelred the Unready, Edward II, Henry VI – and, in Scotland, for Robert II and even Robert III. For it is literally the case that Mary as ruler achieved nothing. Of how many other well-known European monarchs in the pre-modern age can this be said with so little fear of contradiction?

There is great appropriateness in Mary's motto, 'in my end is my beginning'; for she has given people far more pleasure, and far less pain, after her death, when reality ended and legend began, than ever she did in life. Yet it would be quite wrong to finish on so dismissive a note. A pervasive tradition in European culture, which took life from Homer, insists that heroes are usually tragic, and tragedy is necessarily heroic. The weakness of this tradition, as applied to rulers, is that it leaves no room for the merely pathetic. Mary *was* a tragic figure: tragic not because she was young and female, nor because her kingdom was Scotland, nor even because she could be personally delightful (she could be personally odious too). She was tragic because she was one of the rare – strangely rare – cases of someone born to supreme power who was wholly unable to cope with its responsibilities.

Historians have learned to be careful of 'praising famous men'. It may be that they should be equally careful of damning famous failures – even those where it is hard to find compensating

Bibliography

The quantity of writing about Mary Queen of Scots is voluminous in the extreme. Chapter 1 of this book has already outlined the scale and range of Marian works, and referred to some of the more important books. All that will be done here is to direct attention to the printed source material, and to the most useful recent writing on Mary. The major contemporary sources for Mary's government are *The Acts of the Parliaments of Scotland*, eds T. Thomson and C. Innes (Edinburgh, 1814–75), vol. ii; *The Register of the Privy Council of Scotland*, eds J. H. Burton and others (Edinburgh, 1877–), vol. i; *The Register of the Great Seal of Scotland*, ed. J. M. Thomson (reprint, Edinburgh, 1984), vol. iv; *The Register of the Privy Seal of Scotland*, eds M. Livingstone and others (Edinburgh, 1908–), vols iii–v; *The Accounts of the Lord High Treasurer of Scotland*, eds T. Dickson and J. Balfour Paul (Edinburgh, 1877–1916), vols xi–xii. For foreign affairs, and for information about events in Scotland, a goldmine is the *Calendar of the State Papers relating to Scotland and Mary Queen of Scots, 1547–1603*, eds J. Bain and others (Edinburgh, 1898–1969), vols i–ix, and also the *Calendar of State Papers Foreign: Elizabeth*, eds J. Stevenson and others (London, 1863–1950). Also A. Teulet, *Papiers d'Etat relatifs à l'Histoire de l'Ecosse au 16ᵉ siècle* (Bannatyne Club, Edinburgh, 1852–60) and *Relations politiques de la France et de l'Espagne avec l'Ecosse au 16ᵉ siècle* (Paris, 1862); and *The State Papers and Letters of Sir Ralph Sadler*, ed. A. Clifford (Edinburgh, 1809). For Mary of Guise, see *The Scottish Correspondence of Mary of Lorraine*, ed. A. I. Cameron (Scottish History Society, Edinburgh, 1927), and for her foreign correspondence, the *Balcarres Papers*, ed. M. Wood (Scottish History Society, Edinburgh, 1923–5).

Contemporary accounts of the reign include Robert Lindesay of Pitscottie, *The Historie and Cronicles of Scotland* (Scottish Text Society, Edinburgh, 1899–1911) and Sir James Melville of Halhill, *Memoirs of his own Life* (Bannatyne and Maitland Clubs,

Edinburgh, 1827); both are splendidly entertaining reading. There is also the outrageous attack on Mary by George Buchanan, *The Tyrannous Reign of Mary Stewart*, ed. and trans. W. A. Gatherer (Edinburgh, 1958), and the equally hostile account in vol. ii of his *History of Scotland*, ed. and trans. J. Aikman (Glasgow, 1827). And there is the towering and often malevolent prose of John Knox, *History of the Reformation in Scotland*, ed. W. C. Dickinson (Edinburgh, 1949; translated into English); this, in its Scottish form, and other writings are in *The Works of John Knox*, ed. D. Laing (Edinburgh, 1846–64). For Mary's religious activities – or lack of them – there are the *Narratives of Scottish Catholics under Mary Stuart and James VI*, ed. W. Forbes-Leith (Edinburgh, 1885) and *Papal Negotiations with Mary Queen of Scots, 1561–1567*, ed. J. H. Pollen (Scottish History Society, Edinburgh, 1901); and Pollen also edited *Mary Queen of Scots and the Babington Plot* (Scottish History Society, Edinburgh, 1922). For a rather gentler topic, see *Inventaires de la Royne Descosse Douairière de France*, ed. J. Robertson (Bannatyne Club, Edinburgh, 1863). Finally, there are the seven volumes of *Lettres et Mémoires de Marie, Reine d'Ecosse*, ed. A. Labanoff (London, 1844) and also the *Lettres de Marie Stuart*, ed. A. Teulet (Paris, 1859).

Among modern works, the obvious starting-point is Antonia Fraser, *Mary Queen of Scots* (London, 1969), by far the best, and most detailed, biography of the queen. But there is still much of value in an older work, D. Hay Fleming, *Mary Queen of Scots* (London, 1897), not least because of the remarkable fact that the footnotes are almost twice as long as the text, and packed with interest. Gordon Donaldson's *The First Trial of Mary Queen of Scots* (London, 1969) and *Mary Queen of Scots* (London, 1974) are both fairly brief, but balanced and sober accounts; and his *All the Queen's Men: Power and Politics in Mary Stewart's Scotland* (London, 1983) is a real tour de force, breaking new ground in its detailed discussion of the political and religious positions of the queen's supporters and enemies; this book is a 'must' for anyone interested in the reign. Another 'must' is the masterly and sensitive analysis by Maurice Lee Jr, *James Stewart, Earl of Moray* (New

York, 1953) which brought a perspective to the reign which has not been sufficiently followed up. Another indispensable and fascinating book is J. E. Phillips, *Images of a Queen: Mary Stuart in sixteenth century literature* (Los Angeles, 1964), which traces the growth of the totally conflicting legends, the Catholic martyr and the Protestant whore and murderess. Less indispensable, but worth reading – especially for those who find the Casket Letters important – is M. H. Armstrong Davison, *The Casket Letters* (London, 1965). Alison Plowden, *Two Queens in One Isle: the deadly relationship of Elizabeth I and Mary Queen of Scots* (Brighton, 1984) is a more serious book than its rather over-sensational title suggests; some of the analysis is distinctly shrewd, though not sufficiently worked out. I. B. Cowan, *The Enigma of Mary Stuart* (London, 1971) is a useful collection of extracts from books on Mary, showing the violently opposing interpretations of her actions and character. Among more 'popular' works, G. M. Thomson, *The Crime of Mary Stuart* (London, 1967) has the merit of being fast-moving and quite exciting. Books by, for example, Jean Plaidy and Madeleine Bingham may have their place on bedside tables, but should scarcely appear on the bookshelves of those who wish to take the reign of Mary Stewart seriously.

Those who do should, of course, go beyond even the reputable works cited here on Mary herself, and read more widely in order to put her into context. General books covering the period in Scotland are G. Donaldson, *Scotland: James V–VII* (Edinburgh, 1965); T. C. Smout, *A History of the Scottish People* (London, 1969); W. Ferguson, *Scotland's Relations with England: a Survey to 1707* (Edinburgh, 1977); J. Wormald, *Court, Kirk and Community: Scotland, 1470–1625* (London, 1981). More specific studies which are of undoubted relevance to the subject are G. Donaldson's seminal *The Scottish Reformation* (Cambridge, 1960); the different view of the early stages of Scottish Protestantism in the introduction to J. Kirk, *The Second Book of Discipline* (Edinburgh, 1980); and also J. Cameron, *The First Book of Discipline* (Edinburgh, 1972) and I. B. Cowan, *The Scottish Reformation* (London, 1982). M. Lynch, *Edinburgh and the Reformation* (Edinburgh, 1981) is essential reading, opening up the crucial theme of the queen's relations with the capital, and offering much more besides. Margaret Sanderson, *Cardinal of Scotland: David Beaton, c. 1494–1546* (Edinburgh, 1986) is an excellent study of one of the most influential churchmen and politicians in mid sixteenth-century Scotland. J. Wormald, *Lords and Men in Scotland: Bonds of Manrent 1442–1603* (Edinburgh, 1985) includes discussion of the political and religious bonds of the reign. The important article on political language and attitudes by R. A. Mason, and also those by Lynch and Wormald, in *Church, Politics and Society: Scotland, 1408–1929,* ed. N. Macdougall (Edinburgh, 1983) should also be consulted. Despite its title, Helena M. Shire's *Song, Dance and Poetry of the Court of Scotland under James VI* (Cambridge, 1969) in fact illuminates the whole subject of the sixteenth-century court, and therefore adds a crucial dimension to our understanding of Mary's reign. And the record 'Musik Fyne: songs and dances of the Scottish court' (Scottish Records no. 33, SR 133) is essential listening.

This bibliography should not only be confined to Scotland. G. R. Elton, *Reformation Europe, 1517–1559* and J. H. Elliott, *Europe Divided, 1559–1598* (both in the Fontana History of Europe series, 1963 and 1968) admirably create the necessary context for Mary's reign. J. H. M. Salmon, *Society in Crisis: France in the Sixteenth Century* (London, 1975) is a very good introduction to the kingdom which Mary preferred to her own. Roy Strong, *Art and Power: Renaissance Festivals, 1450–1650* (Woodbridge, 1984) is a brilliant evocation, magnificently illustrated, of the visual world of monarchy. For England, the reader should begin with Penry Williams, *The Tudor Regime* (Oxford, 1979) and A. G. R. Smith, *The Emergence of a Nation State: the Commonwealth of England, 1529–1660* (London, 1984), both excellent works. On Elizabeth herself, J. E. Neale, *Queen Elizabeth* (London, 1934) is a book which has certainly stood the test of time, but which must now be read alongside W. T. MacCaffrey, *The Shaping of the Elizabethan Regime* and *Queen Elizabeth and the Making of Policy, 1572–1588* (Princeton, 1968 and 1981) and *The Reign of Elizabeth I,* ed. C. Haigh (London, 1984). R. B. Wernham, *Before the Armada* (London, 1966) and G. Mattingly, *The Armada*

(Boston, 1959) both contain superb analyses of the problem of Mary Stewart; and Mattingly's description of the execution, with which his book opens, has never been bettered.

Finally, there is the publishing boom created by the anniversary of that execution. The result is a mixed bag. Rosalind K. Marshall, *Queen of Scots* (HMSO, 1986) and D. and J. Steel, *Mary Stuart's Scotland* (London, 1987) are, particularly in the case of the first, lavishly and beautifully illustrated, and therefore a pleasure to the eye, but sadly do not advance our understanding of the sixteenth-century political figure. D. Breeze, *A Queen's Progress* (HMSO, 1987), likewise beautifully illustrated, has rather more to offer because of its particular emphasis on the importance of understanding the architectural settings in which the queen lived out her life. I. B. Cowan, *Mary Queen of Scots* (Saltire Society Pamphlets 9, 1987) is of course a work by an acknowledged expert; but lack of space is a major problem here, for compression has caused a certain lack of clarity of interpretation. The real successes are: first, Margaret Sanderson's *Mary Stewart's People* (Edinburgh, 1987), a delightful and splendidly researched collection of essays on a range of people, from aristocrat to tailor, who lived during her reign; and second, the catalogue of the exhibition in the Scottish National Portrait Gallery, *The Queen's Image*, by Helen Smailes and Duncan Thomson, which not only reproduces contemporary pictures (from which there emerges the revealing fact that she had herself painted in France and England, but not in Scotland) but also the quite staggering series of nineteenth-century romantic portraits of the dramatic incidents in her life, from her departure from France to her execution. It is not only in books, but also in art, that the legend of Mary Queen of Scots has had excessive expression. But one need not despair. The length of this bibliography itself, while the merest fraction of the whole, is a reminder that the 'romance, sex and violence' school is not the only one.

This was reinforced by the publication of *Mary Stewart: Queen in Three Kingdoms*, ed. Michael Lynch (Oxford, 1988), an impressively wide-ranging collection of essays, each one of which made a notable contribution to the historical understanding of Mary Queen of Scots. That was the last of the works brought out at the time of the anniversary; since then, there has been a lull. But two further studies are worth noting: Michael Lynch's masterly article 'Queen Mary's Triumph: the baptismal celebrations at Stirling in December 1566', *Scottish Historical Review* 69 (1990), which shows the queen's real sureness of touch in staging celebrations with a clear political message in what was one of the most brilliant court festivals of the later sixteenth century; and Jayne Elizabeth Lewis, *Mary Queen of Scots: Romance and Nation* (London, 1998), which struck out on a highly original line, tracing the enduring fascination of Mary Queen of Scots down to modern times.

a romantic tragedy queen'.[2] John Guy, a renowned Tudor historian, has applied extensive work in English archives to a forensic unpicking of the insurmountable obstacles which William Cecil, Elizabeth's keenly Protestant Secretary, placed in Mary's way, frustrating any fruitful relationship with Elizabeth. His scheming also undermined Mary's relationships with her Protestant nobility on whom she was reliant to govern.[3] Broadening our understanding of Mary's reign has been helped by others writing on its major players: Jane Dawson on Knox, Amy Blakeway on the regents, Rosalind Marshall on *Queen Mary's Women: Female relatives, servants, friends and enemies*, and Keith Brown on noble power;[4] and by studies of significant people and periods either side of the reign, most notable here Wormald's own work on rehabilitating James VI and I, which gave her a yardstick against which to measure Mary's performance. James had to face similarly crisis-filled years, long years of minority, irascible regents, rambunctious nobles, and a Kirk far more established than in Mary's time, containing a strident Presbyterian faction determined to fashion itself outwith royal control.[5]

Retha Warnicke's comprehensive and measured biography of Mary makes good use of the expanding body of work being done not just on the queen herself, but on specific aspects of her reign.[6] Outstanding here are Michael Lynch on the infant James's baptismal celebrations at Stirling in 1566, Alasdair MacDonald and Alan MacDonald on Mary's official Entry of 1561, and Theo van Heijnsbergen on the literature of advice to princes in relation to that notorious Entry and Alexander Scott's subsequent poem 'Ane New Yeir's Gift'.[7] Giving the reign context are important works by Roger Mason on political thought and rights of resistance theory; Alec Ryrie, Margo Todd and Alan MacDonald on the social and political impacts of Protestantism; and Elizabeth Ewan and others on the social and judicial effects of their gender on women in post-Reformation Scotland.[8] Warnicke rightly points to the importance of considering these cultural contexts (the arts, gendered, religious and political cultures), and the uses of inter-disciplinary methodologies to enhance our interpretation of the well-picked-over evidence. Her own work considers Mary within the research on 'a wide range of cultural rituals, mores and behaviour' that shaped her actions, such as court customs and protocol, gender relations and familial networks. She reminds us 'of the limited range of choices, specific to their culture, which individuals have when responding to personal crises'.[9] An analysis of the gendering of such responses is attempted by Kristen Post Walton in her monograph on Mary, and the politics of gender and religion.[10]

It will be within those cultural contexts that the most fertile areas lie for future work, developing an understanding of how they shaped Mary's actions. To those already listed, we could add performance studies, literary analysis, material culture, psychology and medicine – and more. As importantly, this should be done within an intimate understanding of the nature of Scottish monarchy, government and society. As Wormald demonstrated, it is not enough simply to apply methodologies or theories developed elsewhere to what appears to be happening in Scotland. Those theories need to be tested against the specifically Scottish contexts of the subject, and using the original primary sources. Increasingly accessible through digitization and the internet, these sources allow scholars to re-engage directly with the words of Mary and her contemporaries, rather than relying excessively on the synthesized and rehashed interpretations of modern historians. New forms of machine-enabled analysis will allow for larger-scale linguistic and lexicographical analysis (of major significance for the 'Casket Letters' for example). Owing to constraints of space, what follows now is a limited attempt to look at existing and potential areas of research – gender and female authority, the political challenges of religious reformation, negotiating authority and the performance of power – and how they might improve our understanding of the age in which Mary was born to rule, and hence, our evaluation of she fared.

Wormald's Legacy in the Historiography of Power in Early Modern Scotland

But first, future scholarship on Mary needs to take full account of Wormald's work – and that of her successors – on the nature of

Stewart personal monarchy, noble power, society and government in Scotland.[11] Where historians predominantly schooled in ideas of the Tudor state point to the 'tribal politics' (John Guy) of bellicose Scottish noblemen with which they allege Mary had to contend, we need instead research that more rigorously tests whether Mary should have been able to use – as her son did – those nobles' cooperation, and the extensive kinship networks that they controlled. Here Wormald's seminal book *Court, Kirk and Community* is essential reading. No Tudor-based historian has fully understood yet the implications of this specifically Scottish background for any assessment of Mary's reign, or the significance of Keith Brown's work on the nobles' acquiescence in the (eventual) suppression of the feud in James VI's reign. It has been all too easily assumed that the challenge that noble power and faction presented meant that it was inevitable Mary would fail when confronted with it. Wormald knew this interpretation was flawed, and her judgement of Mary is predicated on an understanding of the potential effectiveness of personal monarchy dependent on a cooperative nobility. In this, bonding was crucial, as Wormald explained in her influential *Lords and Men in Scotland: Bonds of Manrent, 1442–1603*: 'political bonds . . . were made for political purposes' and therefore 'they made a very conscious attempt to show that those who entered into them were imbued with political responsibility and desire to serve the state'. Julian Goodare has built on this work to show that those nobles who signed the Ainslie bond with Bothwell meant what they said when they made it, despite their desertion of his cause so swiftly afterwards: the bond was made for honourable reasons to reconcile factions amongst the nobility, no matter how self-interested those reasons might also be.[12]

Tudor historians also get confused by what was represented by the existence of feud in Scotland, seeing it as confirmatory evidence that Scottish nobles acted outside monarchical control within a society in which it was difficult to impose the law. How on earth was Mary supposed to cope with this? But such a view misses the full picture. In her seminal *Past and Present* article 'Bloodfeud, Kindred and Government in Early Modern Scotland', Wormald demonstrated instead the less detrimental aspects of the 'peace within the feud': the informal means of justice that the feud represented, and the codified nature of its conduct, arbitration, settlement and compensation.[13] This meant that even in the Borders, where feuding was legendary, a monarch had the power structures there to suppress it. Wormald's work on the feud has been drawn on by Mark Godfrey and Anna Groundwater to support the premise that a system existed, in which any lines demarcating formal and informal justice blurred, to exercise justice if a monarch was determined to. Did Mary then have the means to govern at her fingertips – or not?[14] What did the rebellion of Moray and his cronies suggest of the reliability of the usually cooperative nobility, and how much of a challenge was this to Stewart monarchy? What went wrong in Mary's case: was it down to her own political insensitivity or mishandling of the monarchical-noble relations? Or were there forces affecting Scotland's political culture over which she was powerless?

Gender and Power in a Patriarchal Society

Arguably one of the main areas in need of further work, and which Wormald deliberately sidestepped, is that of gender. Wormald insisted that Mary's success or failure should be judged on her abilities as a monarch, not merely as a female monarch. That point still stands. It allows us to focus on her acts of government within their specifically Scottish context, a point that Tudor historians have repeatedly missed. However, had Wormald been coming new to the subject in today's historical landscape, she might have looked more closely at the impact of contemporary social mores and cultural constructs of a patriarchal society on Mary's behaviour, questioning how far the actions for which she is criticized as a monarch might have been shaped by her gender. Would a king have taken the same actions? Was he subject to the same constraints? Would he have received the same criticism?

The effects of Mary's gender have not yet been fully addressed, though several writers have begun to acknowledge some of them: on the problems of marrying a foreign prince who might then interfere in the independent government of Scotland; her physical frailty; her 'vulnerability'. These characteristics take it as read, but often without interrogating it further, that she was dependent on men to rule and for protection, and that powerful men would not allow it otherwise. Some have dug deeper. In particular, Post Walton uses the contemporary literature of the *Querelles des Femmes* to demonstrate some of the expectations and constraints within which Mary acted. However, unfortunately, Post Walton's somewhat limited understanding of the workings of Scottish monarchy and government blind her to the difference between what would have been expected of a male monarch in any case, and that which was specifically because Mary was a woman. Most notably, Post Walton observes that Mary was willing 'to operate largely within the traditional boundaries of being female', displaying a 'reluctance to take over the complete governance', because of her gendered upbringing and surroundings. This resulted in her monarchical power being 'challenged subtly by her advisers', who wished 'to maintain their own power by placing themselves in an advisory role' to her, in particular her over-reliance on Moray. Mary's 'reluctance to govern without male advice and support' meant that she 'allowed herself to limit her own authority as queen'.[15] Warnicke similarly observes that contemporarily a queen regnant would have been expected to take that male advice, noting the English agent Sir Nicholas Throckmorton's relief that it appeared Mary 'would be ruled by good counsel and wise men'.[16]

It should be remembered, however, that all Scottish monarchs, whether male or female, were expected to listen and take advice from counsellors. Noble and clerical elites insisted on their voices being heard, and there is a hefty 'advice to princes' literature that articulates this, and is itself part of that expectation. We need but to look at the poems of John Bellenden, Richard Maitland and David Lyndsay addressed to Mary's father James V on the subject. The poems of welcome, and advice, by Maitland, Alexander Scott and Buchanan on Mary's return to Scotland are in this same literary and political tradition.[17] Scott's advice on attracting the support of her governing elites is non-gender-specific:

Foirgifaniss grant, with glaidnes and gude will,
Gratis till all into yor parliament;
Syne stabill statuis, steidfast to stand still,
That barrone, clerk, and burges be content;
Thy nobillis, erlis and lordis consequent,
Treit tendir, to obtene thair hartis inteir;
That thai may serve and be obedient
Vnto thy Grace aganis this gude new yeir.[18]

More gendered however, was his advice on, and his apparent hopes of, Mary attracting a suitable husband:

Latt all thy realme be now in reddines
With coistlie clething to decoir thy cors . . .
Agane thy Grace gett ane guid man this yeir.[19]

This advice was more carefully expressed than that offered by the burgh council four months previously at Mary's formal Entry into Edinburgh, and did something to mitigate the harmful effects of that event's stridently Protestant message. Welcoming their sovereign to her principal city with a book of metrical psalms and a vernacular bible, the council told Mary that in these books

. . . your grace may reade and vnderstand
The perfytt waye vnto the heavens hie,
And how to rewle your subiectis and your land,
And how your kingdome establyshed shalbe.[20]

What was offensive here to Mary was the overtly Protestant framing of this otherwise unexceptionable advice. The audacity of the burgh council's staging of the entry lay in its overtly anti-Catholic pageantry, rather than in the presumption it had in addressing its monarch thus. Such events formed part of an ongoing dialogue between the monarch and her subjects, particularly the civic, noble and clerical elites – a dialogue which both allowed them to voice their opinions, and enabled Mary to display monarchical power.

For Mary to have ignored such consultative devices or mechanisms of dialogue would have been perilous. As Alan MacDonald has shown for Mary's son James VI's reign, the 'central role of counsel' was pivotal within personal monarchy – since 'monarchs had ultimate responsibility for decision-making, mechanisms for counsel-giving were crucial to the functioning of government'. In this the daily engagement of the monarch with government, and the role of the court was important, as were the 'points of contact' provided by meetings of parliament, conventions of estates, and of royal burghs – and royal entries.[21] Monarchs may have been criticized, as Warnicke notes, for accepting evil counsel, but that criticism was within a tradition that held listening to counsel as an integral part of negotiating and securing royal authority. As Jacqueline Rose observes, '[c]ounsel was a fundamental element of the conceptual basis political framework and daily workings of the late medieval and early modern polity'; the 'obligation to take counsel was widely accepted', and it served 'practical functions' in consensus-building, amongst others.[22] The point is that leaning on advisers was not necessarily a gendered issue. It was one crucial way in which Scottish monarchs encouraged the cooperation of those they needed to support their policies, and govern for them in the regions. All monarchs did so. It is breathtaking, then, to find Post Walton relying on a misapprehension to claim, about Mary's and Elizabeth's reigns, that the 'rule of queens in both kingdoms influenced the establishment of governmental systems that included the participation of members of the political nations'.[23]

Nonetheless, a closer look is needed at Mary's choices, and how these were shaped by the patriarchal society in which she lived. Some historians have tried to get more tightly to grips with the mentalities of the period that would have conditioned how she was perceived and what she did. Here the *Querelles* literature provides entertaining evidence, its very existence implying that there was a contemporary understanding of the constraints on a woman's freedom of action. As David Parkinson elucidates, the heightened political and religious tensions of Mary's reign transformed what may have been a more courtly pastime of polite debate on the merits or otherwise of women, into something more hostile. Problematically for Mary, he notes 'the literature circulating within the civic body – especially among mercantile and professional households in the capital, Edinburgh – dwells much upon femininity as unresolvably, even fixedly, controversial'.[24] So might Wormald have taken into consideration that contemporary literature? What might she have made, for instance, of the prevalence of strictures on wives evident in George Buchanan's poetic advice on wifely obedience to Mary on her marriage to the dauphin? Here Buchanan recommends that although the dauphin

> should yield to you the sceptre of royalty, and declare you with tender countenance his [co-equal] lady,
>
> Yet acknowledge your station in life as a woman, and accustom yourself to your husband's authority,
>
> Putting your royal authority aside to this extent.
>
> Learn to bear the [marital] yoke, but together with a beloved husband,
>
> Learn to be subject to your husband's direction . . .[25]

The implications of this for the tensions between royal authority and wifely obedience in Mary's marriage to Darnley make this a fruitful area for further scholarship.

As significantly, however, and despite Buchanan's strictures, Mary was never to grant Darnley the crown matrimonial. So how does this display of female regal power complicate our understanding of patriarchal society in sixteenth-century Scotland? May it have been more complex than both Post Walton and Warnicke suggest? Noting the 'complex, varied, uneven and changing articulation of patriarchal authority', Amanda Flather has shown for early modern England that what may have been preached was not always practised. Recent work on gendered relations, she says, has 'exposed the ways that contradictions and tensions [existed] between the ideal model of gender relations disseminated through the pulpit and prescriptive literature, and the practices of everyday life'; the black and white image of wifely obedience to a dominant male authority needs shading in to reflect how 'the intersection of gender with other social factors such as age, social and marital status, created arenas for female agency'. 'Gender roles as actually lived were a product of complex interactions of ideas and material circumstances.'[26] Similarly, on Scottish women's history, Esther Breitenbach notes the need to 'generate identities of historical women that will reflect the complexity and variety of women's experiences'. Some necessary work has already been done, but as Elizabeth Ewan has concluded these 'findings need to be integrated into the historical picture: . . . how consideration of the role of gender might change perceptions, even the framework of the Scottish past'.[27] What then are the implications of Mary's monarchical status, almost from birth, and the different upbringing she will have had from other women of lesser status; how may these have counter-balanced the constraints of being female?

And what does Mary herself demonstrate of the effects of her gender, unconsciously or otherwise? For this, we are lucky enough to have an extensive range of her correspondence and literary efforts. As Cristy Beemer reminds us, Mary was writing with 'an eye toward posterity', her letters intended as a memorial of both their content and the image she presented within them. In a long supplication to Elizabeth in 1582, Mary wrote that this letter was 'a perpetual testimony and engraving upon your conscience'.[28] The rhetorical techniques she used in phrasing such writings were shaped by her education in the works of Cicero, Plato, Aristotle, Erasmus and Quintilian. For Beemer, Mary like other 'female monarchs [was] prepared for rule by the same texts that guided male monarchs'. Given 'they lacked a history of female rule . . . reigning women adapted classical rhetorical strategies to fit their unique rhetorical situations. The rhetorical artifacts of these women leaders comprise a unique collection of powerful, political, and public performances'.[29] In Mary's letters to Elizabeth, she repeatedly reminds her cousin of her own monarchical status, of their consanguinity, inviting her to take pity on a fellow queen: in her last letter to Elizabeth, she reiterates that 'I know that you, more than any one, ought to feel at heart the honour or dishonour of your own blood, and that, moreover, of a queen and the daughter of a king.'[30] Of course Mary also used the trope of the vulnerable woman to attract pity, or aid: for instance, in response to Philip II's sympathies expressed on the death of her first husband, she writes that she had been 'comforted by your letters [as] the most afflicted poor woman under heaven'. But such phrases can be interpreted as simply one more weapon in her rhetorical armoury, her letters also containing implicit or overt displays of force which utilized male rhetorical strategies. She ends that letter to Philip II reiterating their shared monarchical status, bidding farewell 'monsieur my good brother . . . Your very good sister, Marie R'.[31]

On Mary's literary writings, some work has been done on what they display of gender in relation to monarchical power by Lisa Hopkins in her *Writing Renaissance Queens* and in Peter Herman's edited volume *Reading Monarchs' Writing*. The evidence Hopkins found is not of a woman feeling limited by her gender, but one who, even in the depths of her distress in the 1580s, writes as acutely aware of and insistent on her monarchical status. Mary was raised and treated as a monarch; she knew nothing else, and expected nothing less. Furthermore, for Peter Herman, 'Mary not only wrote from a monarchic perspective, but her political stature allowed her both the freedom and the language to create those texts.'[32] That in itself was a form of power out of the reach of most women. This type of literary analysis has been limited to Mary's poetry and is not comprehensive, while Beemer focuses only as yet on the 'letters of mercy'. The same close reading applied systematically to Mary's correspondence would be necessary to get closer to what effect contemporary social constructs of gender had on the way she acted, or felt that she could.

Also needed is a more exhaustive analysis of the gendering of her portrayal in contemporary literature, memoirs and correspondence, both before and after the crises. Here the significance of the representation of three aspects relating to being female are considered: sexual reputation, the link made between female inconstancy and female inability to rule, and physical vulnerability. In all these, maintaining a good reputation was crucial to the maintenance of authority. For a king, his reputation did not necessarily have to be squeaky clean (though keeping up appearances was preferred), but it did have to promote a belief that what that person did in their official capacity was done for the good of the kingdom. Buchanan did not mince his words on the importance of exemplary behaviour to the infant James:

> Thus do the people fasten their gaze on the king,
> And they love him, and they model their lives on his;
> They strive to fashion themselves and their characters from the mirror, as it were, which he holds up for them . . .

> But if the king should contaminate this image by shameful vices . . .
> God himself will exact a bloody punishment for such a sacrilege.[33]

Promoting a good reputation was therefore important. Here, gender very much raises a problem, for the reputation of a female monarch, as with women more generally, was more susceptible to criticism and more easily damaged.

Firstly, a woman was supposed to be virtuous, and to maintain sexual propriety; not only should she do this, but she had to be seen to be protecting that reputation with her decorous behaviour. Buchanan, commenting on Mary's virtues in 1558, before it all went so wrong, wrote that the dauphin was attracted not merely to her beauty,

> Rather it was virtue greater than her sex, prudence greater than her years,
> And comely behaviour suiting to her beauty, and modesty joined to royal authority,
> An ideal gracefulness uniting all these qualities in a secret bond.[34]

In a queen's case this was particularly important given her responsibility to produce an heir, about whom there should be no whiff of illegitimacy. Thus the rumours circulating about Mary's relationship with Rizzio, though baseless, enabled the conspirators to fire up Darnley in defence of his honour. Later on, in his celebration of the infant king's accession, Thomas Maitland was to bewail the way that Bothwell, 'an infamous adulterer [drew] the widowed queen to himself to associate in the marriage bed with deathly consequence for all' in 'losing the kingdom and her reputation forever'.[35] For Warnicke, Mary was forced to acquiesce in the marriage to Bothwell in order to 'suppress all references to the sexual violation', because she ran the risk of appearing immodest and to have brought the attack on herself.[36] Subsequent literature was often to use allegations of immorality to demonstrate her unfitness to rule, and to legitimize her deposition (veiling the attack on her Catholicism which formed much of its motivation).[37] Allegations of sexual misconduct were more damaging to Mary's reputation than they would have been for a male monarch, and thus to her political authority.

Secondly, women were portrayed as peculiarly vulnerable to their lusts, and therefore unable to control their emotions. To the sixteenth-century mind, it was potentially catastrophic to couple this supposed unreliability with access to power. Knox's *First Blast against the Monstrous Regiment of Women* is part of a wider literature that equated the inconstancy of women with an inability to make good decisions: thanks to their 'naturall weakness and their inordinat appetites', 'whersoever women beare dominion, there must nedes the people be disordred, living and abounding in all intemperancie . . . in the end, that they must nedes come to confusion and ruine'.[38] Women with power upset the natural order. George Buchanan ran into this problem in his poetic attempts to ingratiate himself initially with both Mary and Elizabeth I. Detailing the qualities of an ideal monarch, he could not bring himself at first to credit them to Elizabeth herself, but described them instead as 'My notion of such a king as I should wish for' making it clear that he was in fact describing Elizabeth's virtues. One way to get around the problem of female power was to make a female monarch celestial, not human, and thus able to combine the merits of masculinity with her feminine attributes. Of Elizabeth, Buchanan wrote:

She is a goddess – why hesitate? – in whom there breathes a union
Of masculine power, smiling grace, and celestial honour.
Or if she is not a goddess, she is the power presiding in England,
In genius, countenance, and character, an equal to the gods.[39]

He had done this too for Mary in the early days of her personal
rule, coupling her with Elizabeth in a new Golden Age:

It will redound to the praise of the Goddesses
By whose power peace dwells in the fields of Britain.[40]

Such deference to monarchical authority, though somewhat
conflicted, will have helped to counteract the detrimental effects
of a patriarchal mindset; despite this, Mary as a queen regnant
was still unsettling. Knox cautioned of other queens that they had
'burned with such inordinat lust' that 'they have betrayed to
strangiers their countrie and citie', and killed their children and
husbands.[41] Mary's decision-making was seen to be problematically
subject to her female emotions, specifically lust. The placards that
appeared shortly after Darnley's murder on the streets of Edinburgh
targeted Mary's alleged sexual immorality, one portraying her as a
mermaid (a symbol of promiscuity), linking that to her complicity
in her husband's killing.[42] Ultimately, for Tricia McElroy, the
perception of Mary's 'female passion – specifically recalls the
definition of a bad ruler. As a woman, she is the feminized tyrant,
rash and histrionic'.[43] Maintaining a good reputation was all the
more important if she was to prove her fitness to rule.

And, finally, women were viewed as physically weaker and thus
vulnerable to male advances. Conversely this also meant that they
were dependent on men for protection, which is precisely what
the thuggish, hard-riding Bothwell may well have appeared to
offer Mary. Her apologists were to seize on this perceived weakness
in the case for her defence following the murder of Darnley and
her unfortunate third marriage:

noted originally, '[i]deological commitments now affected political ambitions' creating a 'major shift in political life' in which increasingly 'faction was based on commitments other than the purely personal', of 'considerations of foreign policy and religious belief'.[46] This more than anything else was what Mary had to deal with when she returned to Scotland. That is not to say that the people of Scotland, or at least those with the power to do so, were to challenge her right to rule, or the institution of monarchy itself. But a monarch's power had been successfully challenged in terms of defining the religion of that country, and theorists were considering the limitations of monarchical power; potentially this threatened Mary with what Conrad Russell has called the problem of 'diminished Majesty' in relation to Charles I.[47] When monarchy was so 'personal', the perception of a ruler's authority was paramount for it to be effective. Where it had been successfully overruled, that might impinge on the abilities of that, or a successive monarch to rule.

Moreover, the Calvinist form of Protestantism adopted by the new kirk brought additional challenges to monarchical authority in Scotland. The insistence of the Scottish Presbyterians on parity within religious spheres (which did not extend to the position of women in relation to men), and within ecclesiastical hierarchies, negated the elevated position of the monarch within the kirk, in which they were just a subject. Although the kirk recognized the monarch's authority in the temporal realm, and was happy to use it to ratify acts for its establishment, the more strident Presbyterians denied the monarch's right to intervene in the kirk's affairs. Mary's distressed and outraged reactions to Knox's apparent indifference to her royal status, where their discussions related to her religion and marriage, were early examples of affronted Stewart monarchy, which as Wormald also observes, later had to endure Andrew Melville tugging James VI's sleeve to remind him that, in the eyes of the Presbyterian kirk, he was but a subject.[48] For further on the fraught relationship between the kirk and the Stewarts, Alan MacDonald's *Jacobean Kirk*, and related work, is essential reading; arguably similarly forensic work is still needed for the kirk's earlier relationship with Mary as queen.

Similarly essential reading, in terms of the social and religious changes that Mary was encountering, includes Michael Lynch's *Edinburgh and the Reformation* and other writings, and Margo Todd's *The Culture of Protestantism in Early Modern Scotland* for understanding the wider effects of the new doctrines (they do not always agree).[49] Lynch notes the uneven pace of conversion, as opposed to outward conformity, to the new doctrines that took several generations to embed widely. So, whilst Mary had to endure Knox, he was not the voice of the whole people. This is important because, for Wormald, Mary's reluctance to pursue the re-establishment of the Catholic church in Scotland, given the potential fragility of the new Protestant kirk, was emblematic of her wider failure to rule. However, others have questioned just how possible it would have been for Mary to do this in the face of strong support amongst the nobility for Protestantism; they point instead to Mary's *real politik* tolerance which allowed her to ride out the first couple of years of her reign until she was able to begin to assert her own authority more effectively, particularly following her marriage to Darnley.

Which takes us to another important point on gender, and its relation to the new Protestant doctrines which have been thought to reinforce the patriarchal system. In Scotland, these put the male leader of the household as the person responsible for catechizing those in his care, and found expression in the particularly gendered nature of the accusations and sentences deliberated over by the kirk sessions.[50] Some historians, including Christina Larner, have argued that the Reformation saw the 'criminalization' of women, who now became responsible under the law for their actions. That said, Elizabeth Ewan cautions that there is not enough work yet to conclusively prove such criminalization, noting that '[a]lthough women's formal legal status was inferior to that of men, in practice women both before and after 1560 were able to overcome many of their legal disabilities'; and Helen Dingwall's work shows that in Edinburgh female-heads of households were far from unusual.[51] The vehement nature of the clerical response to Mary's alleged implication in Darnley's murder, and adultery (if true) with

Bothwell, may have been fuelled by wider fears over female agency and criminal responsibility in a post-Reformation world – or perhaps not, and it is here that more work is needed. Couple Mary's gender with her Catholic faith, and you have dynamite in such a world: as Dunnigan observes, the 'political and religious climate of mid-sixteenth-century Scotland was only too willing to perceive the very facts of Mary's femininity and her devout Catholicism as crimes'. 'Her excess of [feminine] passion . . . helped foster in 1560s Scotland the fierce ideological power of anti-Catholicism and anti-feminism.'[52]

And on top of this, the insistence on the foundation of Protestant doctrines on the scriptures saw polemical writers scrambling to find biblical justification for the subjection of women, and a denial of the acceptability of the female right to rule. Where social order itself had been challenged in the Reformation, concern was voiced over the disturbance and potential breakdown to natural and divine order that female government might pose. Thus Knox quoted from St Paul's first letter to the Corinthians (XIV:34), 'let women kepe silence in the congregation, for it is not permitted to them to speake'. Augustine and Chrysostom were also marshalled to back his argument, Knox paraphrasing Augustine on women's subjection to men, having 'none authoritie, nether to teache, nether to be witnesse, nether to judge, muche lesse to rule or beare empire'.[53] Warnicke observes that to 'clerics, especially, it also seemed critical for the queens regnant to accept male advice' given that they ruled 'over tiers of religious institutions mostly staffed by men'.[54] For Dunnigan, Mary's 'monarchical passion' only confirmed what her Protestant critics believed of her unfitness to rule.[55] That heady combination of religious revolution and political rebellion, and the major challenge this made to Mary's government, have not yet been thoroughly unpicked. As Arthur Williamson observed in 1989, and still holds true for any assessment of Mary, more research is needed into the 'extraordinary energy and creativity of revolutionary Scotland, one of the most intellectually and political vital moments in the history of the country'. 'The contemporaneous revaluation of traditional social ties and their history in vocabularies at once classical and Calvinist laid the foundations of Scottish public culture. Scholars who slight this dynamic context . . . do so at their peril. Scotsmen did indeed feel a powerful attachment to the Stewart dynasty' but this did not necessarily preclude other stimuli.[56]

Most significant perhaps for consideration in relation to Mary are the writings by such as Knox and Buchanan on the nature of kingship, and the right to resist tyrannical authority; for Knox, the Old Testament was a useful source of legitimacy and authority for both his opinions and the constraints on early modern kingship. In the decades since Wormald wrote of Mary's failures as ruler, much work has been done by Roger Mason and others on, to quote Mason, 'the way in which sixteenth-century Scots perceived and articulated the changing nature of the relationship between the king and the political community over which he presided'. Of the political tracts that resulted, for Mason, Buchanan's *De Jure Regni apud Scotos Dialogus* is the 'most significant', arguing as it does that 'the people's duty to the commonwealth must take precedence over their allegiance to the king'. Buchanan's 'theory of popular sovereignty' had a 'central premise [which] was that kings were appointed by the people to perform on their behalf a set of well-defined functions. It followed that if they failed to carry out their duties satisfactorily', they broke their contract with the people who thus 'had the right to depose them'. 'Monarchy, in short, was an elective form of government and kings were accountable to those who elected them.'[57] Earlier in 1558, with more overtly biblical rhetoric, Knox, in his *Appellation to the Nobility and Estates of Scotland*, and *Letter to the Commonalty of Scotland*, spelled out his theories on legitimate resistance to tyranny. (That said, Mason somewhat tempers the radical impression that Knox gives in his forceful writings.) While Buchanan's *Dialogue* did not appear in print until 1579, it was conceived much earlier, probably in 1567, to justify the deposition of Mary.[58] The thinking that shaped it, and Knox's 'Letters', will have also shaped Buchanan's political allies' response to, and portrayal of, Mary's actions. New political thinking was conditioning the circumstances in which

Mary was having to act, not the least in her four confrontations with Knox, and the way in which she would subsequently be presented in the historical record.

These opinions resonated in literature other than that on political theory. The demonization of Mary in the publication in 1571 of Buchanan's *Ane Detectioun of the duinges of Marie Quene of Scottes* combined Buchanan's indictment of Mary with the 'evidence' of the Casket Letters, inviting the audience to make an 'impartial' judgement on her morality, and by extension her fitness to rule. In this, as Tricia McElroy so illuminatingly writes, 'Buchanan crafted what would become the standard narrative about her descent into criminality'; at the same time 'his intellectual interests and political theories pervade the summary of Mary's misdeeds and give force to the evidence against her'. Its 'interlocking pieces . . . collaborate to produce an implicit political argument'.[59] For McElroy, in this dramatic account Buchanan had found 'a fitting literary form in which to work out his ideas about kingship and tyranny, hypocrisy and theatricality'; crucially however 'in the *Detectioun* the presentation of those ideas has real political consequences. No longer aimed at theoretical or educational debate, the literary deployment of his political ideas now targets with deadly seriousness the specific goal of justifying the deposition of Mary Queen of Scots.' The *Detectioun*'s very language 'performs' to 'characterize Mary's tyrannical behaviour, and the result is a narrative that puts his ideas about kingship and popular sovereignty into action'.[60] Such a close reading of the myriad of tracts of this nature concerning Mary is needed for a fuller understanding of the changes underway in the political culture of Scotland, its wider European contexts, and how these may have presented new problems that traditional models of royal authority in Scotland had not previously encountered.

Negotiating Authority: the Power of Performance

How was Mary to respond to these potential challenges? For early modern England, Kevin Sharpe, Mike Braddick, John Walter *et al.*

have emphasized the negotiated nature of authority: in Sharpe's words, the 'series of negotiations and exchanges over images of rule, and a dialogue about and for authority' that was heavily dependent on the elites' capacity to present a credible figure of legitimate power. For Sharpe, evidence for this lies in the 'recent interdisciplinary work on theatre and poetry, painting and pageant, vital to historians of politics', which forms an indispensable arena for more traditional historians to plunder. In particular, 'central to early modern as to contemporary politics were rhetoric, powerful oratory, the right image, the capacity to rebrand (after the Reformation of 1688, for example): that is the texts and arts of persuasion. Persuasion is at the heart of the exercise of all authority'.[61] If we are to assess Mary as a monarch, we need to understand the mechanisms that she had available to negotiate her authority in the performance of monarchy during court rituals, and entertainments, as much as her own actions on progresses, or with her council. As Sir John Hayward was to recall of her cousin Elizabeth's entry into London, 'that in [such] pompous ceremonies a secret of government doth much consist, for that the people are naturally both taken and held with exterior shewes'.[62] Equally, her audience, that is her subjects, her noble, burghal and clerical elites could also act as principal agents in creating a stage for that display of monarchy. In doing so they could influence the presentation of that power, and their relationship to it – most notably within Mary's formal entry of 1561 to Edinburgh, organized by the newly and aggressively Protestant burgh council, intended to assert its own stridently anti-Catholic message.[63] For Sharpe, 'the vitality of ritual and symbol and the power of representation and procession' were a crucial part of that negotiation of authority: 'simultaneously mystical and democratized, it starkly demonstrated the reciprocity in all state ritual . . . even the superior force of popular will'.[64]

Mary was more than aware of the political potency of image and performance, Sarah Carpenter noting the permeability of the line between 'recreational relaxation and political statement', in which Mary's court like those of France and England demonstrated its 'familiarity with the sixteenth century's language of performance in spectacle, allegory and image'.[65] Michael Lynch's rich article likewise explores her use of the 'extraordinary spectacle' of the baptismal celebrations for her son James at Stirling in December 1566. The baptism was to be employed to promote a cult of monarchy, but was also part of a longer-term 'process of internal reconciliation', to retrieve the political consensus lost following Moray and his allies' rebellion over the Darnley marriage, and the Rizzio murder.[66] As Lynch notes, the celebrations took place in the midst of a series of remissions to those implicated, and soon after her death scare at Jedburgh, where Mary had beseeched those present 'to haue charitie, concorde and loue amongis your selfis'. The three days of masques, jousting, banquets and fireworks were 'carefully constructed to convey a number of political images, including the promise of a renewed and more glorious Stewart monarchy', in which 'the monarch was portrayed as both hero and reconciler of a divided kingdom'. The culmination of the Stirling celebrations saw the successful defence of a mock fortress from marauding Moors and wild Highland men, reasserting the triumph of Stewart monarchy over these divisions that beset it. As Patrick Adamson memorialized it: 'Our leader has transposed Mars ablaze with civil war into peace in our time' heralding a new 'golden age'.[67] For Lynch, the 'collective symbolism of Mary's Renaissance fête at Stirling suggests the need to reconsider the policy of her reign'.[68]

What too are we to make of the way Mary presented herself, as when she dressed as a man to serve at table during a dinner to honour the French ambassador in February 1566, or to wander incognito around Edinburgh? For David Parkinson, her boldness was intended to convey an image of manliness: '[p]laying the man enables Mary to draw on strength and leadership otherwise, perhaps, unavailable to her'. As author of her own parts, a literary patron and commissioner of royal festivities, Mary was able to shape that image, to use it to counter the less convincing aspects of her femininity, and to manipulate it to maximize her political effectiveness. However, her 'loss of agency' by 1568 was mirrored by, in Parkinson's words, 'her subjection to an increasingly politically charged *querelle des femmes*'.[69] Problematically for Mary, he contends that her 'literary patronage [was] embattled, at least from the outset of her personal reign: those genres and questions through which the queen's authority is furthered are subject to appropriation by her opponents'; thus literary representations of Mary developed to 'cast censorious eyes upon the queen herself'.[70] In this the challenge of gender had raised its ugly head. It was inevitable: Mary was, as Louis Montrose writes of Elizabeth, 'subject to those pervasive cultural perceptions of female weakness and disability that called into question the propriety and effectiveness of her authority'. Mary's gender therefore 'had a profound impact upon the relations of power and upon their representation', such representations being themselves constructions of gender. Like Elizabeth, Mary was subject to the early modern 'cultural logic' that would shape any representation she made of herself, or was made of her.[71]

Studies of specific occasions, as with those of the 1561 Entry, have been factored into the assessment of her reign by Goodare and Warnicke, in particular, but a more systematic consideration is still needed in which this display and negotiation of monarchy is brought together with Mary's more day-to-day performance of power, and the gendering of it – and set within its specifically Scottish historical and historiographical context. Work has been done on such a scale for Elizabeth, most notably by Roy Strong, David Howarth, and perhaps most comprehensively by Louis Montrose. When the modern audience thinks of Elizabeth, we see her through the magnificent representation of monarchy in her portraits, a carefully crafted legacy that for Strong helped her, and her allies, to build a 'mythology of monarchy' that continues to 'exert a hypnotic hold upon the imagination'.[72] Royal portraits were used to convey a political message: for Howarth, Elizabethan portraiture was one way in which to claw back the stability of the Tudor monarchy in a 'country rife with potential chaos', thus 'through her portraits [she] tried to invent the myth that hers was an unchanging regime'.[73] In these she counter-balances the problems of her gender by emphasizing her chastity, as well as the more usual tropes of monarchy: a 'complex programme with mottoes celebrating her powers of discernment and terrestrial globes prognosticating expansions of her empire' to create 'an object of veneration whose destiny is both mysterious and great'. At the time, those portraits will have been seen by a limited few, though they were increasingly reproduced as etchings on handbills.

Somewhat problematic for this type of assessment of Mary is the paucity of visual images from her personal reign. The ones we remember her by (as Scottish, rather than French queen) are mostly posthumous, and modelled on portraits done during her English captivity.[74] These tend to convey the political message of patrons keen to rehabilitate her reputation, clothed in seemly black, a rosary dangling, the 'martyrized' scene of her execution. Foremost amongst these is her son's tribute in the pure white marble of her tomb at Westminster Abbey. None of these, however, capture her as queen-in-action, from 1561 to 1567, with which Wormald's book is mainly concerned. But, as Strong reminds us, portraiture was just one tool in 'that strange repertory which makes up the Idea of Monarchy which includes ceremonial and pageantry, eulogistic literature and poetry besides emblems and devices. All contributed to the increase in mystique.'[75] In this Elizabeth, for Montrose, 'was a privileged agent in the production of the royal image, but she was not its master'. As powerfully, she was 'consciously and systematically fashioned by those Elizabethan subjects who were engaged in producing the texts, pictures and performances in which the Queen was variously represented to her people, to her court, to foreign power'. And as significantly, her subjects also 'participated in a ceaseless and casual process of producing and reproducing "the Queen" in their daily practices – in their prayers and oaths, their gossip and their fantasies'.[76] The similar types of evidence on which to base our understanding of what Mary had to contend with, and how well she did it, thus widens.

And finally what does Mary's own performance (outside those formalised rituals and representations considered above) suggest of the cultural forces shaping the language she used, her self-presentation, and the reception she anticipated? How was the behaviour of those who surrounded her determined by their interaction with her, and the message they intended to convey? How significant was the earl of Moray's manner of dealing with her? According to Mary, in Thomas Randolph's words, 'Lord James deals after his nature, "rudelye, homelye, and bluntlye".' Though Lethington dealt 'more delicatlye and fynelye', as would be expected of his less elevated social status, he 'in effect swerves not' from Moray. How forceful was this partnership thus presented? How did the 'performance of nobility' impact on the way Mary could act?[77] What for instance do we read into the torrents of tears with which Mary greeted Knox's effronteries? Was she simply given to 'womanlike' over-emotion (to quote a Spanish ambassador on Elizabeth); or was there something more knowing than this? As Randolph observed 'As well you knowe, there be of that sexe that wyll do that, as well for anger as for greef, thoughe in thys the Lord James wyll dysagre with me.' What exactly did he mean by this? Were Mary's tears born of 'anger', sheer frustration at Knox's behaviour? What was the 'emotional script', or perhaps 'semi-improvisation' being followed here, what is the significance of the 'language of emotion'?[78] Was Mary merely doing what she thought would be expected of her to draw attention to her slighted honour, as both monarch and woman, or was this the kind of instance where, as Burke has remarked, the 'strategy of studying the gap between "script" and practice remains a valuable one'?[79] How much was Mary playing to her audience beyond the council chamber: those overhearing it in the court, those who would be told of it, including Elizabeth? What should we make of their reaction to her 'performance'? Though Knox in his reporting of it was to use the weeping to evidence the righteousness of his words in her frailty, for others Knox's outspoken virulence endangered the Protestant cause. Mary's carefully chosen words in response to Knox can be analysed as 'performative utterances': the sarcastically edged observation 'my subjects shall obey you, and not me . . . and so must I be subject to them, and not they to me' was at odds with the vulnerability also displayed, and more like the 'crafty wit' Knox accusingly ascribed to her.[80]

Using a combination of her femininity and monarchy like this, however, was a double-edged sword for Mary. The pathetic figure she presented in bedraggled serving-womenswear as she was led back into Edinburgh after the Carberry Hill confrontation was greeted by howls of derision and contempt, from a crowd that will have also witnessed the damning placards on display after Darnley's murder. What do their insults suggest of the way in which Mary had allowed the veil of monarchy to become so torn? But that again is not the whole story, for others in the crowd shouted out against such treatment of a queen. As Michael Lynch reminds us, many in Edinburgh were still loyal to her; and for many Mary's religion was not necessarily an issue, since Edinburgh's populace were nothing like as Protestant as the burgesses might have hoped.[81] Any public event like this inescapably allowed for a multiplicity of meanings, and could create 'a theatre of far greater fluidity' than those orchestrating it might have planned (in Thomas Laqueur's words on executions).[82] The fevered reporting of English agents, as much as more formal literary representations or the glimpses we get of Mary in the few extant contemporary diaries, are fertile ground for this sort of performative and linguistic analysis.

To Conclude

Wormald was one of the few Scottish historians to engage closely with such evidence in relation to Stewart Scottish monarchy, a fact reflected in one of her honours courses at the University of Edinburgh, 'Scottish Literature and Politics in early modern Scotland', on which I was lucky enough to teach. The constraints of the series in which her 'Mary' was originally published probably precluded such a close engagement with the material then – and much of the research mentioned above by others was yet to come.

A wealth of primary material, and a growing body of secondary contextual work, is there now for the exploiting, to give Mary's personal reign the close reading it still needs. Many of the pieces exist: from James Emerson Phillips' survey of her literary represen-tations, to others on the court and civic rituals, literary, political and religious cultures, and their gendering, and the display or castigation of her monarchical abilities or personal virtues. We are beginning to see the cultural conditions in which she operated and was judged. Tricia McElroy's forthcoming work *Executing Mary Queen of Scots: Strategies of Representation in Early Modern Scotland* promises to fill in the gaps further. As Williamson called for, that 'public culture' has been increasingly painted in to provide a richer understanding of the age in which she lived. Conversely, we also should ask how much did Mary herself contribute to the generation of that culture, to the burgeoning publishing industry, the intellectual firmament in which George Bannatyne began to compile his literary collections, and Sir James Balfour and David Chalmers their treatises on Scots law? We also have now a wider range of lenses through which to view how early modern monarchs could act, and the mechanisms available to them to rule effectively – the significance of negotiated authority, the use of space, and the performative interaction between subject and monarch, monarch and monarch, husband and wife. We now need to apply such approaches systematically to Mary's actions, words, images – within their proper Scottish historiographical contexts – and, yes, within their British and European contexts too.

That Scottish historiographical context (and for James VI, the British and European contexts) was set up in no small measure by Jenny Wormald. Her relentless determination to unpick sloppy Tudor-based interpretations of Scottish monarchical, political and social systems helped to establish a new rigour in the study of Scottish history. *Mary Queen of Scots: a Study in Failure* is as much a product of that steely insistence as a stimulus for the reinvigorated analysis of Mary that followed. For the ongoing study of the 'daughter of debate' in the years to come, it is a great sadness that it will not include the acute voice of Jenny, that great queen of debate.

Notes

1   Wormald, *Mary Queen of Scots*, 198. Many thanks are due to colleagues, too numerous to mention and especially amongst the Scottish Medievalists, for stimulating conversations on the subject of Mary. My biggest thanks are to Jamie Reid-Baxter for his insightful comments on a draft of this chapter. Any errors as ever are mine.

2   Julian Goodare, 'Mary (1542–1587)', *Oxford Dictionary of National Biography* (Oxford, 2004; online edn, May 2007); Julian Goodare, 'The First Parliament of Mary, Queen of Scots', *Sixteenth Century Journal*, 36:1 (2005), pp. 55–75.

3   John Guy, *My Heart Is My Own: The Life of Mary Queen of Scots* (London, 2004).

4   For details of these, see Additional Bibliography.

5   Jenny Wormald, 'James VI and I (1566–1625)', *Oxford Dictionary of National Biography* (Oxford, 2004; online edn, Sept 2014).

6   Retha M. Warnicke, *Mary Queen of Scots* (London, 2006).

7   Michael Lynch, 'Queen Mary's Triumph: The Baptismal Celebrations at Stirling in December 1566', *Scottish Historical Review*, 69 (1990), pp. 1–21; Alasdair A. MacDonald, 'Mary Stewart's Entry to Edinburgh: An Ambiguous Triumph', *Innes Review*, 42 (1991), pp. 101–10; A. R. MacDonald, 'The Triumph of Protestantism: The Burgh Council of Edinburgh and the Entry of Mary Queen of Scots, 2 September 1561', *Innes Review*, 48 (1997), pp. 73–82; Theo Van Heijnsbergen, 'Advice to a Princess: The Literary Articulation of a Religious, Political and Cultural Programme for Mary Queen of Scots, 1562' in Julian Goodare and Alasdair A. MacDonald (eds), *Sixteenth-century Scotland: Essays in Honour of Michael Lynch* (Leiden, 2008), pp. 99–122.

8   For details of these see Additional Bibliography.

9   Warnicke, *Mary Queen of Scots*, 6, 7.

10 Kristen Post Walton, *Catholic Queen, Protestant Patriarchy: Mary Queen of Scots and the Politics of Gender and Religion* (New York, 2007).

11 For a full list of Jenny Wormald's writings to 2014, and a summary introduction to her work, see Steve Boardman and Julian Goodare (eds), *Kings, Lords and Men in Scotland and Britain, 1300–1625: Essays in Honour of Jenny Wormald* (Edinburgh, 2014).

12 Wormald, *Lords and Men in Scotland: Bonds of Manrent, 1442–1603* (Edinburgh, 1985), 145; Julian Goodare, 'The Ainslie Bond', in Boardman and Goodare (eds), *Kings, Lords and Men in Scotland and Britain*, pp. 301–319, at 302–3, 317.

13 Jenny Wormald, 'Bloodfeud, Kindred and Government in Early Modern Scotland', *Past and Present*, 87 (1980), pp. 54–97.

14 Steve Boardman and Julian Goodare, 'Introduction: Kings, Lords and Jenny Wormald', in Boardman and Goodare, *Kings, Lords and Men in Scotland and Britain*, pp. 1–17, at 2–5, 15.

15 Post Walton, *Catholic Queen, Protestant Patriarchy*, 96–100, quotes at 96, 100.

16 Warnicke, *Mary Queen of Scots*, 12.

17 Theo van Heijnsbergen, 'Advice to a Princess', 111–14; poems include Sir Richard Maitland, 'Off the Quenis Arryvale in Scotland', *The Maitland Folio Manuscript*, ed. W. A. Craigie (Scottish Text Society, Edinburgh, 1919) p.34. See also James Emerson Phillips, *Images of a Queen: Mary Stuart in Sixteenth-Century Literature* (Berkeley, CA, 1964), 22–3.

18 Alexander Scott, 'Ane New Yeir's Gift', in *The Poems of Alexander Scott*, ed. James Cranstoun (Scottish Text Society, Edinburgh, 1896), 1–8, ll. 161–8.

19 *Ibid.*, ll. 177–8, 180.

20 'Welcome, our soueraine, welcome, our natyue quene', ll. 9–12, printed in Macdonald, 'Mary Stewart's Entry to Edinburgh: An Ambiguous Triumph', 109–10.

21 Alan R. MacDonald, 'Consultation, Counsel and the "Early Stuart Period" in Scotland', in Jacqueline Rose (ed.), *The Politics of Counsel in England and Scotland 1286 to 1707* (Oxford, 2016), pp. 193–210, at 194–9, quote at 194.

22 Jacqueline Rose, 'The Problem of Political Counsel in Medieval and Early Modern England and Scotland', in Rose, *The Politics of Counsel in England and Scotland 1286 to 1707*, pp. 1–43, at 1, 38, 37.

23 Post Walton, *Catholic Queen, Protestant Patriarchy*, 173, see also 173–7.

24 David Parkinson, '"A Lamentable Storie": Mary Queen of Scots and the Inescapable Querelle des Femmes', in L. A. J. R. Houwen, A. A. MacDonald and S. L. Mapstone (eds), *A Palace in the Wild: Essays on Vernacular Culture and Humanism in Late-Medieval and Renaissance Scotland* (Leuven, 2000), pp. 141–60, at 142–4, 146, quote at 142.

25 George Buchanan, 'Epithalamium for Francis of Valois and Mary Stewart of the Kingdom of France and Scotland', in P. J. McGinnis and A. H. Williamson (eds), *George Buchanan's Political Poetry* (Edinburgh, 1995), pp. 126–46, quote at 140.

26 Amanda Flather, *Gender and Space in Early Modern England* (Woodbridge, 2007), 4–8, 13–16, 37–8, 73–4, 174, 176, 178, quotes at 4, 8.

27 Esther Breitenbach, 'Curiously Rare? Scottish Women of Interest or the Suppression of the Female in the Construction of National Identity', *Scottish Affairs*, 18 (1997), pp. 82–94, at 92–3; Elizabeth Ewan, 'A Realm of One's Own? The Place of Medieval and Early Modern Women in Scottish History', in Terry Brotherstone *et al.*, *Gendering History: Scottish and International Approaches* (Glasgow, 1999), pp. 19–36, at 29.

28 Cristy Beemer, 'God Save the Queen: Kairos and the Mercy Letters of Elizabeth I and Mary, Queen of Scots', *Rhetoric Review*, 35:2 (2016), pp. 75–90, at 82.

29 *Ibid.*, 75–6, quotes at 75.

30 *Ibid.*, 86.

31 *Letters of Mary, Queen of Scots . . .*, ed. Agnes Strickland, vol. 1 (1942), 6–7.

32 Lisa Hopkins, *Writing Renaissance Queens: Texts by and about Elizabeth I and Mary Queen of Scots* (Newark, DE, 2002), especially ch. 4 'Writing to Control: The Verse of Mary, Queen of Scots', pp. 72–85; Peter C. Herman, '"mes subjectz, mon ame assubjectie": The Problematic (of) Subjectivity in Mary Stuart's Sonnets', in Peter C. Herman (ed.) *Reading Monarch's Writing: The Poetry of Henry VIII, Mary Stuart, Elizabeth I and James VI/I* (Tempe, AZ, 2002), pp. 51–78, quote at 57. See also Sarah M. Dunnigan, 'Sacred Afterlives: Mary Queen of Scots, Elizabeth Melville and the Politics of Sanctity', *Women's Writing*, 10:3 (2003), pp. 401–24.

33 Buchanan, 'A Celebration of the Birth of James VI, King of Scots' ('Genethliacon'), in McGinnis and Williamson, *George Buchanan's Political Poetry*, 154–60, at 156, 160.

34 Buchanan, 'Epithalamium for Francis of Valois and Mary Stewart of the kingdom of France and Scotland', *Political Poetry*, 126–46, at 128.

35 Thomas Maitland, *Sylva I: The Consecration of James VI, King of Scots*, in 'Bridging the Continental Divide: Neo-Latin and its Cultural Role in Jacobean Scotland, as Seen in the *Delitiae Poetarum Scotorum* (1637)', ll. 144–50: http://www.dps.gla.ac.uk/

36 Warnicke, *Mary Queen of Scots*, 154.

37 *Calendar of State Papers relating to Scotland and Mary Queen of Scots* [*CSP Scot*], vol. 2, pp. 178, 185, 191, 205; Phillips, *Images of a Queen*, 43–5, 49–51.

38 *The Works of John Knox*, ed. David Laing (Edinburgh, 1895), vol. 4, pp. 363–422, at 376.

39 Buchanan, 'To Thomas Randolph, an Englishman', and 'To Elizabeth, Queen of England', *Political Poetry*, 148, 112.

40 Buchanan, 'For Lord Walter Haddon, Master of the Court of Requests of the Most Serene Queen of England', *Political Poetry*, 150–2, at 152.

41 *Works of John Knox*, vol. 4, 476.

42 Phillips, *Images of a Queen*, 41–2.

43 Tricia McElroy, 'Performance, Print and Politics in George Buchanan's *Ane Detectioun of the duinges of Marie Quene of Scottes*', in Roger Mason and Caroline Erskine (eds), *George Buchanan: Political Thought in Early Modern Britain and Europe* (Aldershot, 2012), pp. 49–70, at 67.

44 Anon., 'Rhime in Defence of the Queen of Scots: the Double Dealing of the Rebells, in Scotland', in Phillips, *Images of a Queen*, 50.

45 Sarah M. Dunnigan, *Eros and Poetry at the Courts of MQS and James VI* (Basingstoke, 2002), 1, 7–11, chs 1 and 2, quote at 8.

46 Wormald, *Mary Queen of Scots*, 44, 50.

47 Conrad Russell, *The Causes of the English Civil War* (Oxford, 1990), 24.

48 Jenny Wormald, 'Godly Reformer, Godless Monarch: John Knox and MQS', in Roger A. Mason (ed.), *Knox and the British Reformations* (Aldershot, 1998), pp. 220–41, at 221–2.

49 Michael Lynch, *Edinburgh and the Reformation* (Edinburgh, 1981); Margo Todd, *The Culture of Protestantism in Early Modern Scotland* (New Haven, 2002).

50 See, for example, Michael Graham, *The Uses of Reform: 'Godly Discipline' and Popular Behaviour in Scotland and Beyond, 1560–1610* (Leiden, 1996), especially 'Sexuality' and 'Gender: Was There a Double Standard?', 280–86, 286–89 (he concludes not).

51 Ewan, 'A Realm of One's Own?', 24.

52 Dunnigan, *Eros and Poetry*, 7.

53 See, for instance, C. M. Harker, 'John Knox, *The First Blast* and the Monstrous Regiment of Gender', in Theo van Heijnsbergen and Nicola Royan, *Literature, Letters and the Canonical in Early Modern Scotland* (East Linton, 2002), 35–52. *Works of John Knox*, vol. 4, 379, 383.

54 Warnicke, *Mary Queen of Scots*, 13.

55 Dunnigan, *Eros and Poetry*, 7.

56 Arthur H. Williamson, review of Wormald, *Renaissance Quarterly*, 42:2 (1989), pp. 320–2, at 321, 322.

57 Roger A. Mason, *Kingship and the Commonweal: Political Thought in Renaissance and Reformation Scotland* (East Linton, 1998), 1–8, 191–2, quotes at 1, 2, 191.

58 *Ibid.*, 6, 139–64, 191.

59 McElroy, 'Performance, Print and Politics', 49, 54.

60 *Ibid.*, 64, 50.

61 Kevin Sharpe, 'Representations and Negotiations: Texts, Images, and Authority in Early Modern England', *Historical Journal*, 42:3 (1999), pp. 853–81, at 853, 854.

62 Sir John Hayward, quoted in Louis Montrose, *The Subject of Elizabeth: Authority, Gender, and Representation* (Chicago and London, 2006), 229.

63 See Alasdair A. MacDonald, 'Mary Stewart's Entry to Edinburgh' and A. R. MacDonald, 'The Triumph of Protestantism'.

64 Sharpe, 'Representations and Negotiations', 878.

65 Sarah Carpenter, 'Performing Diplomacies: The 1560s Court Entertainments of Mary Queen of Scots', *Scottish Historical Review*, 82:214 (2003), pp. 194–225, at 195.

66 Lynch, 'Queen Mary's Triumph', 1, 3–4, 8, quotes at 1, 4.

67 *Ibid.*, 4–5, 6–8, 10, 11–13, quotes at 5, 6, 13.

68 *Ibid.*, 16.

69 Parkinson, '"A Lamentable Storie"', 149–51, 155–6, quotes at 149, 156.

70 *Ibid.*, 143.

71 Montrose, *The Subject of Elizabeth*, 1.

72 Roy Strong, *The Tudor and Stuart Monarchy: Pageantry. Painting. Iconography*, vol. II, *Elizabethan* (Woodbridge, 1995), 15.

73 David Howarth, *Images of Rule: Art and Politics in the English Renaissance, 1485–1649* (Houndmills, 1997), 104.

74 For instance, Jeremy L. Smith, 'The Sheffield Portrait Types, their Catholic Purposes, and Mary Queen of Scots's Tomb', *British Catholic History*, 33:1 (2016), pp. 71–90.

75 Strong, *The Tudor and Stuart Monarchy*, vol. 2, 5.

76 Montrose, *The Subject of Elizabeth*, 2.

77 Thomas Randolph to William Cecil, 7 Sept. 1561, *CSP Scot*, vol. 1, no. 1017. See D. M. Posner, *The Performance of Nobility in Early Modern European Literature* (Cambridge, 1999).

78 Randolph to Cecil, *CSP Scot*, vol. 1, no. 1017; See Peter Burke, 'Performing History: The Importance of Occasions', *Rethinking History*, 9:1 (2005), pp. 35–52, at 40–1.

79 Burke, 'Performing History', 42.

80 *Ibid.*, 41. John Knox, *History*, vol. 2, 13–20, at 17. See Jane Dawson, *John Knox*, 213–16, 236–7.

81 Lynch, *Edinburgh and the Reformation*, 120.

82 T. W. Laqueur quote in Burke, 'Performing History', 42.

Additional Bibliography

Jenny Wormald on Mary Queen of Scots

For full list of Jenny Wormald's writings to 2014, and a summary introduction to her work, see Steve Boardman and Julian Goodare (eds), *Kings, Lords and Men in Scotland and Britain, 1300–1625: Essays in Honour of Jenny Wormald* (Edinburgh: Edinburgh University Press, 2014).

Jenny Wormald, 'Resistance and Regicide in Sixteenth-century Scotland: The Execution of Mary Queen of Scots', *Majestas* [Köln], 1 (1993), 67–87

Jenny Wormald, 'Godly Reformer, Godless Monarch: John Knox and Mary Queen of Scots', in Roger A. Mason (ed.), *John Knox and the British Reformations* (Aldershot: Ashgate, 1998), 220–41

Jenny Wormald, 'James VI and I (1566–1625)', *Oxford Dictionary of National Biography* (Oxford: Oxford University Press, 2004; online edn, Sept 2014)

Jenny Wormald, 'Mary Queen of Scots Passes on her Jinx', *Sunday Times*, 10 August 2008, p.15

T. M. Devine and Jenny Wormald (eds), *The Oxford Handbook of Modern Scottish history* (Oxford University Press: Oxford, 2012) – especially their introductory chapter, 'The Study of Modern Scotland', 1–18, and Wormald, 'Reformed and Godly Scotland?', 204–19

Jenny Wormald, 'Confident Stuart Scotland' (Book review of *Crown of Thistles: The Fatal Inheritance of Mary Queen of Scots*; *Fatal Rivalry: Henry VIII, James IV and the Battle for Renaissance Britain – Flodden 1513*), *Times Literary Supplement*, 5788, 7 March 2014, p.5

Bloody Queens: Elizabeth and Mary, BBC (2016), on Youtube: https://www.youtube.com/watch?v=Y7dtcbzphiM

Some Reviews of the Original Publication of Wormald's *Mary Queen of Scots*

M. Lee, 'The Daughter of Debate: Mary, Queen of Scots, After 400 years', *Scottish Historical Review*, 68 (1989), 70–9

Michael Lynch, 'Mary, Queen of Scots: A New Case for the Prosecution', *Journal of Ecclesiastical History*, 41 (1990), 69–73

N. M. Sutherland, review, *English Historical Review*, 106 (1991), 452

Arthur H. Williamson, review, *Renaissance Quarterly*, 42:2 (1989), 320–2

Books about and Biographies of Mary Queen of Scots, in Reverse Order of Publication

Rosalind K. Marshall, *Mary, Queen of Scots*, catalogue for exhibition 'In My End is My Beginning' at National Museum of Scotland, Edinburgh, June–November 2013 (Edinburgh: National Museum of Scotland, 2013)

Rosalind K. Marshall, *Mary Queen of Scots: Truth or Lies* (Edinburgh: St Andrew Press, 2010)

John D. Staines, *The Tragic Histories of Mary Queen of Scots, 1560–1690: Rhetoric, Passions and Political Literature* (Farnham: Ashgate, 2009)

Michael Bath, *Emblems for a Queen: The Needlework of Mary Queen of Scots* (London: Archetype Publications, 2008)

Roderick Graham, *An Accidental Tragedy: the Life of Mary, Queen of Scots* (Edinburgh: Birlinn, 2008)

Susan Doron, *Mary Queen of Scots: An Illustrated Life* (London: The British Library, 2007)

Julian Goodare, 'Mary (1542–1587)', *Oxford Dictionary of National Biography* (Oxford: Oxford University Press, 2004; online edn, May 2007)

Kristen P. Walton, *Catholic Queen, Protestant Patriarchy: Mary Queen of Scots and the Politics of Gender and Religion* (New York: Palgrave Macmillan, 2007)

Rosalind K. Marshall, *Queen Mary's Women: Female Relatives, Servants, Friends and Enemies of Mary, Queen of Scots* (Edinburgh: John Donald, 2006)

Retha M. Warnicke, *Mary Queen of Scots* (London: Routledge, 2006)

John Guy, *My Heart Is My Own: The Life of Mary Queen of Scots* (London: Fourth Estate, 2004)

Alexander S. Wilkinson, *Mary Queen of Scots and French Public Opinion, 1542–1600* (Basingstoke: Palgrave Macmillan, 2004)

Alison Weir, *Mary, Queen of Scots and the Murder of Lord Darnley* (London: Jonathan Cape, 2003)

Harry Potter, *Bloodfeud: The Stewarts and the Gordons at War in the Age of Mary Queen of Scots* (Stroud: Tempus, 2002)

A. E. MacRoberts, *Mary, Queen of Scots and the Casket Letters* (London and New York: I. B. Tauris, 2002)

Lisa Hopkins, *Writing Renaissance Queens: Texts by and about Elizabeth I and Mary Queen of Scots* (Newark, DE: University of Delaware Press, 2002), especially ch. 4 'Writing to Control: The Verse of Mary, Queen of Scots', 72–85

Susan Watkins and Mark Fiennes, *Mary Queen of Scots* (New York: Thames & Hudson, 2001)

Marcus Merriman, *The Rough Wooings: Mary Queen of Scots, 1542–1551* (East Linton: Tuckwell Press, 2000)

James Mackay, *In My End is My Beginning* (Edinburgh: Mainstream, 1999)

Jayne Elizabeth Lewis, *The Trial of Mary Queen of Scots: A Brief History with Documents* (Boston: St Martin's, 1999) with texts of nine documents related to Mary's trial and execution.

Jayne Elizabeth Lewis, *Mary Queen of Scots: Romance and Nation* (London and New York: Routledge, 1998)

Michael Lynch (ed.), *Mary Stewart, Queen in Three Kingdoms* (Oxford: Basil Blackwell, 1988)

And in the pipeline: Tricia McElroy, *Executing Mary Queen of Scots: Strategies of Representation in Early Modern Scotland* (forthcoming)

Contextual Books

Stephen Alford, *The Early Elizabeth Polity: William Cecil and the British Succession Crisis, 1558–1569* (Cambridge: Cambridge University Press, 1998)

Amy Blakeway, *Regency in Sixteenth-Century Scotland*, St Andrews Studies in Scottish History (Woodbridge: Boydell Press, 2015)

Keith M. Brown, *Noble Society in Scotland: Wealth, Family and Culture, from Reformation to Revolution* (Edinburgh: Edinburgh University Press, 2000)

Keith M. Brown, *Noble Power in Scotland from the Reformation to the Revolution* (Edinburgh: Edinburgh University Press, 2011)

R. Crawford, *Scotland's Books: the Penguin History of Scottish Literature* (London: Penguin, 2007)

Jane Dawson, *The Politics of Religion in the Age of Mary Queen of Scots: The Earl of Argyll and the Struggle for Britain and Ireland* (Cambridge: Cambridge University Press, 2002)

Jane Dawson, *Scotland re-formed: 1488 to 1587* (Edinburgh: Edinburgh University Press, 2007)

Jane Dawson, *John Knox* (New Haven: Yale University Press, 2015)

Sarah M. Dunnigan, *Eros and Poetry at the Courts of MQS and James VI* (Basingstoke: Palgrave Macmillan, 2002)

Sarah M. Dunnigan and C. Marie Harker (eds), *Women and the Feminine in Medieval and Early Modern Scotland* (Basingstoke: Palgrave, 2004)

John Durkan, *Scottish Schools and Schoolmasters 1560–1633*, ed. Jamie Reid-Baxter (Woodbridge: Scottish History Society, 2013)

Julian Goodare and Alasdair A. MacDonald (eds), *Sixteenth-century Scotland: Essays in Honour of Michael Lynch* (Leiden: Brill, 2008)

Michael Graham, *The Uses of Reform: 'Godly Discipline' and Popular Behaviour in Scotland and Beyond, 1560–1610* (Leiden: Brill, 1996)

Theo van Heijnsbergen and Nicola Royan (eds), *Literature, Letters and the Canonical in Early Modern Scotland* (East Linton: Tuckwell, 2002)

L. A. J. R. Houwen, A. A. MacDonald and S. L. Mapstone (eds), *A Palace in the Wild: Essays on Vernacular Culture and Humanism in Late-Medieval and Renaissance Scotland* (Leuven: Peeters, 2000)

R. D. S. Jack (ed.), *The History of Scottish Literature, Volume 1: Origins to 1660 (Mediaeval and Renaissance)* (Aberdeen: Aberdeen University Press, 1988)

Michael Lynch, *Scotland: a New History* (London: Pimlico, 1992)

Alasdair A. MacDonald and Kees Dekker (eds), *Rhetoric, Royalty, and Reality: Essays on the Literary Culture of Medieval and Early Modern Scotland* (Paris: Peeters, 2006)

Sally Mapstone and Juliette Wood (eds), *The Rose and the Thistle: Essays on the Culture of Late Medieval and Renaissance Scotland* (East Linton: Tuckwell, 1998)

Roger A. Mason (ed.), *Kingship and the Commonweal: Political Thought in Renaissance and Reformation Scotland* (East Linton: Tuckwell, 1998)

Roger A. Mason (ed.), *John Knox and the British Reformations* (Aldershot: Ashgate, 1998)

Roger A. Mason and Caroline Erskine (eds), *George Buchanan: Political Thought in Early Modern Britain and Europe* (Aldershot: Ashgate, 2012)

Roger A. Mason and M. S. Smith (eds), *A Dialogue on the Law of Kingship among the Scots: A Critical Edition and Translation of George Buchanan's De Jure Regni Apud Scotos Dialogus* (Aldershot: Ashgate, 2004).

Louis Montrose, *The Subject of Elizabeth: Authority, Gender, and Representation* (Chicago, IL, and London: University of Chicago Press, 2006)

Jamie Reid-Baxter, Michael Lynch and E. Patricia Dennison, *Jhone Angus: Monk of Dunfermline and Scottish Reformation Music* (Dunfermline: Dunfermline Heritage Community Projects, 2011), containing CD of Reformation sung psalms

Jacqueline Rose (ed.), *The Politics of Counsel in England and Scotland 1286 to 1707* (Oxford: Oxford University Press, 2016)

Nicola Royan and Kevin McGinley (eds), *The Apparelling of Truth: Literature and Literary Culture in the Reign of James VI: A Festschrift for Roderick J. Lyall* (Newcastle: Cambridge Scholars Press, 2010)

Alec Ryrie, *The Origins of the Scottish Reformation* (Manchester: Manchester University Press, 2010)

Margo Todd, *The Culture of Protestantism in Early Modern Scotland* (New Haven: Yale University Press, 2002)

Sebaastian Verweij, *The Literary Culture of Early Modern Scotland: Manuscript Production and Transmission* (Oxford: Oxford University Press, 2016)

J. Hadley Williams and J. Derrick McClure (eds), *Fresche Fontanis: Studies in the Culture of Medieval and Early Modern Scotland* (Newcastle upon Tyne: Cambridge Scholars, 2013)

Mary Queen of Scots Related and Contextual Articles

Cultural

Cristy Beemer, 'The Female Monarchy: A Rhetorical Strategy of Early Modern Rule', *Rhetoric Review*, 30:8 (2001), 258–74

Cristy Beemer, 'God Save the Queen: Kairos and the Mercy Letters of Elizabeth I and Mary, Queen of Scots', *Rhetoric Review*, 35:2 (2016), 75–90

Sarah Carpenter, 'Performing Diplomacies: The 1560s Court Entertainments of Mary Queen of Scots', *Scottish Historical Review*, 82:214 (2003), 194–225

Forrest P. Chisman, 'The Portraits of Mary, Queen of Scots, "En Deuil Blanc": A Study in Copying', *British Art Journal*, 6:2 (2005), 23–7

Douglas Gray, 'The Royal Entry in Sixteenth-century Scotland', in Sally Mapstone and Juliette Wood (eds), *The Rose and the Thistle: Essays on the Culture of Late Medieval and Renaissance Scotland* (East Linton: Tuckwell, 1998), 10–37

Giovanna Guidicini, 'Scottishness on Stage: Performing Scotland's National Identity during Triumphal Entries in the Sixteenth and Early Seventeenth Centuries', in Jodi Campbell, Elizabeth Ewan and Heather Parker (eds), *The Shaping of Scottish Identities: Family, Nation, and the Worlds Beyond* (Guelph: Centre for Scottish Studies, 2011), 113–27

Alasdair A. MacDonald, 'Mary Stewart's Entry to Edinburgh: An Ambiguous Triumph', *Innes Review*, 42 (1991), 101–10

Charles McKean, 'A Cult of Mary Queen of Scots?', *Architectural Heritage*, 18:1 (2007), 55–72

Kevin Sharpe, 'Representations and Negotiations: Texts, Images, and Authority in Early Modern England', *Historical Journal*, 42:3 (1999), 853–81

Jeremy L. Smith, 'Mary Queen of Scots as Susanna in Catholic Propaganda', *Journal of the Warburg and Courtauld Institutes*, 73:1 (2010), 209–20

Jeremy L. Smith, 'The Sheffield Portrait Types, their Catholic Purposes, and Mary Queen of Scots's Tomb', *British Catholic History*, 33:1 (2016), 71–90

Marguerite A. Tassi, 'Martyrdom and Memory: Elizabeth Curle's Portrait of Mary, Queen of Scots', in Debra Barrett-Graves (ed.), *The Emblematic Queen: Extra-Literary Representations of Early Modern Queenship* (New York: Palgrave, 2013), 101–32

Gender

Esther Breitenbach, 'Curiously Rare? Scottish Women of Interest or the Suppression of the Female in the Construction of National Identity', *Scottish Affairs*, 18 (1997), 82–9

Elizabeth Ewan, 'A Realm of One's Own? Women in the History of Medieval and Early Modern Scotland', in Terry Brotherstone *et al.*, *Gendering History: Scottish and International Approaches* (Glasgow: Cruithne Press, 1999), 19–36

Elizabeth Ewan, 'A New Trumpet? The History of Women in Scotland, 1300–1700', *History Compass*, 7:2 (2009), 431–46

C. M. Harker, 'John Knox, *The First Blast* and the Monstrous Regiment of Gender', in Theo van Heijnsbergen and Nicola Royan (eds), *Literature, Letters and the Canonical in Early Modern Scotland* (East Linton: Tuckwell, 2002), 35–52

Caroline Hibbard, 'Early Modern Queens Revived and Revised', *Journal of Women's History*, 22: 2 (2010), 181–190 (Review article of Doran, Post Walton, Montrose, Mears, etc.)

Anne Mclaren, 'Gender, Religion, and Early Modern Nationalism: Elizabeth I, Mary Queen of Scots, and the Genesis of English Anti-Catholicism', *American Historical Review*, 107:3 (2002), 739–67

Evelyn S. Newlyn, 'Images of Women in 16th-Century Scottish Manuscripts', in Elizabeth Ewan and Maureen Meikle (eds), *Women in Scotland, c.1100–1750* (East Linton: Tuckwell, 1999), 56–66

David Parkinson, '"A Lamentable Storie": Mary Queen of Scots and the Inescapable *Querelle des Femmes*', in L. A. J. R. Houwen, A. A. MacDonald and S. L. Mapstone (eds), *A Palace in the Wild* (Leuven: Peeters, 2000), 141–60

Literary

Marguérite Corporaal, 'Mary Stewart and Mary Beaton: The Construction of a Female Poetic Voice', in Alasdair A. MacDonald and Kees Dekker (eds), *Rhetoric, Royalty, and Reality: Essays on the Literary Culture of Medieval and Early Modern Scotland* (Paris: Peeters, 2006), 151–63

Jane Donawerth, 'Women's Poetry and the Tudor-Stuart System of Gift Exchange', in M. E. Burke *et al.* (eds), *Women, Writing, and the Reproduction of Culture in Tudor and Stuart Britain* (New York: Syracuse University Press, 2000), 3–18

Sarah M. Dunnigan, 'Sacred Afterlives: Mary, Queen of Scots, Elizabeth Melville and the Politics of Sanctity', *Women's Writing*, 10:3 (2003), 401–24

Sarah M. Dunnigan, 'Marian and Jacobean Literature', *Literature Compass*, 2 (2005)

Juanita Feros Ruys, 'Experience and the Courteour: Reading Epistemological Revolution in a Sixteenth-century Text', in Hadley Williams and J. Derrick McClure (eds), *Fresche Fontanis: Studies in the Culture of Medieval and Early Modern Scotland* (Newcastle upon Tyne: Cambridge Scholars, 2013), 249–69

Ryoko Harikae, 'Kingship and Imperial Ideas in the *Chronicles of Scotland*', in Williams and McClure (eds), *Fresche Fontanis*, 217–30

Peter C. Herman, 'Introduction', and '"mes subjectz, mon ame assubjectie": The Problematic (of) Subjectivity in Mary Stuart's Sonnets', in Peter C. Herman (ed.), *Reading Monarchs' Writing: The Poetry of Henry VIII, Mary Stuart, Elizabeth I, and James VI/I* (Tempe: Arizona Center for Medieval & Renaissance Studies, 2002), 1–10, 51–78

Tricia McElroy, 'Imagining the "Scottis Natioun": Populism and Propaganda in Scottish Satirical Broadsides', *Texas Studies in Literature and Language*, 49:4 (2007), 319–39

Tricia McElroy, 'A "Litle Parenthesis" to History: The *Memoirs* of Sir James Melville of Halhill', in Nicola Royan and Kevin McGinley (eds), *The Apparelling of Truth: Literature and Literary Culture in the Reign of James VI: A Festschrift for Roderick J. Lyall* (Newcastle: Cambridge Scholars Press, 2010), 148–61

Tricia McElroy, 'Performance, Print and Politics in George Buchanan's *Ane Detectioun of the duinges of Marie Quene of Scottes*', and 'Introduction', in Roger Mason and Caroline Erskine (eds), *George Buchanan: Political Thought in Early Modern Britain and Europe* (Aldershot: Ashgate, 2012), 49–70

Kevin J. McGinley, '"That Every Man May Knaw": Reformation and Rhetoric in the Works of Sir David Lyndsay', *Literature Compass*, 2:1 (2005)

Jamie Reid-Baxter, 'Philotus: The Transmission of a Delectable Treatise", in T van Heijnsbergen and N. Royan (eds), *Literature, Letters and the Canonical in Early Modern Scotland* (East Linton: Tuckwell Press, 2002, 52–68

Cathy Shrank, '"This Fatall Medea," "This Clytemnestra": Reading and the Detection of Mary Queen of Scots', *Huntington Library Quarterly*, 73:3 (2010), 523–41

Rosalind Smith, 'The Case of Mary Queen of Scots, Lord Darnley and Lord Bothwell: Initiating the Literature of Husband-Murder in Sixteenth-Century England', *Notes and Queries*, 59:4 (2012), 498–501

Danila Sokolov, 'Ane Detectioun of Mary Stewart, Queen of Scots, and the Languages of Royal Imprisonment in Medieval and Early Modern England and Scotland', *Journal of Medieval and Early Modern Studies*, 44:2 (2014), 321–44

Politics and Political Culture

K. M. Brown and A. R. MacDonald (eds), *The History of the Scottish Parliament, Volume III: Parliament in Context, 1235–1707* (Edinburgh, 2010)

Articles in Boardman and Goodare (eds), *Kings, Lords and Men in Scotland and Britain, 1300–1625*, including:

Boardman and Goodare, 'Introduction: Kings, Lords and Jenny Wormald', 1–17

Roger A. Mason, 'Beyond the Declaration of Arbroath: Kingship, Counsel and Consent in Late Medieval and Early Modern Scotland', 265–82

Julian Goodare, 'The Ainslie Bond', 301–19

Julian Goodare, 'The First Parliament of Mary, Queen of Scots', *Sixteenth Century Journal*, 36:1 (2005), 55–75

Theo van Heijnsbergen, 'Advice to a Princess: the Literary Articulation of a Religious, Political and Cultural Programme for Mary Queen of Scots, 1562' in Julian Goodare and Alasdair A. MacDonald (eds), *Sixteenth-century Scotland: Essays in Honour of Michael Lynch* (Leiden: Brill, 2008), 99–122

Michael Lynch, 'Queen Mary's Triumph: The Baptismal Celebrations at Stirling in December 1566', *Scottish Historical Review*, 69 (1990), 1–21

Roger A. Mason, 'James VI, George Buchanan, and the True Lawe of Free Monarchies"', in Roger A. Mason (ed.), *Kingship and the Commonweal* (East Linton: Tuckwell, 1998), 215–41

Roger A. Mason, 'George Buchanan's Vernacular Polemics, 1570–1572', *Innes Review*, 54:1 (2003), 47–68

A. R. MacDonald, 'The Triumph of Protestantism: The Burgh Council of Edinburgh and the Entry of Mary Queen of Scots, 2 September 1561', *Innes Review*, 48 (1997), 73–82

A. R. MacDonald, 'Ecclesiastical Representation in Parliament in Post-Reformation Scotland: The Two Kingdoms Theory in Practice', *Journal of Ecclesiastical History*, 50 (1999), 38–61

Glyn Parry, 'The Monarchical Republic and Magic: William Cecil and The Exclusion of Mary Queen of Scots', *Reformation*, 17:1 (2012), 29–47

Jenny Wormald, 'Bloodfeud, Kindred and Government in Early Modern Scotland', *Past and Present*, 87 (1980), 54–97

Primary Sources Available Online, Open Access

The Records of the Parliaments of Scotland to 1707, Keith M. Brown *et al.* (eds), Manuscript images and transcriptions of Acts of Parliament, searchable by reign, subject or person: http://www.rps.ac.uk

Sir David Lyndsay, *The Satyre of the Thrie Estaitis*, performed at Linlithgow in 2013. Filmed performance and text at 'Staging and Representing the Scottish Court': http://stagingthe scottishcourt.brunel.ac.uk/filmed-performances/index.html

Many printed volumes of primary sources published in the last two centuries, and now out of copyright, are available freely at the 'Internet Archive': https://archive.org. These include:

Letters of Mary, Queen of Scots, and documents connected with her personal history now first published, with an introduction, ed. Agnes Strickland,
  vol. 1 (1842): https://archive.org/details/lettersofmaryque01mary
  vol. 2 (1843) https://archive.org/details/lettersofmaryque02mary
  vol. 3 (1843) https://archive.org/details/lettersofmaryque03mary

Calendar of State Papers relating to Scotland and Mary, Queen of Scots, ed. J. Bain *et al.* (Edinburgh, 1898); vol. 1, 1547–1563: https://archive.org/stream/calendarstatepa00baingoog#page/n564/mode/2up

Calendar of the State Papers relating to Scotland, ed. Markham John Thorpe (London, 1858),
  vol. 1: 'The Scottish Series of the Reigns of Henry VIII, Edward VI, Mary, Elizabeth, 1509–1589': https://archive.org/details/cu31924091754360
  vol. 2: 'The Scottish series of the reign of Queen Elizabeth, 1589–1603; an Appendix to the Scottish series, 1543–1592; and the state papers relating to Mary Queen of Scots during her detention in England, 1568–1587': https://archive.org/details/calendarstatepa00thorgoog

Extracts from the Records of the Burgh of Edinburgh: vol. 3, 1557–1571, ed. J. D. Marwick (Edinburgh: Scottish Burgh Records Society, 1875): https://archive.org/details/extractsfrom reco03edin

Edinburgh Records: The Burgh Accounts of Edinburgh, vol. 2, 'Dean of Guild's Accounts, 1552–1567', ed. Robert Adam (Edinburgh, 1899): https://archive.org/details/edinburgh record00edigoog

David Calderwood, *The History of the Kirk of Scotland*, ed. Rev. Thomas Thomson (Edinburgh: Wodrow Society, 1842–3):
  vol. 1 to 1560: https://archive.org/details/historyofkirkofs01cald
  vol. 2 to 1570: https://archive.org/details/historyofkirk02cald
  vol. 3 to 1583: https://archive.org/details/historyofkirkofs03cald
  vol. 4 to 1588: https://archive.org/details/historyofkirkofs04cald

The Works of John Knox, ed. David Laing (Edinburgh, 1846–95), including Knox's *History of the Reformation* in vols 1 and 2:
  vol. 1 to 1559: https://archive.org/details/cu31924092463029
  vol. 2: https://archive.org/details/worksofjohnknox2knox
  vol. 4, containing the *First Blast of the Trumpet against the Monstrous Regiment of Women*: https://archive.org/details/worksofjohnknox04knox

John Knox, *The History of the Reformation*, ed. C. J. Guthrie (Edinburgh, 1898): https://archive.org/details/JohnKnox HistoryOfTheReformationOfReligionWithinTheRealmOf Scotland

James Melville of Halhill, *Memoirs of his Own Life* (Edinburgh 1827): https://archive.org/details/MemoirsOfHisOwnLife

The Poems of Sir Richard Maitland of Lethingtoun, ed. J. Bain (Glasgow, 1830): https://archive.org/details/poemsof sirrichar00mait

The Poems of Alexander Scott, ed. James Cranstoun (Scottish Text Society, Edinburgh 1896), including 'Ane New Yeir Gift', 1–8 https://archive.org/details/poemsalexanders01scotgoog

Robert Sempill *et al.*, *Satirical Poems of the Time of the Reformation*, ed. James Cranstoun (Edinburgh: Scottish Text Society, 1901–3), 2 vols: https://archive.org/details/satirical poemst03churgoog; https://archive.org/details/satirical poemst02churgoog

George Buchanan's Political Poetry, ed. P. J. McGinnis and A. H. Williamson (Edinburgh: Scottish History Society, 1995) at National Library of Scotland: http://digital.nls.uk/126160656

An Analytic Bibliography of On-Line Neo-Latin Texts, ed. Dana Sutton, at 'The Philological Museum' online, hosted by University of Birmingham. This includes poems by George Buchanan and others: http://www.philological.bham.ac.uk/bibliography/index.htm

Primary Sources Available Online, Subscription Access (through a Library)

Medieval and Early Modern Sources Online (MEMSO) (TannerRitchie Publishing)

Accounts and Papers relating to Mary Queen of Scots, ed. Allan J. Crosby, John Bruce (Camden Society, Old Series, XCIII; digital edition, TannerRitchie Publishing, 2011)

Inventaires de la Royne Descosse douairiere de France. Catalogues of the Jewels, Dresses, Furniture, Books, and Paintings of Mary Queen of Scots, 1556–1569, ed. Joseph Robertson (Edinburgh: Bannatyne Club, 1863; digital edition, TannerRitchie Publishing, 2011)

Collections Relating to the History of Mary Queen of Scotland in Four Volumes; Containing a Great Number of Original Papers Never before Printed, ed. James Anderson (1662–1728) (Edinburgh, 1727; digital edition, TannerRitchie Publishing and University of St Andrews, 2008)

Index

abbeys 54, 57–9, 114, 180, 198, 230
Abercromby, Walter 47
Aberdeen 23–5, 109, 129, 187
  bishop of 25
  cathedral (St Machar's) 25
  grammar school 45
  university 23–4
Aberdeenshire, Protestants in 46
Adamson, Patrick 228
adultery xi, 3, 6, 88, 127, 183, 223
Æthelred the Unready, king of
     England (978–1016) 199
Ainslie Tavern Bond 169–71, 210
Albany, 3rd duke of (Alexander
     Stewart) 45
Albany, 4th duke of (John Stewart) 42
Aleandro, Girolamo 24
Alesius, Alexander 24, 47
Alexander III, king of Scotland
     (1249–86) 23, 56
Alva, duke of (Fernando de Toledo)
     156–7, 174, 193
Amboise, Pacification of 143; Tumult
     of 101
Ancrum, battle of (1545) 59
Anderson, James 6
Anet, Palace of 73
Angus, Protestants in 84, 88
Angus, 6th earl of (Archibald
     Douglas) 42, 52, 54, 55, 59, 150
Anne, queen of Britain (1702–14) 1
architecture 30–1, 38, 71, 124, 205
  French 71
  and politics 31, 124
Argyll, 4th earl of (Archibald
     Campbell) 44, 52, 54–5, 57, 85–7
Argyll, 5th earl of, also lord Lorne
     (Archibald Campbell, son of
     above) 93–4, 98, 101, 112, 118,

121, 154, 159, 162–3, 165, 171, 176,
    179–80, 189
Armada 4, 35
Armstrong, Johnnie 33
Armstrong Davison, M.H. 8, 203
Arran, 2nd earl of, duke of
     Châtelherault (James
     Hamilton) 62, 85, 92, 100–1,
     105, 138, 151, 154, 155, 182
  bonds of 48–50, 61
  French duchy 62, 77–8
  heir presumptive 47, 54, 56
  marriage alliances proposed for son
    54, 60–2, 100, 114, 144
  regency of 47, 57, 60–1, 67, 78–9,
    150
Arran, 3rd earl of (James Hamilton,
     son of above) 54, 60–2, 99–100,
     1064, 114, 144
artillery 16, 29, 30, 59, 82
Ashley, Catherine 75
Atholl, 4th earl of (John Stewart) 118,
    120, 159, 162, 164–5, 171, 176
Auld Alliance 24–5, 57, 63, 65, 68, 71,
    79, 109–10
Ayala, Pedro d' 19–20
Ayrshire, Protestants in 46, 84, 88, 154

Babington Plot 7, 185, 196
Balfour, Henry 44
Balfour, Sir James of Pittendreich 161,
    171, 233
Balliol, John 53
Bannatyne, George 233
Bannockburn, battle of (1314) 22
Barbour, John 22
Bastian (valet of Mary Queen of
     Scots) 167
Bayonne, treaty of (1565) 156

Gordon, Alexander of Strathdon 48
Gordon, George *see* Huntly, earls of
Gordon, lady Jean (first wife of
    Bothwell) 169
Gordon, John *see* Sutherland, earl of
Gordon, Sir John 129
Goring, Rosemary xiv
Gouda, Fr Nicholas de 132–3
Gowrie, 1st earl of (William Ruthven)
    185
Graham, William *see* Menteith, earl of
    and Montrose, earl of
Gray, Patrick, 4th lord 50
Great Council of the Realm 103, 112
Greenwich, Treaty of (1543) 54, 56, 62
Grey, Henry *see* Kent, earl of
Grey, Lady Jane 73, 79
Greyfriars (Edinburgh) 88; (Perth) 92
Gueldres, county of 32
Guise family 76, 81, 91, 94, 98, 101,
    106, 143–5, 148, 198
Guise, Antoinette duchess of 76
Guise, Charles, cardinal of Lorraine
    76, 91, 94, 98, 143–4
Guise, Francis duke of 76–7, 91, 94,
    98, 143
Guise, Henry duke of 144, 195
Guise, Mary of *see* Mary of Guise
Guy, John xv, 208, 210

Haddington 59, 62; Treaty of (1548)
    62
Haggai (prophet) 111
Hailes, David lord 6
Hale, J.R. 27
Hamilton (town) 179–80
Hamilton family 34, 47, 53, 61, 95, 98,
    100, 105, 150, 159, 175
Hamilton, James, 1st lord 44
Hamilton, James, duke of
    Châtelherault 98 *see also* Arran,
    earls of
Hamilton, James of Bothwellhaugh
    188
Hamilton, Sir James of Finnart 33
Hamilton, John, abbot of Paisley,

    later archbishop of St Andrews
    52, 56, 78, 86–7, 128, 133, 145,
    188–9
  reforming councils and *Catechism*
    78, 86–7
Hamilton, Patrick, Protestant martyr
    46
Hamilton, Thomas of Drumcairn 121
Hamilton archives *see* Lennoxlove
Hapsburg, house of 72, 81, 143–4,
    148–9, 152
Hardwick, Bess of 194
Hardyng, John 18
Harryson (or Henderson), James 64
Hay, Fr Edmund 133
Hay, George *see* Errol, earl of
Hayward, Sir John 227
Heal, Felicity xvii
Heijnsbergen, Theo van 208
Henri II, king of France (1547–59) 13,
    40, 50, 62, 72–5, 83, 90–1, 94,
    103
Henri III, king of France (1574–89) 4,
    74, 132
Henrietta Maria (wife of Charles I of
    Britain) 158
Henri IV, king of France (1589–1610)
    134–5
Henry IV, king of Castile (1454–74)
    34
Henry VI, king of England (1422–61,
    1470–1) 34, 199
Henry VII, king of England (1485–
    1509) 25, 29, 45, 191
Henry VIII, king of England
    (1509–47)
  attempt to dominate Scotland 25,
    43, 51–60, 63–5, 68, 83, 150
  conniving in Beaton's murder 67
  death of 43–4, 159
  marriages of 2, 4, 42, 152
  megalomania of 30, 53, 56, 64, 74,
    125, 140
  offering pension to Glencairn 50
  religious policy of 41, 45, 65
Hepburn family 41